"This Teacher's Guide is a must-have resource for educators. It offers practical, research-based strategies for fostering positive, inclusive classrooms. With realistic scenarios, it supports both new teachers and seasoned veterans in effectively implementing preventive strategies to teach and maintain positive behaviors. Implementing these strategies allow educators to spend less time managing intensive behaviors and more time creating inclusive classrooms where every student can thrive."
    Heather Griller Clark, *PhD Arizona State University*

"The book *Improving Student Behavior and Cultivating Meaningful Relationships: A Teacher's Guide to Positive and Preventive Approaches in Inclusive Classrooms* is a source for pre-service and in-service teachers can use when establishing community classrooms that promotes active student engagement. From a practitioner lens, this book provides a step-by-step process for pre-service and in-service teachers to consider while building a foundation for their community inclusive classrooms."
    William C. Hunter, *EdD University of Memphis*

"This is the book that I wish I would have had as a new teacher. While these strategies are not typically taught in teacher preparation programs, Collins, Landrum, and Sweigart have created a survival manual of sorts. The strategies and considerations discussed represent our current science of effective classroom management, presented in an accessible and user-friendly manner."
    Terry Scott, *PhD University of Louisville*

Improving Student Behavior and Cultivating Meaningful Relationships

This comprehensive guide offers simple and effective strategies for supporting and improving the classroom behavior of all your students, including those with intensive behavior support needs. Applicable across all K–12 contexts, with recommendations for whole classes as well as individual supports, each practical strategy builds on a foundation of research-supported behavioral approaches. The authors emphasize how each strategy can help build and maintain positive relationships between students and educators, which has been shown to be a key predictor of individual student success. With a myriad of helpful visuals, ready-to-use planning templates, and easy-to-try ideas, this book is key reading for all general or special education teachers, school support staff, and instructional coaches.

Lauren W. Collins, Ph.D., is an associate professor of special education at San Diego State University. Her work focuses on the dissemination of practical, evidence-based strategies for students with disabilities, with an emphasis on early literacy and behavioral interventions.

Timothy J. Landrum, Ph.D., is a professor of special education at the University of Louisville. He is a leading scholar in the field of emotional and behavioral disorders who specializes in the translation of research into practice.

Chris A. Sweigart, Ph.D., is a special education consultant in Kentucky and the creator of Limened, a website for teachers to support students with a variety of challenges.

Other Eye on Education Books
Available from Routledge
(www.routledge.com/eyeoneducation)

Fostering Parent Engagement for Equitable and Successful Schools: A Leader's Guide to Supporting Families and Students
Patrick Darfler-Sweeney

Sparking Change to Promote Equity: Implementing Culturally Responsive Leadership Practices in Gifted and Advanced Programs
Javetta Jones Roberson and Kristina Henry Collins

Where Is the Teacher? The 12 Shifts for Student-Centered Environments
Kyle Wagner

Relational Inclusivity in the Elementary Classroom: A Teacher's Guide to Supporting Student Friendships and Building Nurturing Communities
Christoforos Mamas, Shana R. Cohen, and Caren Holtzman

Improving Your School One Week at a Time: Building the Foundation for Professional Teaching and Learning, Second Edition
Jeffrey Zoul and Spiri Diamantis Howard

Improving Student Behavior and Cultivating Meaningful Relationships

A Teacher's Guide to Positive and Preventive Approaches in Inclusive Classrooms

Lauren W. Collins, Timothy J. Landrum, and Chris A. Sweigart

Routledge
Taylor & Francis Group
NEW YORK AND LONDON

Designed cover image: © Getty Images

First published 2025
by Routledge
605 Third Avenue, New York, NY 10158

and by Routledge
4 Park Square, Milton Park, Abingdon, Oxon, OX14 4RN

Routledge is an imprint of the Taylor & Francis Group, an informa business

© 2025 Taylor & Francis

The right of Lauren W. Collins, Timothy J. Landrum, and Chris A. Sweigart to be identified as authors of this work has been asserted in accordance with sections 77 and 78 of the Copyright, Designs and Patents Act 1988.

All rights reserved. No part of this book may be reprinted or reproduced or utilised in any form or by any electronic, mechanical, or other means, now known or hereafter invented, including photocopying and recording, or in any information storage or retrieval system, without permission in writing from the publishers.

Trademark notice: Product or corporate names may be trademarks or registered trademarks, and are used only for identification and explanation without intent to infringe.

ISBN: 978-1-032-74514-5 (hbk)
ISBN: 978-1-032-74233-5 (pbk)
ISBN: 978-1-003-46959-9 (ebk)

DOI: 10.4324/9781003469599

Typeset in Palatino
by KnowledgeWorks Global Ltd.

To all the students whose challenging behaviors made our jobs meaningful and fun. We thank you for the impact you had on our profession and our lives.

Contents

List of Figures..................................... xi
List of Tables.................................... xiv
Meet the Authors.................................. xv
Preface xvii

Part I: Introduction 1

1 Behavioral Interventions and Student-Teacher Relationships 3

Part II: Teaching Behavior 13

2 Establishing Expectations............................15

3 Explicit Instruction 31

Part III: Encouraging Appropriate Behavior 49

4 Positive Greetings at the Door........................51

5 Behavioral Momentum...............................69

6 Instructional Choice 86

7 Increasing Opportunities to Respond...................103

8 Precorrection 124

9 Precision Requests..................................140

Part IV: Maintaining Appropriate Behavior 163

10 Behavior-Specific Praise 165

11 Token Economies 180

12 Positive Group Contingencies 198

Part V: Responding to Intensive Behavior Support Needs 215

13 Differential Reinforcement 217

14 Check-In Check-Out 246

15 Behavior Contracts 265

16 Informal Functional Behavioral Assessment 281

Part VI: Closing Thoughts 303

17 Final Takeaways 305

Figures

2.1	Completed Example of Establishing Expectations Planning Template	24
2.2	Establishing Expectations Planning Template	29
2.3	Establishing Expectations Implementation and Self-Assessment Checklist	30
3.1	Completed Example of Explicit Instruction Planning Template	45
3.2	Explicit Instruction Planning Template	47
3.3	Explicit Instruction Implementation and Self-Assessment Checklist	48
4.1	Completed Example of Positive Greetings at the Door Planning Template	63
4.2	Positive Greetings at the Door Planning Template	66
4.3	Positive Greetings at the Door Guiding Questions	67
4.4	Positive Greetings at the Implementation and Self-Assessment Checklist	68
5.1	Completed Example of Behavioral Momentum Planning Template	81
5.2	Behavioral Momentum Planning Template	84
5.3	Behavioral Momentum Implementation and Self-Assessment Checklist	85
6.1	Completed Example of Instructional Choice Planning Template	97
6.2	Instructional Choice Planning Template	101
6.3	Instructional Choice Implementation and Self-Assessment Checklist	102
7.1	Completed Example of Opportunities to Respond Planning Template	119
7.2	Opportunities to Respond Planning Template	122
7.3	Opportunities to Respond Implementation and Self-Assessment Checklist	123

8.1	Completed Example of Precorrection Planning Template	135
8.2	Precorrection Planning Template	138
8.3	Precorrection Implementation and Self-Assessment Checklist	139
9.1	Completed Example of Precision Requests Planning Template	156
9.2	Precision Requests Planning Template	160
9.3	Precision Requests Implementation and Self-Assessment Checklist	161
10.1	Completed Example of Behavior-Specific Praise Planning Template	173
10.2	Behavior-Specific Praise Planning Template	178
10.3	Behavior-Specific Praise Implementation and Self-Assessment Checklist	179
11.1	Completed Example of Token Economy Planning Template	193
11.2	Token Economy Planning Template	196
11.3	Token Economy Implementation and Self-Assessment Checklist	197
12.1	Completed Example of Positive Group Contingencies Planning Template	209
12.2	Positive Group Contingencies Planning Template	213
12.3	Positive Group Contingencies Implementation and Self-Assessment Checklist	214
13.1	Completed Example of Differential Reinforcement Planning Template	238
13.2	Example of Differential Reinforcement Student Data	240
13.3	Differential Reinforcement Planning Template	244
13.4	Differential Reinforcement Implementation and Self-Assessment Checklist	245
14.1	Completed Example of Check-In Check-Out Planning Template	257
14.2	Check-In Check-Out Planning Template	262
14.3	Check-In Check-Out Implementation and Self-Assessment Checklist	263

14.4	Check-In Check-Out Daily Progress Report Example	264
15.1	Completed Example of Behavior Contract Planning Template	273
15.2	Behavior Contract Planning Template	278
15.3	Sample Behavior Contract	279
15.4	Behavior Contract Implementation and Self-Assessment Checklist	280
16.1	Completed Example of Informal Functional Behavioral Assessment Planning Template	294
16.2	Informal Functional Behavioral Assessment Planning Template	300
16.3	Informal Functional Behavioral Assessment Implementation and Self-Assessment Checklist	301

Tables

7.1	Forms of Opportunities to Respond	107
8.1	Steps in Planning and Implementing Precorrection	129
8.2	Sample Precorrection Statements	132
9.1	Components and Characteristics of Precision Requests	143
13.1	Example of Behaviors to Target in DRI	225
13.2	Examples of Alternative Behaviors that Might Be Reinforced in a DRA Implementation	226
13.3	Examples and Nonexamples of Effective Differential Reinforcement	232
13.4	Planning for the Use of DRI, DRA, DRL, and DRO	233
14.1	Core Components of CICO	251
16.1	Student Examples of Functions of Behavior	284
16.2	Sample A-B-C Chart	288

Meet the Authors

Lauren W. Collins, Ph.D., is an associate professor of special education at San Diego State University, where she prepares future educators to support students with mild to moderate disabilities. She earned her B.A. and M.T. from the University of Virginia and her Ph.D. from Old Dominion University. Lauren's experience in special education began as an elementary school teacher supporting students with learning disabilities, emotional and behavioral disorders, and autism. Her current work focuses on practical, evidence-based strategies, with a particular interest in early literacy and behavioral interventions. In addition, Lauren founded *ResearchED and PracticED*, where she provides direct support to students with and at risk for disabilities, offers professional development to teachers, and collaborates with families to improve student outcomes.

Timothy J. Landrum, Ph.D., is a professor of special education at the University of Louisville. He began his career teaching children with autism in a residential setting and later students with emotional and behavioral disorders (EBD) in self-contained classes in public schools in Virginia. He has contributed as author or editor to more than 100 publications and is co-author with James M. Kauffman of *Characteristics of Emotional and Behavioral Disorders of Children and Youth* (2018), now in its 11th edition. His research interests include EBD, classroom and behavior management, the identification of evidence-based practices, and the translation of research into practice.

Chris A. Sweigart, Ph.D., is a special education consultant and the creator of Limened, a website for teachers to support students with a variety of challenges. He has an extensive background of work with at-risk youth facing serious challenges from mental health and behavior disorders and academic failure to homelessness and involvement with the criminal justice system. Chris currently trains, coaches, and supports educators across 14 Kentucky school districts to address a range of challenges faced by students. Chris has served previously as a director of outreach for a community youth center for at-risk youth, program coordinator for a housing and mentoring program for homeless young adults and youth with disabilities, teacher of adolescent students with emotional and behavioral disorders, and postdoctoral fellow at the University of Louisville where he previously received his doctorate in Curriculum and Instruction and Special Education.

Preface

We include in every college course we teach – or professional development session we deliver – examples from our own experiences as classroom teachers. We do this for a few reasons. First, we want teachers to know we have been there. We know firsthand what it's like to have to plan instruction and interventions for a diverse set of students across different settings – but then often have our planning periods evaporate as we deal with behavioral outbursts. We know what it's like to have only 23 minutes to eat lunch to begin with, only to see that, too, disappear when a student has a meltdown or crisis. And we know how unhealthy and stressful it is to find that there is literally no time in a school day for a restroom break. We also know that even when the logistics run well, teaching can be stressful. The best planned lesson can go south in a hurry if just one student doesn't get it, or doesn't seem to want to get it. Add in that it's very easy for that one student to set off one or more of his classmates, and – well, we know well that sinking feeling of "uh-oh… I'm losing control of this class …."

Another reason we share personal experiences is that we think (and actually research is beginning to support) that teachers find it easier to understand and then *use* strategies when they're described with stories (compared to, say, reading a research report on effective practices). In this book, we describe lots of examples of what the strategies in each chapter look like in classrooms. We can say that while these are fictional, nearly all are based on experiences we had as public school teachers, or saw elsewhere in our school buildings. But we know that stories alone are not enough. In fact, we find ourselves worrying sometimes that good story-tellers may influence practice a lot – even when some of the practices or interventions they describe are not actually effective practices. For this reason, we have strategically selected approaches for improving student behavior that are *actually* effective – they are all supported by extensive research.

When we were teachers, we also gained firsthand experience teaching students with severely challenging behaviors. All three of us mostly taught kids identified with, or at risk for, emotional and behavioral disorders (EBD) who were served in a variety of settings, including co-taught classrooms. We add this part – that we've taught students with some of the most challenging behavior there is – because one element of resistance we sometimes hear when we describe interventions like those featured in this book is "Look, that sounds good on paper, but that stuff would never work with *my* kids, in *my* classroom ...." One of the things we learned as teachers was that these strategies – those we describe in this book – do work. And they can work even with most kids whose behavior may seem unmanageable. But there are two important points we like to make here when we're working with teachers. First, the strategies have to be implemented well, or correctly, as well as consistently. Using behavior-specific praise one day (say, for hand raising), but then seeing Johnny shout out answers without raising his hand the next day does not mean praise doesn't work. It simply takes time and consistent implementation.

A second point here is that we say these strategies work (when implemented well) with *most* kids. This book focuses on positive, mostly preventive (antecedent) strategies, and this was intentional as research tells us these are not used nearly often enough in classrooms. But we're not naive. Some students will definitely need more. We touch on a few interventions for more seriously challenging behavior in the last section of this text, but we need to be honest – this book is about strategies we think all teachers can and should use, or at least have available to them, in virtually all classrooms. Not only does using these strategies increase the effectiveness of the more intensive interventions, we are convinced that for the vast majority of teachers, the strategies we present here will help the vast majority of students more consistently meet basic expectations. And we think this addresses what are far and away the most common behavioral concerns teachers see on a daily basis.

We like to think we learned most of this as teachers, but in truth it was more validated as we moved into graduate school and dug deeper into research on what goes on in classrooms, and what really works in terms of consistent research evidence. We all had a series of *aha* moments as we became researchers and teacher educators – we *knew* that stuff worked for us as teachers, then we learned the *why* behind it. And now we spend most of our time training teachers and supporting professionals in translating research into practice around effective methods for teaching and supporting students who experience behavioral challenges, including those with and at risk for EBD. As we work with teachers to implement the practices we describe in this book, we are guided by something we learned early in graduate school, which completely matched our experience as teachers, and which guides what we do now in all our work: some interventions are simply better than others.

As you read this book, we hope that you will notice a few things we have done to make this resource as useful as possible in meeting your needs. First, we have done our best to streamline information. As such, some chapters are brief because the strategy is relatively straightforward, while others are a bit more lengthy because the strategy is more nuanced. You may also notice that we have used very few references; this was a strategic decision, as our hope is that this book is more of a practical guide than an academic textbook. That said, we were careful and thoughtful in selecting strategies we know to be supported by strong research evidence and to ensure that the references we have used are from reliable, peer-reviewed resources.

You may also notice that we have stayed away from technical terms as much as possible. At least we tried. We also know that in lots of earlier writings on classroom and behavior management, terms like appropriate and inappropriate, or positive and negative were used to describe behavior, and we recognize that these terms have varied meanings and connotations across cultures. We admit that we fall into using these terms sometimes ourselves, so we preface this book with the caveat that if we use those terms, we use them with an implied message: behavior can only be interpreted in context, and in light of cultural and contextual norms. Our discussions about school-related behaviors and recommendations about them must be interpreted as they apply to *your* students in *your* classroom. We want to be clear; our goal is to help students meet the expectations of whatever contexts they find themselves in, including in school, family, community, and ultimately employment and independent living contexts. We also know that these contexts will include varying family, cultural, and community norms and expectations. Our goal in all our work has been to work directly with students and families or caregivers to identify those contexts most important to them, in both near and long terms, and then to help them develop the skills needed to be successful and meet the expectations of those environments. We try to use terms like negative or inappropriate only when referring to behaviors on which there is probably universal agreement (e.g., we believe that physical aggression should be reduced or eliminated).

Another facet of this book that we hope you will notice is that we have provided supplemental resources at the end of each chapter to help in your planning and implementation of the strategies we present. We know well that teachers are short on time and in our experience, few things are more frustrating than attending a professional development or reading about a new strategy, and then having to spend hours of additional time finding or creating additional resources or materials before we can implement what we learned. Therefore, the templates we've included at the end of each chapter are ready to use. Of course, you may want to modify or tweak them in some way, but at the very least, we've provided a jumping-off point for planning and data collection. Each chapter includes a blank planning template as well as a completed planning template as an example. In addition, we have included a self-assessment checklist in each chapter. The idea is that this checklist can serve two purposes. First, it can be a guide to help you know you are implementing the steps in a given strategy correctly – with *fidelity*, as researchers say. As we noted earlier, any strategy must be implemented the way it was designed and tested (i.e., correctly, or with fidelity) if we want to see its positive effects. The checklist may also serve as a simple way for you to assess and identify steps that might need some extra attention in your teaching practice. We know that interventions are most effective when teachers implement them with high rates of fidelity (at least 80%), so we encourage you to utilize these checklists as a way to ensure that you are implementing the various strategies with as much fidelity as possible.

Speaking of data collection, you may also notice that we don't spend much time in this book talking about *methods* for collecting data. This is not because we don't think data collection is important – we absolutely do, and we encourage teachers to collect data and use that data to make instructional decisions. However, we think there are already some excellent, and free, resources available to support teachers in data-based decision-making (e.g., https://iris.peabody.vanderbilt.edu/; https://ruralsmh.com/intervention-hub/) and our goal was to streamline information about the implementation of effective behavior management strategies and how these strategies can be used to help build positive student-teacher relationships. We encourage readers to exercise their own professional judgment in regard to their need for information on data collocation and to utilize some of the resources we've mentioned as needed. The planning templates provided in Parts III, IV, and V of this book include a space for collecting student data, with tips related to how to focus data collection efforts in the most efficient way for monitoring how students are responding.

This book is organized into four sections: teaching behavior, encouraging appropriate behavior, maintaining appropriate behavior, and responding to intensive behavior support needs. We believe the approaches presented in the Parts II, III, and IV (Chapters 2–12) are things that all teachers should have in their repertoire and use in their classroom management routines for all students. However, given our own teaching experience and research, we know that some students will need a bit more. In Part V (Chapters 13–16), we describe interventions that are slightly more intensive and are generally intended primarily for students with behavior that has proven a bit more resistant to change. It is important to note that many of the strategies in this book can be used simultaneously and that the interventions in Part V will be most effective if the strategies in Parts II–IV are in place.

As a final thought, we need to be clear that (unfortunately) none of the strategies presented in this book provide a universal remedy for challenging behavior. No strategy will work every time, for every student. However, scores of research studies across many decades indicate that some strategies are more likely to work than others. Our goal in writing this book is to provide you with a toolbox of some of the strategies that have the greatest *probability* of improving student behavior and that are the most likely to facilitate the establishment of positive student-teacher relationships. We learned early in our careers that progress can be slow, but everything we have learned as teachers, as graduate students, as researchers, and as teacher educators continues to point to a few key takeaways. First, behaviorally oriented approaches work but are underused in most classrooms. Some of this, we think, lies in the idea that positive, preventive behavioral strategies are not placed front and center as they should be; we fear too many schools and classrooms fall back on punitive-only approaches when concerns about behavior mount. Second, relationships matter. There is growing evidence that kids are more successful in school when they experience positive relationships with teachers. But what does this mean for instruction, or classroom and behavior management? We have heard some professionals question whether a behavioral approach "works," or is the right thing to do when the importance of relationships is increasingly clear. An underlying message we have sensed is that a relationship focus should replace a behavioral orientation (e.g., "If you develop a good relationship with students, then their behavior will change"). We disagree! We sincerely hope that the chapters in this book accurately convey how positive, preventive behavioral strategies are in fact *very* consistent with the exact things that make up a positive teacher-student relationship (e.g., a sense of warmth, security, and respect for autonomy and individual differences and preferences). In short, we are convinced that positive, preventive strategies both improve behavioral outcomes *and* enhance relationships between teachers and students. It was our intention and is our hope that this book captures these takeaways in ways that are easy to understand, and thus will be easier to implement in classrooms. We think we would have really liked to have a book like this when we were teachers, and we hope it's useful to others as well.

Part I
Introduction

1

Behavioral Interventions and Student-Teacher Relationships

In this chapter, we describe the importance of using positive and preventive strategies to support student behavior and the impact that such approaches have on student learning and student-teacher relationships. We emphasize the importance of keeping students in the learning environment to maximize academic, behavioral, and social success, with specific attention to avoiding the cycle of exclusionary discipline and missed instruction. Finally, we define the characteristics of positive student-teacher relationships and explain why it matters, especially for students with challenging behavior.

Anyone who has ever been a teacher or had a teacher does not need to be convinced of the impact that a teacher can have on the life of a student – for better or for worse. If asked to name a teacher who had a positive impact on your life, it is very likely that you can name at least one person who was meaningful to you when you were a student, no matter how many years have passed. On the other hand, if asked to name a teacher with whom you had a negative experience, you could almost certainly (and maybe even more quickly) also identify that person by name. There is no question that teachers impact the lives of the students they teach, and there is little question that having a positive student-teacher relationship increases the magnitude of that impact for the better. The question, then, is *how* do teachers build a positive relationship with the students they teach, and especially with those who may be harder to connect with due to chronic and challenging behaviors? Just like there is no question that student-teacher relationships are important, there is also little question that difficult student behaviors are among the most commonly reported problems that teachers face. In fact, both research and our experience indicate that students who demonstrate challenging behaviors can be the toughest to teach and that building positive relationships with these students can be especially difficult.

During our years in the classroom teaching students with and at risk for emotional and behavioral disorders, and in more years supporting teachers to do the same, we often hear the belief that if teachers can just connect with students – if they can build relationships with them – students will be more likely to demonstrate the behaviors that are expected of them. While we agree that a positive student-teacher relationship is a great thing, and for some students may help them demonstrate positive behaviors, we have a slightly different perspective. Decades of research indicate that students who have significant behavioral needs require specific behavioral interventions and supports in order to be successful in a classroom environment. Put simply, these students need *more* than a positive student-teacher relationship. Further, these students are likely among those who need positive relationships with their teachers more than others but who, by nature of their behavioral challenges, are typically the least likely to establish such a relationship. From our perspective, if teachers utilize positive and effective strategies to support student behavior, they are more likely to build a positive student-teacher relationship with even those students whose behavior is most challenging. Rather than needing a relationship to improve student behavior, we see behavioral interventions as a key entry point for building that relationship (Collins & Landrum, 2023).

In this introductory chapter, we begin by discussing behavioral interventions – specifically, the foundational characteristics of the most effective interventions for improving student behavior and the reasons that these interventions are effective.

We also discuss the connection between student behavior and achievement, as the overarching goal of teaching is to help students learn new skills. Finally, we conclude with a discussion about what actually makes a positive student-teacher relationship, and why these relationships matter.

What Are the Most Effective Behavioral Interventions?

The philosophy that guides our teaching and research is that the best behavioral interventions are those that are positive, preventive, and instructional in nature and that are also supported by a sound body of research evidence. This approach is often described in the context of antecedent-behavior-consequence (A-B-C) logic, which we describe in more detail in Chapter 15. In this way of thinking about behavior, the antecedent (A) includes what happens before a behavior (B) in question occurs, and the consequence (C) is whatever happens immediately after the behavior. Using this logic, it is often easy to see how consequences influence the occurrence of behavior – if a consequence the student likes or desires consistently follows a certain behavior (contingently, in the language of behavior analysis), that behavior becomes likely to occur more often – and indeed we may have discovered the *function* of this behavior. Put another way, the consequence has provided reinforcement for the behavior. For example, consider a teacher who presents a math worksheet to a student (the antecedent). The student rips up the worksheet, throws it on the ground, and yells an expletive at the teacher (the behavior). The student is then sent to the office (the consequence). If the function (or purpose) of the student's behavior was to escape the task, he was successful! The consequence of sending that student to the office has likely reinforced the student's behavior – which means he is now more likely to engage in similar behavior the next time an undesirable task is presented. Another example is a teacher who asks a student to put their materials away (the antecedent), the student successfully completes the task (the behavior), and then the teacher praises the student, saying "You did an excellent job getting your materials put away" (the consequence). If we see that "successfully putting materials away" increases, we can conclude that the teacher's praise served as a reinforcer for that behavior.

While we are certainly big advocates of using positive reinforcement as a consequence-based strategy (we include various ways to use this in several chapters throughout this book), we believe that the most effective approach is to use antecedent-based interventions to *prevent* challenging behavior from occurring in the first place, and to then follow-up with positive reinforcement when the student demonstrates the desired behavior. Antecedent interventions, as you'll see in the chapters on things like behavioral momentum (Chapter 5), instructional choice (Chapter 6), and precorrection (Chapter 8), involve teachers manipulating the A side of the behavioral equation – doing something slightly different *before* the behavior occurs, with the specific goal of encouraging a more appropriate response (e.g., asking for help) instead of the behavior that has become problematic (e.g., tearing up a paper).

Once a student begins to engage in challenging behavior, it is significantly more difficult to get that student back on track and, in many cases, instructional time is lost because now the teacher must turn their attention to managing the behavior problem and its fallout. Another common problem with the use of consequence-based strategies is that they are often reactionary and exclusionary. Exclusionary discipline is problematic for many reasons, but especially because more often than not, it worsens the behavior and negatively impacts a student's overall trajectory (Collins & Landrum, 2023). In 2008, the American Psychological Association examined the impacts of Zero Tolerance discipline, which is the most extreme application of exclusionary discipline in which students are suspended or expelled for behavior, with little to no consideration of the context in which that behavior occurs. The findings of this examination revealed that exclusionary discipline does more harm than good, including that students who are suspended or expelled are more likely to eventually drop out of school. Moreover, exclusionary discipline disproportionately impacts students with disabilities and students of color. Specifically, students with emotional and behavioral disorders are suspended and expelled at disproportionate rates, as are students of color, especially black boys. Even worse, students of color who receive special education services are the most likely to be disproportionately suspended or expelled. These disproportionate rates of exclusionary discipline occur even though students of color are not any more likely than white students to engage in behavioral offenses. Therefore, the use of antecedent-based strategies and interventions may be especially important for these populations of students.

Put simply, students cannot learn if they are not in the classroom. Exclusionary approaches that lead to removal from the learning environment ultimately place students even more behind and create a cycle that leads to even worse academic challenges. Think about the student who had disruptive behavior when given a math worksheet – perhaps the behavior was an indication that the student does not have the skills needed to complete the assignment and therefore requires additional instruction (more on that in a moment). When the student is removed from the learning environment, they lose *all* access to instruction. When they return, they may well be presented with new work that requires application of the skills that were taught when they were not even in the classroom. And because their disruptive behavior was reinforced before, the student is more likely to engage in that behavior again in order to escape the next difficult task. On the other hand, if the student had remained in the classroom, the teacher could have worked on improving both behavioral skills (i.e., how to communicate a need for support) and the actual academic content (i.e., math skills).

Another benefit of antecedent-based strategies is that they decrease the amount of time spent dealing with challenging behavior because they prevent those behaviors from occurring in the first place. And let's be clear – antecedent strategies don't just stop behavior from occurring. A key reason that these strategies prevent challenging behaviors is because many of them include explicit teaching components – modeling behavioral expectations, prompting students with reminders of what they need to do, giving them opportunities to practice behavioral skills. When students are provided with an opportunity to learn and practice behavioral expectations, they are more likely to receive positive reinforcement for successfully demonstrating the behaviors that are expected. As you might imagine, this creates a cycle that is quite the opposite of the negative, exclusionary cycle we just described.

What Is the Connection between Student Behavior and Achievement?

In the previous section, we described how challenging student behavior can lead to removal from the classroom, ultimately creating a cycle that impedes academic achievement. Another issue that should be considered when examining student behavior and achievement is that sometimes, behavioral interventions will not be enough. Although the focus of this entire book is on behavioral strategies, it is important for us to briefly discuss that even though behavioral interventions can be necessary, they are not sufficient for promoting academic achievement and other skills (e.g., social, functional, behavioral).

We believe that at the core, student behavior is a mechanism for communication. In most cases, students are communicating that they are trying to access something (usually attention or a desired task, object, or activity; in some cases, sensory input) or to avoid or escape something (usually attention or an undesirable task, object, or activity; in some cases, sensory input). When students are engaging in behavior as a way to avoid or escape a task or activity, it is critical that teachers consider whether or not students have the skills needed to complete the task. If not, the first step is to provide additional instruction and support by teaching the student what they need to know and be able to do to carry out the task. Think back to the student with the math worksheet and how differently things may have turned out had the teacher proactively provided some additional instruction before asking the student to complete the worksheet independently.

To underscore this point, we often tell teachers we work with that no matter how powerful the reinforcement might be, we could not be positively reinforced into effectively performing open-heart surgery or sending a rocket to outer space and ensuring that all the astronauts arrive home safely. Someone could provide us with a combination of every strategy described in Chapters 4–8 of this book, like behavioral momentum or instructional choice (antecedent interventions), and offer us reinforcement in the form of one million dollars (a consequence) for successfully completing this task, and we would still fail at meeting the expectation (the behavior). The reason we would not succeed is that we have never been taught *how* to perform these tasks.

Therefore, we encourage teachers to consider a student's skills when responding to behavior that appears to be refusal or noncompliance. In some cases, the student may very likely have the skills to complete a task and in those cases, the teacher should absolutely move forward with implementing antecedent-based strategies and using positive reinforcement. However, in other cases, the student may not have *learned* the skills needed to complete the task. Note here that we used the term "learned" rather than the phrase "the student may not have been taught" because – as you very likely know – just because a student has been taught how to do something does not mean that they have *learned* how to do it. In these cases, teachers should start with providing additional instruction and then, once students have demonstrated that they can perform the skill, begin to implement antecedent-based strategies and positive reinforcement.

What Makes a Positive Student-Teacher Relationship and Why Does It Matter?

A positive student-teacher relationship is often easy to identify but harder to define. Many people can identify a teacher who has impacted their life in a positive way, and many teachers could name students with whom they believe they had a positive relationship. However, when asked *why* that relationship was a good one, or *what* about the relationship made it so positive, it might be more difficult to identify specific characteristics, particularly from the perspective of the teacher. When we think about positive student-teacher relationships from our own time as students, words like *trust, compassion, dependability,* and *accountability* come to mind. When we think about it from our perspective as the teacher, there is more pause, and we tend to say things like "I *think* the student felt safe in my classroom" or "It *seems like* they trusted me."

Almost every teacher will have their own approach to building positive student-teacher relationships because at the crux of it, these relationships are personal and individualized, just like the other types of relationships we have in our lives. Although they will be different across teachers and students, and even though we may know exactly what we do as teachers to create these relationships, several researchers in the field (Cook et al., 2018; Kennedy & Haydon, 2021; Pianta et al., 2003; Sutherland et al., 2019) have identified a few defining characteristics of positive student-teacher relationships. In a positive student-teacher relationship, there is consistent engagement (either verbal or nonverbal); warmth; reciprocal and effective communication; closeness; security; and overall high-quality interactions. Pianta et al. (2003) summarized a high-quality, positive student-teacher relationship to be one where there is increased closeness and decreased conflict; we would assert that for students with challenging behavior, there may be more conflict than with others, but that the student and teacher know how to effectively navigate these conflicts in ways that are positive and therapeutic. When these relationships are in place, students benefit in virtually every aspect of their lives. They have better relationships with their peers; demonstrate more desirable classroom behavior; have increased engagement and, consequently, improved academic outcomes; and an increased sense of belonging, which may be particularly true for students of color (Cook et al., 2018).

Final Thoughts

In this chapter, we discussed the foundational concepts for this book: effective behavioral interventions and positive student-teacher relationships. We described why the most promising and most effective behavioral interventions are those that prevent challenging behaviors from occurring and increase demonstration of expected behaviors. We also briefly described what it means to have a positive relationship between student and teacher, or at least what some of the characteristics of a positive relationship may look like. We hope it is clear that we see the use of positive, preventive, antecedent behavioral strategies and interventions as not only consistent with a relationship focus in classrooms, but as a starting point for building those relationships. Accordingly, throughout the chapters in this book, we have tried to make clear how each strategy we describe both improves student behavior and connects back to the defining characteristics of a positive student-teacher relationship.

References

American Psychological Association Zero Tolerance Task Force. (2008). Are zero tolerance policies effective in the schools? An evidentiary review and recommendations. *American Psychologist, 63*, 852–862.

Collins, L. W., & Landrum, T. J. (2023). Using behavioral interventions to build relationships with students with challenging behavior. *TEACHING Exceptional Children, 55*(3), 188–197.

Cook, C. R., Coco, S., Zhang, Y., Duong, M. T., Renshaw, T. L., & Frank, S. (2018). Cultivating positive teacher-student relationships: Preliminary evaluation of the establish-maintain-restore (EMR) method. *School Psychology Review, 47*(3), 226–243.

Kennedy, A. M., & Haydon, T. (2021). Forming and sustaining high-quality student-teacher relationships to reduce minor behavioral incidents. *Intervention in School and Clinic, 56*(3), 141–147.

Pianta, R. C., Hamre, B., & Stuhlman, M. (2003). Relationships between teachers and children. *Handbook of Psychology*, 199–234.

Sutherland, K. S., Conroy, M. A., McLeod, B. D., Kunemund, R., & McKnight, K. (2019). Common practice elements for improving social, emotional, and behavioral outcomes of young elementary school students. *Journal of Emotional and Behavioral Disorders, 27*(2), 76–85.

Part II
Teaching Behavior

2

Establishing Expectations

In this chapter, we explain how and why we establish behavioral expectations with students. We begin by providing a definition and description of this practice, followed by a brief overview of the research that supports the use of this practice. Next, we explain how establishing expectations can build positive relationships with students, particularly those who demonstrate challenging behaviors. Finally, we describe how to implement this practice and provide two examples of what this practice might look like in a classroom. The supplemental resources for this chapter include a planning template (one blank for your use and one completed as an example) and a self-assessment checklist to support implementation fidelity.

What Does It Mean to Establish Expectations?

Most people would agree that one of the most important foundations for any classroom – one of the very first things a teacher needs to do – is to establish clear rules and expectations. Everyone, including all adults and students, needs to be on the same page with regard to expected behavior. More specifically, it is essential that students have a solid understanding of what their behavior should *look like* in order for them to be successful. Without these common understandings about basic expectations, it is less likely that any other interventions a teacher may try (like those described throughout his book) will have a positive impact. It may be helpful to think about the importance of clear rules and expectations as similar to the importance of laying a solid foundation for a house before it is built. If there are any problems with the foundation, no matter how small or how much repairing is done to issues that arise, the likelihood of bigger problems down the line as the rest of the house is built increases. As another example, it may be helpful to think of trying to fill a cup with water. If there are holes in the bottom of a cup, no matter how much water is poured in, the cup will never fill. In education, these foundational supports are sometimes called "Tier 1" or "universal" supports – meaning that they are in place for *all* kids, regardless of whether they show any signs of risk for academic or behavioral concerns. A teacher could implement all of the other strategies covered in this book, but if basic behavioral expectations for the classroom have not been explicitly defined and taught, many of the other efforts will fall short of making lasting behavioral change.

Note that we said above that it's critical that behavioral expectations are defined and taught. This word choice is very intentional! In the context of schools and classrooms, it is important to recognize that establishing expectations involves both of these things. Put simply, it's more than just telling students what to do, or merely telling them what the rules are. To be clear, the first step really is simply establishing what the expectations are – in other words: what are the rules? There are several recommended steps to establishing rules, and we discuss those in the next section. There we also emphasize that a teacher should not just present a list of rules already set in stone, but engage students in helping to establish classroom rules, along with a common understanding of what they mean. But an important element that some teachers may miss in establishing expectations involves the next step, which is actively teaching the behaviors that will allow students to successfully meet the expectations these rules have established. So, while it is important that students learn the rules – that they can remember and even recite the classroom rules – the more important element is that they have learned and can consistently display the behaviors that follow these rules. Think of obvious examples; it is one thing for a student to be able to state that a classroom rule is that students must raise their hand and wait to be called on in the middle of a lesson, and quite another thing for a student to actually do this instead of shouting out ("I need help!") every time they get stuck on a math problem. We discuss both of these elements in the section below, "How Do I Implement Establishing Expectations in My Classroom?"

Another element that requires some thought when teachers establish expectations is that while consistency in expectations is important, there are also subtle differences in the specific behaviors students need to learn and demonstrate in order to meet expectations at different times throughout the day, and in different contexts. For example, the behavioral expectations during a whole group lesson (e.g., raise your hand and wait to be called on before speaking) may be different from the expectations during a collaborative group activity (e.g., wait until it is your turn to speak). Imagine, too, the differences children need to understand in how they are responsible, or demonstrate 'responsibility,' in math class versus the cafeteria.

A final note that most teachers probably have seen frequently is that schools have historically been very good at making clear what students should *not* do in the classroom. Classroom rules from years ago (and, probably, still too often today) were often no more than a list of prohibited behaviors (no running, no talking during class, no gum-chewing, and so on). However, we have learned that effectively establishing expectations is more than just telling students what behaviors to avoid. Rather, the emphasis should be on making sure that students understand what they *should* do. Once students know what is expected, they can be taught how to demonstrate the behaviors that are most compatible with those expectations across different activities throughout their day.

How Do I Know Establishing Expectations Works?

The benefits of establishing expectations is supported by decades of research (Hester et al., 2009), as this practice helps create a predictable environment and is effective for students of all ages, as well as for students with and without disabilities. As we described, establishing expectations is an integral component of Tier 1 supports, and this strategy is consistently found in schools that utilize a Positive Behavioral Interventions and Supports (PBIS) framework (Robbie et al., 2022). Importantly, in schools that implement Tier 1 PBIS supports with a high-level of fidelity (i.e., they actually implement the Tier 1 strategies just as they are intended to be used), students with disabilities are less likely to be suspended (Simonsen et al., 2022).

The professional guidance related to this strategy is clear: if teachers use student friendly language, state expectations positively, and provide examples and non-examples when teaching students how to meet those expectations, students are more likely to be successful (e.g., Myers et al. 2017). Alter and Haydon (2017) conducted a review of research on this very topic and found that in classrooms with clear rules and expectations, student behavior improved, particularly when paired with other supports such as positive reinforcement. As a final note, it is important to remember that establishing expectations is also important for virtual teaching environments (Croce & Salter, 2022); teachers can establish, teach, and support students in meeting expectations in these environments just as they would in traditional, face-to-face learning environments.

How Does Establishing Expectations Build Positive Relationships with My Students?

Much like establishing expectations lays the groundwork for overall classroom management, it is also a foundational component of building a positive student-teacher relationship. One reason this practice is helpful in building positive relationships involves the recommended strategies for establishing expectations. For example, it is best practice for a teacher to take the time to explain classroom expectations in a way that acknowledges that classrooms are made up of students who are diverse in many ways, and whose behavioral norms in their home environment may differ greatly from the expectations in classroom environments. A rule or expectation is not presented as the "right" way (or, by implication, the "wrong" way) to accomplish something. Rather, the teacher works with students in a classroom to talk through what everyone needs to do in order to feel safe, to get their work done, and to learn as best they can *in this context*. Establishing expectations is also helpful for students who may need support in understanding the "hidden curriculum;" that is, some of the basic norms and expectations that many students – but not all – quickly pick up simply from being in an environment (things like taking turns, lining up for certain transitions, respecting one another's personal belongings or personal space).

Students with disabilities and students from culturally or linguistically diverse backgrounds may benefit especially when teachers take time to talk through expectations in ways that encourage student input, and ensures that all students have a shared understanding of what the expectations are and why they are important. In addition to acknowledging the diversity and different needs of individual students, when teachers set clear expectations, the likelihood that students will engage in behavior that sets them up for success increases, which in turn provides opportunities for teachers to positively reinforce students (e.g., "I really appreciated how safe you were on the playground today when you climbed up the stairs to get to the slide, and how respectful you were when you waited in line so that others could have a turn."). The use of clear expectations and consistent acknowledgment when students meet them also increases the likelihood that the classroom environment will be a warm and welcoming place, where students feel secure, all of which are defining characteristics of positive student-teacher relationships (Pianta et al., 2003; Sutherland et al., 2019). More specifically, establishing clear expectations decreases the likelihood of conflict between student and teacher because students are aware of what is expected from the beginning and know that teachers see and appreciate them for meeting those expectations.

Finally, teachers have the choice of involving students in the development of classroom expectations, and this can be valuable in several ways. Involving students in establishing expectations and defining how expectations can be met helps establish students as integral members of the classroom community, and thus has the potential to increase feelings of belonging. This approach also sends the important message to students that their ideas and values are appreciated and heard.

How Do I Implement Establishing Expectations in My Classroom?

The first step in establishing expectations for the classroom is for the teacher to have a general idea of between three and five expectations for the classroom. If you are teaching in a school that already has school-wide expectations, we recommend aligning your classroom expectations with these. It is okay to add a small number of classroom-specific expectations to existing school-wide expectations, but we strongly encourage teachers to limit their expectations to no more than five; a lengthy list of expectations has the potential to confuse or overwhelm students. As an example, we describe the three very common expectations mentioned earlier: be responsible, be respectful, be safe.

Rather than simply telling students what the classroom expectations will be, we suggest starting with a group activity that involves student participation. This strategy helps create student buy-in by giving them some ownership of the process. In this activity, the teacher leads the class in a brainstorming activity by asking students to share what they think should be part of the classroom expectations. As students share, the teacher records ideas using a graphic organizer. It is important to note here that the younger the students, the more support they will need in generating ideas for classroom expectations. Older students have experience in schools and are generally well-equipped to identify basic expectations, such as hanging up a backpack upon entering the room. As you lead your class in this activity, be sure to record what you want students to do, rather than what not to do. For example, if a student suggests "don't call out if you have a question" the teacher would re-state that positively by saying "that's right; instead of calling out we should raise our hand and wait to be called on if we have a question." Then, the teacher would record a shorthand version of that expectation on the graphic organizer (e.g., raise hand).

After students have generated several ideas for classroom expectations, the next step is to group these into categories that align with the three to five expectations the teacher has previously identified. It's helpful to use different colored markers to correspond with each expectation, and teachers should "think aloud" as they group similar items. For example, a teacher might say, "I see a few items on our web that are related to responsibility. Hanging up your belongings when you enter the classroom, completing your work on time, and writing your homework assignments in your planner are all behaviors that demonstrate responsibility. Are there any other behaviors on our web that are related to responsibility?" Depending on students' needs, it may be necessary to define *responsibility* (or whatever the umbrella term is). After circling all of the related behaviors, the teacher should then write the expectation (i.e., Be Responsible) on the chart paper. This procedure should be used until all of the classroom expectations have been covered and the graphic organizer should be posted in the classroom. As a way to further create ownership, some teachers invite students to write or sign their name on the web. It is important to tell students that even if they choose not to sign the web, the classroom expectations still apply.

The next step in establishing expectations is to create an expectation matrix (Robbie et al., 2022); see Figure 2.2 for a matrix template. In this matrix, each expectation is clearly described across a variety of activities and environments. The idea is simple. We've just defined some behaviors that show how to meet a given expectation (e.g., to be responsible). Now we want to make sure students understand how they demonstrate responsibility in different contexts throughout the day. The matrix should include expectations for instructional routines (e.g., independent learning stations, whole group instruction), transition times (e.g., lining up, packing at the end of the day), and other areas of the building as it is appropriate for your students (e.g., cafeteria, hallway, bus). Creating the matrix can be done as an instructional activity with the class; or, the teacher can create the matrix and then review it with students once it is finished. Either way, as we have noted, it is critical that teachers find the time to teach and practice the behavioral expectations, which are covered in Chapter 3. To further support you as you develop your classroom expectations matrix, we have provided a completed planning template (see Figure 2.1). Additionally, we have included a self-assessment checklist (see Figure 2.3) that addresses each step for establishing expectations and leaves room to self-reflect on your implementation efforts.

What Do I Need to Begin Establishing Expectations?

Creating clear expectations requires very little advanced preparation and relatively few materials. The first thing a teacher needs to do to begin is to think about the broad behavioral expectations he or she wants to emphasize in the classroom. We have suggested that students should be active participants in establishing rules and expectations, and their voices should be heard and perspectives valued. Nonetheless, it is quite appropriate for the teacher to think in advance of the broad concepts that probably need to be stressed to create a safe, supportive, respectful, and well-functioning learning environment. Having these broad ideas in mind in advance of the activity involving students will help the teacher shape and guide the discussion. As we also noted, a good starting place would be to connect classroom expectations to broader existing school-wide expectations if possible.

Once the teacher has an idea of the three to five classroom expectations that will be emphasized, all that is needed is a large piece of chart paper, markers, and the expectation matrix template. This activity can also be completed electronically on an interactive board or using a projector, but afterward, teachers should make physical posters of the expectations that can be clearly displayed in the classroom.

Something else to consider when setting expectations is how students will be reinforced for demonstrating the expected behaviors (see Section 3 of this book). We suggest that teachers explain to students how and why they will be reinforced (e.g., earning tickets for demonstrating behaviors in the matrix) and what the reinforcement earns (e.g., time doing a preferred activity). Introducing the class-wide reinforcement system early in the year is ideal for everyone: students are set up for success, and teachers save time by reducing the likelihood that a chaotic or disorderly environment will emerge in their classroom.

What Does Establishing Expectations look Like in a Classroom?

Although establishing expectations will look slightly different across grade levels and classroom environments (e.g., a general education classroom, an art class, a special education classroom), the core components will look very similar. Below, we provide two examples of what it may look like to establish expectations in a classroom. In the first example, Mr. Rodriguez is a second grade inclusion teacher who frequently uses small-group collaborative activities in his classroom. In the second example, Ms. Woodward and Ms. Smith are team teachers in seventh grade, so students spend half of their time in one classroom and half in the other.

Elementary Example
Mr. Rodriguez began the year establishing expectations using the process described in this chapter: he began with a whole-class brainstorming activity, wrote ideas on a web-style graphic organizer, and then grouped the students' ideas into the school-wide expectations – be responsible, be respectful, be safe. For the most part, his students did an excellent job following the expectations that were set at the beginning of the year. However, a few months after school started, Mr. Rodriguez began implementing small-group collaboration activities for his students to do while he led small-group instruction during reading and math. He noticed that the volume in his classroom was increasing during small-group instruction (and things seemed to be getting louder and louder each day). Students began interrupting him while he was teaching small groups more frequently, and minor conflicts between students also began to rise. Mr. Rodriguez realized that it would be beneficial to basically repeat the procedures used for establishing expectations at the beginning of the year, with a focus this time on expectations for small-group instructional time (see Figure 2.1 for a completed sample that includes Mr. Rodriguez's work from the start of the year, as well as a new column focused on small-group expectations).

Expectation Matrix Template

SCHOOL EXPECTATIONS	SETTING/ROUTINE					
	Entering our classroom	Whole Group Instruction	Independent Work	Tests & Quizzes	Dismissal	Small Group Instruction
Be responsible	• Bring all materials • Arrive on time	• Listen actively • Have only needed materials out	• Stay on task • Raise hand to ask for help if needed	• Stay on task • Try your best • Raise hand for help	• Clean your desk/area • Bring materials home	• Follow checklists • Use timer
Be respectful	• Sit in assigned seat • Follow voice level on board	• Follow directions given by speaker • Follow the voice level	• Focus on your own work • Follow voice level	• Focus on your own work • Follow voice level 0	• Wait your turn to leave the class • Follow voice level 2	• Take turns sharing • Use soft voices • Limit interruptions
Be safe	• Keep hands and feet to self • Walk in classroom	• Keep four on the floor • Keep hands and feet to self	• Keep four on the floor • Keep hands and feet to self	• Keep four on the floor • Keep hands and feet to self	• Wait to be dismissed • Walk in the classroom and hallway	• Use materials appropriately • Use timer

FIGURE 2.1 Completed Example of Establishing Expectations Planning Template

Mr. Rodriguez leads a whole-class discussion and brainstorming activity where students share their ideas about what behavior should look like when they are working with their peers. Ultimately, the class generates expectations for small-group instructional time that are anchored in the school-wide expectations. For example, the expectation to "be responsible" means that students use the task checklists that Mr. Rodriguez presents before small group time, and they keep an eye on the classroom timer to monitor their progress toward completing their assignments. To "be respectful" during small-group instruction means that while students don't need to raise their hands to be called on by their peers, they still should take turns sharing ideas by waiting for their classmates to finish talking before they join in and by using soft voices, so it doesn't get too loud. It also means that students respect everyone's learning by limiting their interruptions of Mr. Rodriguez while he is teaching; they should interrupt him only for issues that are related to safety or personal well-being (and they discuss examples of what this is and is not!). Finally, to "be safe" during small-group time, students are reminded that materials such as math manipulatives and scissors are for learning activities only, and that if they are not used properly (e.g., thrown at another student), they could hurt someone. Mr. Rodriguez also implements strategies to support students in their success. For example, to help students "be respectful" regarding the volume of their voice, Mr. Rodriguez decides to play classical music. If students cannot hear the music, it is a signal that the volume in the classroom has become too loud and students need to soften their voices. Mr. Rodriguez briefly reviews the expectations for small-group instruction before every session – this takes less than one minute and is an excellent pre-correction (see Chapter 8). Following this simple review of expectations, and the clarifications about how this applies to small-group instructional time, Mr. Rodriguez is amazed by how quickly the behavior during these instructional times improves. He is pleased with the amount of instructional time he has gained because he is spending less time managing behaviors and more time teaching.

Secondary Example

Ms. Woodward and Ms. Smith teach the same group of eighth grade students – Ms. Woodward teaches English and History, Ms. Smith teaches Math and Science. To help create cohesion across their classrooms, Ms. Woodward and Ms. Smith use the same class-wide reinforcement system (see Chapters 10–12) in which students earn "Dolphin Dollars" for following expectations. Once each quarter, there is a class store where they can purchase items, such as snacks, books, fun school supplies, and other items. However, the expectations across their classroom are slightly different. For example, Ms. Woodward doesn't mind when students socialize and walk around the room as they are entering class, but in Ms. Smith's class, there are often materials for science experiments setup around the room, so she prefers students take a seat at their desks as soon as they enter the classroom. These are small differences, but explicitly setting these expectations ahead of time and explaining to students that the school-wide expectation to "be safe" looks different in a science classroom than in an English classroom sets students up for success.

Final Thoughts

In this chapter, we discussed the importance of establishing clear expectations for students in the classroom and ideally connecting these expectations to school-wide expectations. We described how teachers can engage students in developing expectations, and how teachers can then group students' ideas to create between three and five expectations for their classroom. We talked about the importance of defining how these expectations look across the learning environment (e.g., the difference between expectations during whole-group and small-group instruction).

We hope that we have made it clear that although there is a need for consistency and clarity, there will often be different expectations for different instructional periods. For example, during whole-class instruction, students may be expected to be respectful by remaining in their seat and quietly looking at and listening to the teacher or speaker. In the upper grades, especially, most students spend time in more than one classroom on most days. It is almost certain that the expectations of different teachers across these classrooms will vary, sometimes in significant ways. In this sense, it is easy to see how students come to regard some teachers as more 'strict' than others. And while general consistency across classrooms is a desirable goal, some natural variation in expectations is quite common, and this should not create major problems. For example, some teachers might allow students to quietly talk to others during independent practice, yet other teachers might expect that students who are working independently are not talking at all.

Just as kids come to view some teachers as more strict than others, they also learn very quickly to adapt to these varying expectations across environments. The real key here is that expectations are consistent (or consistently applied, to be more precise) *within* a given context. Working to overtly define and teach expectations for each classroom or context, rather than simply waiting for students to figure them out clearly helps students understand that there are different norms and requirements in different environments. As always, the important element in supporting students is that teachers work to establish these expectations explicitly, and then to reinforce behavior that meets them.

References

Alter, P., & Haydon, T. (2017). Characteristics of effective classroom rules: A review of the literature. *Teacher Education and Special Education*, 40(2), 114–127.

Croce, K. M., & Salter, J. S. (2022, May). Beyond the walls: Establishing classroom expectations in a virtual classroom. *Frontiers in education*, 7, 816007.

Hester, P. P., Hendrickson, J. M., & Gable, R. A. (2009). Forty years later— The value of praise, ignoring, and rules for preschoolers at risk for behavior disorders. *Education and Treatment of Children*, 32(4), 513–535.

Myers, D., Freeman, J., Simonsen, B., & Sugai, G. (2017). Classroom management with exceptional learners. *Teaching Exceptional Children*, *49*(4), 223–230.

Pianta, R. C., Hamre, B., & Stuhlman, M. (2003). Relationships between teachers and children. In W. M. Reynolds & G. E. Miller (Eds.), *Handbook of psychology: Educational psychology*, (Vol. 7, pp. 199–234). John Wiley & Sons, Inc. https://doi.org/10.1002/0471264385.wei0710

Robbie, K., Santiago-Rosario, M. A. R. I. A., Yanek, K., Kern, L., Meyer, B., Morris, K., & Simonsen, B. (2022). Creating a classroom teaching matrix [Practice brief]. Center on Positive Behavioral Interventions and Supports.

Simonsen, B., Freeman, J., Gambino, A. J., Sears, S., Meyer, K., & Hoselton, R. (2022). An exploration of the relationship between PBIS and discipline outcomes for students with disabilities. *Remedial and Special Education*, *43*(5), 287–300.

Sutherland, K. S., Conroy, M. A., McLeod, B. D., Kunemund, R., & McKnight, K. (2019). Common practice elements for improving social, emotional, and behavioral outcomes of young elementary school students. *Journal of Emotional and Behavioral Disorders*, *27*(2), 76–85. https://doi.org/10.1177/1063426618784009

Establishing Expectations ◆ 29

Expectation Matrix Template

SCHOOL EXPECTATIONS	SETTING/ROUTINE					

FIGURE 2.2 Establishing Expectations Planning Template

Establishing Expectations Steps & Self-Assessment			
0→Not in Place 1→Partially in Place 2→Fully in Place			
STEPS	**How Did I do?**		
1. Establish three to five expectations for the classroom, ideally aligned to schoolwide expectations.	☐ 0	☐ 1	☐ 2
2. Collaborate with students to brainstorm possible classroom expectations.	☐ 0	☐ 1	☐ 2
3. Categorize student ideas into the three to five identified classroom expectations.	☐ 0	☐ 1	☐ 2
4. Create an expectations matrix that defines how students can meet each expectation across different contexts and routines.	☐ 0	☐ 1	☐ 2
Notes & Reflection:			

FIGURE 2.3 Establishing Expectations Implementation and Self-Assessment Checklist

3

Explicit Instruction

In this chapter, we explain how and why explicit instruction can be used to teach behavioral expectations. We begin by providing a definition and description of this practice, followed by a brief overview of the research that supports the use of this practice. Next, we explain how explicit instruction in behavioral expectations can build positive relationships with students, particularly those who demonstrate challenging behaviors. Finally, we describe how to implement this practice and provide two examples of what this practice might look like in a classroom. The supplemental resources for this chapter include a planning template (one blank for your use and one completed as an example) and a self-assessment checklist to support implementation fidelity.

What Is Explicit Instruction?

When you read the term "explicit instruction," you may very likely think of teaching academics and wonder why we have selected this as a strategy to highlight in a book about improving student behavior and building positive relationships with students. If the term explicit instruction does prompt you to think about teaching academic skills, that's probably because that is how explicit instruction is most commonly used in education. This association is helpful, though, because thinking about how we teach academic skills is exactly how we encourage teachers to think about teaching behavioral skills. In fact, one of the main points we make when teaching our pre-service college students and delivering professional development to in-service teachers is that behavioral skills should be taught just like academics. This point is so important that we probably make it (more than once) in every class session and professional development where we talk about improving student behavior.

Explicit instruction, also known as direct instruction, is a direct and systematic approach to providing students with the information they need in order to successfully learn a skill. Teachers who use explicit instruction provide modeling, guided practice, independent practice, increased opportunities for students to engage (with the material, the teacher, and one another), and feedback. Rather than telling students what to do, teachers who engage in explicit instruction *show* students how to do it.

One reason explicit instruction is so important for teaching behavior is that it helps students understand exactly what teachers mean when they share behavioral expectations. Unlike academic skills, it is easy to fall into the trap of thinking students come to school knowing how to behave, particularly if they are older. However, as you have likely experienced, students come to school with a wide variety of backgrounds. These backgrounds include cultural and linguistic diversity, disabilities that can impact behavioral performance, and differences in school experiences. Although it is likely that many (probably most) of the students in a classroom will understand what a teacher means when they say "line up at the door for lunch" or "walk safely down the hallway," there are some students who will need more explicit instruction regarding what exactly it means to "line up" (think about an English Learner who might be unfamiliar with the expression) or "walk safely" (consider a student who has never been to school before, and does not realize that safely walking in the hallway means stopping at the corners to make sure no one else is coming). This can become even more complicated with the broader expectations we often share, such as "be respectful" or "be responsible," in which the meaning of those characteristics can vary greatly across different cultures.

To illustrate this point, we share a real-life example from one of our colleagues (with permission of course) that has resonated with us over the years. Our friend was homeschooled for the first few years of her education and in her homeschool community, independence was not only encouraged, but it was expected and reinforced. She began attending public school in second grade, and one day at recess, the ball she was playing with went over the fence, so she climbed the fence and got the ball, but when she returned to the playground she was told that she broke a rule by climbing the fence. She recalls being genuinely confused because she did what would have been expected in her culture: she exerted independence and solved her own problem. The next day, she returned to the playground and again, the ball went over the fence. She remembered from the previous day that climbing the fence was not allowed, so this time, she walked around the fence to get the ball. When she returned to the playground, she learned that yet again, she had violated one of the rules. Our friend was fortunate to have a teacher who recognized that her behavior was not an attempt to be defiant, but rather that she needed a bit more of an explanation about what the rules and expectations were during recess. Her teacher took the time to explain to her that the expectations at school were different from the expectations in her community, and that when she was at school it was okay (and encouraged) to ask an adult for help. She also explained the issue was not really about climbing the fence, but rather that she needed to stay in the enclosed playground area. In her home community, our friend demonstrated responsibility by solving her own problems; at recess, the responsible choice would have been to ask an adult to help retrieve the ball. Once our friend understood the expectations at school, she was able to follow them successfully and did not have any more "behavior problems" moving forward.

Knowing that students have diverse backgrounds and understandings of what constitutes acceptable or appropriate behavior, we advocate for teachers to approach classroom management and behavior with the assumption that all students will benefit from an explanation, rather than waiting for a student to struggle and then correcting the behavior. Beginning with explicit instruction in behavioral expectations provides the foundation for using a positive and preventive approach to behavior management, and it is the most effective way to teach students about the behavior that is expected in the various environments that they will encounter across their school day (see Chapter 2). Of course, just like with academic skills, some students (again, probably most students) will grasp the behavioral expectations the first time they are explained and demonstrated; other students will need additional practice and support.

How Do I Know Explicit Instruction Works

The research supporting the effectiveness of explicit instruction is some of the strongest research in the field of education. When thinking about the research that supports explicit instruction, we think it is important to briefly consider the history of this approach (Mason & Otero, 2021). Direct Instruction (commonly referred to as "big DI") is credited to the work of Siegfried ("Zig") Engelmann and Carl Bereiter in the late 1960s, whose focus was on improving outcomes of students from disadvantaged backgrounds by developing an approach to teaching in which the teacher's behaviors are carefully sequenced to include high rates of student responding. In practice, big DI is typically seen in the form of scripted lessons, in which the instruction, prompting, and feedback that students receive is formally outlined. The characteristics of big DI are reflected in a broader instructional approach known as direct instruction (commonly referred to as "little di"). The origins of little di are often credited to Rosenshine (1976), who identified several teacher behaviors as being the most impactful for student achievement. Specifically, Rosenshine described direct instruction as an approach that includes the systematic organization and presentation of material and lessons that are led in a "business like" (p. 66) format. This format includes clear goals and directions, questions with one correct answer, and immediate feedback. Another characteristic that is especially important for the context of this book is that Rosenshine described little di as being "warm and convivial" (p. 66) because of frequent praise and feedback, despite the high-level organization and seemingly rigid teacher behavior. Research on both big DI and little di has yielded consistently strong and positive effects on student outcomes, and this has been evident for several decades (Mason & Otero, 2021).

Rosenshine (2012) later summarized research on cognitive science, the behavior of master teachers, and cognitive supports to identify ten instructional principles that seemed most consistent with research and effective practice. These principles reflect characteristics of explicit instruction, and can be applied to teaching behavior in the same way they are applied to teaching academics. The ten characteristics are: (1) review background knowledge; (2) deliver instruction in small steps that include opportunities to practice; (3) include several questions and opportunities to respond; (4) model; (5) provide guided practice; (6) frequently assess understanding; (7) teach skills until mastery (e.g., to a high level of accurate responding, typically 80%); (8) use scaffolds; (9) provide independent practice with monitoring and feedback; and (10) include consistent (i.e., monthly or weekly) review of skills.

In contemporary education, the terms "direct instruction" (little di) and "explicit instruction" are used more or less interchangeably (Hughes et al., 2017). Explicit instruction can be defined as

> an unambiguous and direct approach to teaching that includes both instructional design and delivery procedures. Explicit instruction is characterized by a series of supports or scaffolds, whereby students are guided through the learning process with clear statements about the purpose and rationale for learning the new skill, clear explanations and demonstrations of the instructional target, and supported practice with feedback until independent mastery has been achieved.
> (Archer & Hughes, 2010, p. 1)

Archer and Hughes (2010) identified 16 elements of explicit instruction. We interpret those elements as they relate to behavioral instruction to be: (1) instruction is focused on critical skills; (2) skills are taught in a logical sequence; (3) complex skills are broken into small steps; (4) lessons are organized and focused on specific skills; (5) goals and expectations are clearly stated at the beginning of a lesson; (6) prior knowledge is activated or built before instruction; (7) demonstrations are provided using step-by-step modeling; (8) clear and concise language is used; (9) examples and non-examples are provided; (10) guided practice and feedback are provided; (11) high rates of student responses are elicited; (12) student progress is frequently monitored; (13) corrective feedback and specific praise are provided; (14) instruction occurs at a brisk pace; (15) students are supported in organizing and generalizing knowledge; (16) opportunities to practice occur over time and across settings. In the sections that follow, you will see these elements reflected as we discuss the implementation of explicit instruction to teach students behavioral skills.

How Does Explicit Instruction Build Positive Relationships with My Students?

Think back to the example we shared about our friend who needed explicit instruction to demonstrate the behavioral expectations during recess. Upon realizing that our friend was having a hard time, her teacher took the time to talk to her and explicitly teach her the expectations. We think that this reaction shows immense care and concern from the teacher to the student and in fact, our friend often talks about this teacher as being one of the most influential teachers in her life. When teachers use explicit instruction to teach behavior, especially when used proactively and positively (recall the high rates of accurate responding, along with positive feedback on performance), it helps build positive relationships with students in many ways. Specifically, explicit instruction in behavioral expectations can help students feel safe and secure in their environment, as they know what is expected of them and what to expect in return for their behavior (e.g., reinforcement). Moreover, when students know what is expected of them and how to demonstrate those expectations, there are more opportunities for teachers to provide positive reinforcement, which thus increases the number of positive student-teacher interactions.

How Do I Implement Explicit Instruction in My Classroom?

While Rosenshine (2012) and Archer and Hughes (2010) described numerous features, principles, and characteristics of effective instruction, these can be distilled into six elements of effective teaching (Rosenshine & Stevens, 1986) that can be used to guide the implementation of explicit instruction:

1. review prerequisite skills and background knowledge;
2. present the lesson;
3. provide guided practice;
4. provide corrective feedback and praise;
5. provide independent practice; and
6. provide frequent review

We have provided a planning template to help guide you through this process (see Figures 3.1 and 3.2), but it is important to remember that the "cycle" of explicit instruction is not always linear – after modeling and guided practice, for example, a teacher may recognize that she needs to return to the modeling phase and demonstrate the behavior again. Or, if a student is struggling with independent practice, the teacher may need to provide a few more guided practice opportunities. We encourage teachers to use their professional judgment in determining if any of the instructional stages need to be revisited. We have also provided a self-assessment to guide reflection as teachers implement each element of explicit instruction with students (see Figure 3.3). In the sections that follow, we describe how the six elements of explicit instruction (Archer & Hughes, 2010; Rosenshine & Stevens, 1986) can be applied in the classroom.

Element 1: Review prerequisite skills and background knowledge. When using explicit instruction, we suggest that teachers begin by talking about the concept or skill that they are going to teach in student friendly terms, explain why it is important for students to learn the material, and then make a connection to students' background knowledge. If students don't have background information, teachers can provide it in a variety of ways, such as by showing a brief video, reading a story aloud, or sharing pictures. For example, before teaching students about the behavior that is expected in the library, a teacher might say something like "Today we will be going to the library, which is a place we can visit to find books we want to read for fun or to help us learn about new topics. Usually in the library, people are trying to read, so it's important to be respectful by using a quiet voice. I'm going to read a short story about Paul, a little boy who visits the library for the first time. As I read, I want you to think about ways that you might relate to Paul." This process helps students connect the information that they are about to learn to information they already know or to past experiences. This is also a time to review any skills that a student already has that will support them in learning the new behavior. For example, a teacher might say, "I've seen you use a quiet voice in our classroom when you need help while other students are working. This is the same voice you should use in the library."

Element 2: Present the lesson. The presentation of the lesson should begin by clearly stating the learning goals (e.g., "Today we are going to learn...."). After that, there are a few "rules of thumb" for presenting lessons using explicit instruction: skills that a student needs to learn should be chunked into small and manageable steps; the teacher should use clear and concise language and should stick to the main points, rather than digressing into related topics or lengthy explanations.

A critical piece of presenting a lesson using an explicit instruction approach is to use modeling and to provide examples and non-examples. During modeling, the teacher shows students exactly what the behavior should look like by demonstrating examples and non-examples. Consider a common elementary classroom routine of sitting on the carpet during a read-aloud lesson. Prior to inviting students to the carpet, a teacher should explain the purpose of the activity (e.g., tell students why they will be listening to a particular story, such as to compare and contrast characters). The teacher would begin by reviewing expectations, such as pushing in chairs, walking in the classroom, keeping hands in your own space, and raising hands and waiting to be called on. Then, the teacher would demonstrate these behaviors as he thinks through them out loud. For example, the teacher would take a seat near a student's desk and say something like, "I just heard Mr. Tong call my table to the carpet. I'm going to quietly stand up without talking to my friend or making any extra noises with my mouth, push in my chair, and walk to the carpet. Now that I'm on the carpet, I'm going to take a seat and sit criss-cross applesauce. I am going to imagine a small circle around my body. This small circle (Mr. Tong demonstrates with hands) is my personal space. I'm going to show respect to my classmates by keeping my hands and feet to myself, in my personal space so that everyone has room to sit and learn. If my hands and feet are here (Mr. Tong demonstrates), they are in my own space. If my hands and feet are like this (Mr. Tong demonstrates a non-example) or like this (Mr. Tong demonstrates another non-example), they are not in my personal space. When I have a question or a thought about the story I would like to share, I am going to raise my hand like this (Mr. Tong demonstrates) and wait for Mr. Tong to call on me." After modeling, Mr. Tong will demonstrate a few examples and non-examples of the key behaviors (pushing in a chair, walking quietly, keeping hands and feet in personal space, and raising a hand) and ask students to identify if his behaviors align with the expectations.

Notice in this example that Mr. Tong modeled examples and non-examples of the expected behavior – he showed students exactly what it should look like to keep their hands and feet in their own area, as well as what it does not look like. Something else that Mr. Tong did to help students is he thought aloud through the transition of moving from a desk to the carpet area. Thinking aloud through behaviors in this way is helpful for students in a few ways. First, it makes his choices obvious. It could be easy for a student to see him stand up, push in his chair, and start walking but not connect that he is purposely staying quiet. Second, his think-aloud used academic vocabulary to connect his behavior to the overall expectation of being respectful to classmates. These two things – demonstrating examples/non-examples and thinking aloud, are integral to high-quality teacher modeling.

Element 3: Provide guided practice. After explicitly modeling behavioral expectations for students, the next step is to allow students an opportunity to practice with guidance from the teacher. During this phase of instruction, the teacher's goal is to ensure that students have several opportunities to respond and practice behavior successfully (Archer & Hughes, 2010).

For this step, imagine a ninth-grade teacher who is preparing her homeroom to attend a pep-rally for the first time. After teaching students the school cheer, and modeling behaviors expected at the pep-rally, she then gives her students an opportunity to practice what they have learned. The day before the pep-rally, the teacher walks her students to the gym and talks them through the behaviors, saying something like, "Okay, now that we are at the gym, we are going to wait outside until we hear Ms. Davis (the PE teacher) call our class. Let's pretend we just heard her, and now let's enter the gym. Remember, you can clap as you enter, but this isn't a time to yell or cheer." Once the class has entered the gym and walked to the bleachers, the teacher continues, "Alright, now who remembers where our class will sit? Yes, David, that's correct. We are in the third section of bleachers, rows 5 and 6. Go ahead and find your seats, remembering to stay in line. You will probably see your friends from other classes, so if you can give them a quick high-five or fist-bump *without* getting out of line, that's perfectly fine. Otherwise, you'll have to wave." As students take their seats, the teacher then says something along the lines of, "I see everyone is sitting in rows 5 and 6. Who can remind us of the two big rules for sitting in bleachers? Yes, Maya, that's right! We need to refrain from putting our feet on the row in front of us and from leaning back into the row behind us so that everyone has space – it's going to get crowded." After students are seated, the teacher gives them an opportunity to practice the school cheer and then walks them through exiting the pep-rally, highlighting behaviors related to safety, such as walking (not running or jumping) down the bleachers.

Element 4: Provide corrective feedback and specific praise. A very critical component of explicit instruction is that students are provided with feedback on their demonstration of the behaviors, especially in the guided practice and independent practice phases. When students are meeting the behavioral expectations, teachers should use behavior-specific praise, such as "Ruthie, you're doing a great job keeping your hands and feet in your own area" (see Chapter 10). Teachers may also choose to reinforce students individually using a token economy (Chapter 11) or as a whole class using a positive group contingency (Chapter 12). When students do not demonstrate the behavioral expectations, teachers should use immediate and corrective feedback, such as "Parker, I noticed you jumped down the bleachers. Let's try this one more time, focusing on safety by walking down each step – I've seen some bad falls over the years and I don't want that to happen in our class." Notice the difference in the corrective feedback example we just provided, versus a teacher who says something along the lines of "Parker, cut it out" or "Seriously, Parker. Stop goofing-off when you come down the bleachers." In our example, the teacher told the student exactly where the behavioral misstep was, and even gave a quick explanation for why the behavior is important. Corrective and positive feedback is crucial for student learning, and it also supports the formation of a positive, student-teacher relationship.

Element 5: Provide independent practice. During the independent practice phase, students have an opportunity to engage in the behaviors that were just taught. In the examples above, the students would practice transitioning from their seats to the carpet or entering and exiting the gym for a pep-rally. Note here that the practice opportunity (or opportunities if more than one is needed) should occur before the students need to demonstrate the behavior in an applied context. For these examples, this means students would practice before they are actually going to the carpet for a read-aloud and before the pep-rally. The key here is that the first opportunity to demonstrate the expectations in context should not be the first time the students are asked to demonstrate the behaviors on their own.

Element 6: Provide frequent reviews. Maintaining (i.e., continuing to demonstrate) and generalizing (i.e., demonstrating in new settings) new behavioral skills can be especially difficult for students with or at risk for challenging behaviors. Therefore, it is important for teachers to provide opportunities for students to practice the skills they have learned over time, and across settings. The general recommendation for this is that students should have opportunities to review new skills weekly or monthly, depending on where they are in their ability to consistently demonstrate the behavioral expectations. For behaviors that occur more often, students will likely need fewer opportunities for formal review because there are natural opportunities to practice. On the other hand, behaviors that are needed for situations that occur less frequently will likely need to be practiced more.

What Does Explicit Instruction look Like in a Classroom?

Like many of the strategies presented in this book, explicit instruction in behavioral expectations can occur for all students, some students, or individual students, depending on their needs. In this section, we provide two examples of explicit instruction, one at the whole class level because all students can benefit, and one at the individual level.

Elementary Example (Whole Class)

Mrs. Darst is a kindergarten grade teacher who has over a decade of teaching experience at Green Gable Elementary School. The students who attend Green Gable come from a variety of backgrounds and her class is usually a mixture of students who have attended the public school pre-kindergarten program, students who have attended private preschool, and students who have not had any formal schooling experience. To ensure that students are set up for success, Mrs. Darst spends time on the first day of school explicitly teaching the behaviors that students need to know. One behavior that is always challenging for Mrs. Darst's kindergarteners is walking down the hallway in a single-file line. Many of the students have not had to walk down a hallway in a large school before, and even those who had that experience in the public school pre-kindergarten program have not had a lot of it. That said, there are typically a few students who attended public school pre-kindergarten and have a solid understanding of the behavior; while these students still benefit from additional practice, they may also help serve as role models for some of the other students. Since everyone in her class can benefit, Mrs. Darst decides to use explicit instruction to teach her students how to walk down the halls.

She starts by pretending that the front of her classroom is a hallway, using the wall in the front of the classroom to simulate a wall in the hall. Mrs. Darst begins by saying, "Right now, I am pretending that I am in the hallway. Ms. Butler (the teaching assistant) is going to stand in front of me. I want you to notice that my feet are not touching the back of Ms. Butler's feet, but I'm also not really far away from her; I'm about two hands away (Mrs. Darst uses her hands to show the space). My hands are by my side; they are not touching the wall because a lot of times, other teachers will hang their students' work on the wall, and we don't want to mess it up. I am facing forward so that I can see where I am going and so that I don't bump into Ms. Butler if she stops. My lips are going to be closed because it's really important to be quiet in the hallway so that we don't disrupt other students who are trying to learn. Here is what it should look like." Mrs. Darst follows Ms. Butler, walking around the classroom and narrating her behaviors. Then, Mrs. Darst and Ms. Butler provide a few non-examples (e.g., standing too close to one another, running a finger down the wall) and they ask the students to tell them why their behavior didn't match the expectations. After modeling the behavior, Mrs. Darst asks her students to line up at the door to practice walking to the end of the hallway. Before exiting the classroom, she says a rhyme to help them remember the expectations: My hands are by my side, I'm standing straight and tall. Eyes ahead, mouth is closed, I'm ready for the hall. Then, as students begin to walk down the hall, Mrs. Darst states the expectations out loud, provides specific praise to those who are exhibiting the behavioral expectations and corrective feedback for students who need support. After the class has walked up and down the hall a few times with Mrs. Darst's guidance, they return to the classroom. Then, they start from the beginning (including saying the rhyme), and practice walking down the hallway without prompting from Mrs. Darst; Mrs. Darst continues to provide positive and corrective feedback throughout the independent practice opportunity.

Secondary Example (Individual Student)

Elliot is a seventh grade student who has autism; he has attended the same school since kindergarten and has had the same special education teacher. This year, however, Elliot has a new teacher, Mr. Thomas, who notices that when Elliot buys a snack at the snack-bar in the afternoons, he hands the cashier his entire wallet. This has worked for Elliot for a long time because the cashiers who work the snack-bar know him; they are honest and caring people who help Elliot by taking out his money and then returning the wallet to him. While this is fine for school, Mr. Thomas has concerns about the social appropriateness of this behavior and decides that he wants to teach Elliot how to pay for his snacks without giving his entire wallet to the cashier (see Figure 3.1 for Mr. Thomas's completed planning template). Mr. Thomas explains to Elliot that not all cashiers are going to be as honest as the cashiers in his school, so it is important for him to learn how to pay for things without using his entire wallet. That afternoon, Mr. Thomas and Elliot head to the snack-bar and Mr. Thomas models the behavior and says "Okay, it's time to pay. I'm going to take my wallet out of my back pocket, just like you do, Elliot. I'm going to open my wallet and find my money... here it is! I have three dollars in my wallet. My snack is only two dollars, so I am going to only take out the money that I need and leave the rest. Elliot, how many dollars will I take out? That's right, two. And how many dollars will be left? Yes, one dollar will stay in my wallet. I'm going to hand my money to the cashier and put my wallet back in my pocket. Now it's your turn to try." Mr. Thomas verbally prompts Elliot through the same steps as he purchases his snack, and he continues to provide prompting for a few more days until Elliot seems to have the hang of it.

Once Elliot is ready for independent practice, Mr. Thomas goes to the snack-bar but gives Elliot space to try paying on his own. He stays close enough that he can see and hear the

Explicit Instruction Planning Template

Describe the behavioral skill or expectation:
Elliot will learn to appropriately take out his wallet, get out the correct amount of money, and pay the cashier when purchasing snacks.

Elements
Describe all elements in specific detail, including how they will be introduced to the student.

PREREQUISITE SKILLS & BACKGROUND KNOWLEDGE	**Why skill/concept is important:** Social appropriateness; not all cashiers will help Elliot or be honest if given his whole wallet. Paying for purchases appropriately is an important independent living skill. **Methods to activate background knowledge:** Talk with him about times he's been to the store and what he's seen other people do. Watch a video model of someone checking out at a store. **Skills to review:** Basics of money; social story of interactions in the checkout line
LESSON	**Learning goals:** I can check out successfully at the snack bar by getting the appropriate amount of money out of my wallet and giving it to the cashier. **Skill steps:** 1. Submit order at snack bar. 2. Wait for cashier to give the total amount. 3. Take enough money out of wallet. 4. Hand money to cashier. 5. Accept change if any is owed. 6. Put change and wallet away in pocket. **Examples:** / **Non-examples:** Taking just the right amount of money out of the wallet (model different amounts) / Giving entire wallet to cashier. Giving all money to cashier. Giving too little money to cashier.
GUIDED PRACTICE	**Method for providing guided practice:** Go with Elliot to the snack bar and provide some visual cues (e.g., hold up my wallet in my hand) when needed as well as corrective feedback as he checks out.
FEEDBACK	**Reinforcement method:** Behavior specific praise
INDEPENDENT PRACTICE	**Method for providing independent practice:** Fade out my presence, at first standing farther away, then sending Elliot to the snack bar on his own (and checking in with the cashier after to assess his skill performance)
REVIEW	**Timeline for skill review:** Brief weekly review for a few weeks after Elliot is performing the skill independently, then fade to monthly after Elliot has a successful month

FIGURE 3.1 Completed Example of Explicit Instruction Planning Template

interactions and provide corrective feedback if needed, but far enough away that he isn't hovering over Elliot. After a successful transaction, Mr. Thomas provides specific praise to Elliot ("You did a great job taking out the money you need and keeping the rest in your wallet") and after a week of successfully and independently purchasing his snacks, Mr. Thomas decides that Elliot is ready to go to the snack-bar without supervision.

Final Thoughts

In this chapter, we described how explicit instruction can (and should) be used to teach students behavioral expectations. We described the cycle of explicit instruction (modeling, guided practice, independent practice, and feedback) and emphasized three ways to deliver high-quality, explicit instruction: explaining the need for the behavior to students by activating or providing background knowledge; sharing examples and non-examples of the behavior; and thinking aloud while demonstrating the behavior. We provided several examples of what explicit instruction in behavior looks like in a classroom. Although these examples may seem extreme (Do students really need to be taught how to walk down the hallway?), we encourage teachers to remember that students enter their classrooms from a wide variety of backgrounds and experiences, which means that they have different understandings of how to demonstrate the behavior that is expected in school. Providing explicit instruction in behavioral expectations is an excellent way to ensure that all students have the knowledge and understanding of the behavioral skills needed for success.

References

Archer, A. L., & Hughes, C. A. (2010). *Explicit instruction: Effective and efficient teaching.* Guilford Publications.

Hughes, C. A., Morris, J. R., Therrien, W. J., & Benson, S. K. (2017). Explicit instruction: Historical and contemporary contexts. *Learning Disabilities Research & Practice, 32*(3), 140–148.

Mason, L., & Otero, M. (2021). Just how effective is direct instruction?. *Perspectives on Behavior Science, 44*(2), 225–244. https://doi.org/10.1007/s40614-021-00295-x

Rosenshine, B. (1976). Recent research on teaching behaviors and student achievement. *Journal of Teacher Education, 27*(1), 61–64.

Rosenshine, B. (2012). Principles of instruction: Research-based strategies that all teachers should know. *American Educator, 36*(1), 12.

Rosenshine, B., & Stevens, R. (1986). Teaching functions. In M. C. Wittrock (Ed.), *Handbook of research on teaching* (3rd ed., pp. 376–391). Macmillan.

Explicit Instruction Planning Template		
Describe the behavioral skill or expectation:		
Elements *Describe all elements in specific detail, including how they will be introduced to the student.*		
PREREQUISITE SKILLS & BACKGROUND KNOWLEDGE	Why skill/concept is important: Methods to activate background knowledge: Skills to review:	
LESSON	Learning goals: Skill steps:	
	Examples:	Non-examples:
GUIDED PRACTICE	Method for providing guided practice:	
FEEDBACK	Reinforcement method:	
INDEPENDENT PRACTICE	Method for providing independent practice:	
REVIEW	Timeline for skill review:	

FIGURE 3.2 Explicit Instruction Planning Template

Explicit Instruction Elements & Self-Assessment			
0→Not in Place 1→Partially in Place 2→Fully in Place			
ELEMENTS	**How Did I do?**		
1. Review prerequisite skills and background knowledge.	☐ 0	☐ 1	☐ 2
2. Present the lesson.	☐ 0	☐ 1	☐ 2
3. Provide guided practice.	☐ 0	☐ 1	☐ 2
4. Provide corrective feedback and specific praise.	☐ 0	☐ 1	☐ 2
5. Provide independent practice.	☐ 0	☐ 1	☐ 2
6. Provide frequent reviews.	☐ 0	☐ 1	☐ 2
Notes & Reflection:			

FIGURE 3.3 Explicit Instruction Implementation and Self-Assessment Checklist

Part III
Encouraging Appropriate Behavior

4

Positive Greetings at the Door

In this chapter, we explain how and why positive greetings at the door (PGD) can be used to improve student behavior. We begin by providing a definition and description of this strategy, followed by a brief overview of the research that supports the use of this strategy. Next, we explain how PGD can build positive relationships with students, particularly those who demonstrate challenging behaviors. Finally, we describe how to implement this strategy and provide two examples of what this practice might look like in a classroom. The supplemental resources for this chapter include a planning template (one blank for your use and one completed as an example), guide questions for implementation, and a self-assessment checklist to support implementation fidelity.

What Is Positive Greetings at the Door?

Hearing the term "positive greetings at the door" probably makes one think that this must be a really simple strategy: you just greet students at the door in a positive manner, right? While that's partly true, the strategy we're talking about in this chapter includes a little more than that, and in fact was developed and tested with some very specific components. What researchers learned was that if teachers implement PGD following a few simple but specific steps, students tend to engage more quickly in their work or the task at hand (they get to work faster), they persist longer in the work once started (they keep working), and they engage in fewer disruptions and less problematic behavior. The strategy has three components, and importantly begins with the teacher standing at the door as students enter the classroom. We point this out because while a teacher can certainly greet students from anywhere in the room (e.g., sitting at your desk, prepping for a science experiment at the back of the classroom), this strategy depends heavily on this greeting occurring 1:1 *as students enter the classroom*. The next two steps are even more intentional. As we know from our own experience, it is easy to get distracted chatting with another teacher across the hall or next door while "going through the motions" of greeting students. But PGD is intentional, systematic, and individualized. To implement PGD, the teacher stands at the door and:

1. **Greets each student** by name as they arrive with a verbal (e.g., "Hi!" "Good morning, Kendrick") or non-verbal (fist-bump; high-five) greeting.
2. **Provides a positive statement that reinforces the student**, even if in the smallest way (e.g., "thanks for being on time!" "hey, looks like you remembered your book and notebook – nice job").
3. **Provides a prompt or precorrection** about what's going to happen in class that day. We'll say more about these in the next sections, but for now, a *prompt* is simply a suggestion about what the student needs to do first to be successful (e.g., "the challenge problem is on the board; just copy it down for now and you'll be ready to go"). A *precorrection* is a bit more specific, and used mostly when the teacher has seen trouble spots with particular students entering the classroom or getting started successfully. For example, if a student often wanders around the classroom when they first come in, or doesn't settle in well and get ready for class, a precorrect might be "remember to put your backpack in your cubby before you head to your desk with just your notebook."

How Do I Know Positive Greetings at the Door Works?

Some of the first research on PGD focused on some basic outcomes. In short, researchers wanted to know if it would help students engage more quickly and positively in the day's activities. Given the second and third steps in the process (a reinforcing statement and a prompt), this makes sense, and indeed that's exactly what was found. For example, Allday and Pakurar (2007), found that when teachers implemented the three simple steps we outlined above, students' rates of on-task behavior – engagement in their work – increased from about 45% before the procedure was used to over 70% once the teacher started using PGD. As these researchers stated, this is a really simple, easy-to-implement strategy that can result in noticeable and positive results almost immediately.

But, while things like getting to work and staying "on task" are important for kids to be successful, we also know that this is not the only outcome we desire. Partly because of this, researchers also wanted to know what other impacts PGD might have. Especially given that there is increasing evidence that relationships matter in classrooms (more positive relationships between teachers and students are associated with a host of improved academic, behavioral, and social outcomes), this has become a focus of additional research. And this made sense logically as well – wouldn't a positive greeting as kids enter classrooms set a more positive tone generally, and convey a sense of warmth and belonging? In fact, this too has been shown in more recent research. Cook and his colleagues (Cook et al., 2018) found that using PGD not only resulted in the behavioral and engagement outcomes other researchers had found, but that it also enhanced relationships between teachers and students. Given what we have described elsewhere about the importance of relationships in the context of managing classroom behavior in positive ways, PGD is increasingly viewed as a win-win approach. In short, its benefits for students' engagement, on-task behavior, decreased disruptions, *and* improved teacher-student relationships make it a highly recommended strategy.

How Does Positive Greetings at the Door Build Positive Relationships with My Students?

The argument here is pretty simple. By definition, using PGD means that a teacher will be greeting each individual student, by name and in a personal way, each time they enter the classroom. Compare that with what is more likely in classrooms, even with teachers who devote a lot of energy to greeting students in a positive way (e.g., "good morning everyone;" "Great to see you all ready to learn today!"). With PGD, as we describe below, the greetings are both 1:1 – the teacher takes a moment to greet each student individually, rather than the generic "good morning class" – and the greeting is individualized to the greatest extent possible. Noticing and acknowledging something positive about the individual child is highly consistent with what we know about how positive relationships are built and maintained.

How Do I Implement Positive Greetings at the Door in My Classroom?

As we noted, PGD is a simple, three-step strategy that is virtually self-explanatory in its implementation. Again, the teacher simply (1) greets students individually (1:1) at the door as they enter the classroom; (2) provides a positive/reinforcing statement; and (3) provides a prompt or precorrect. The process is described briefly in this section; in the next section we offer additional tips on some simple pre-planning that will help teachers individualize and implement PGD successfully, and then in the final section we offer examples of what PGD might look like in actual classroom scenarios.

The first step in implementing PGD obviously requires that the teacher is at the door! Thus, on any given day the teacher plans to implement this strategy, it is an absolute must that the teacher arranges to be at the doorway *before* any students enter the classroom and is able to stay at the door until all students have arrived. Note that this can be more complicated than it sounds – as any teacher knows, the unexpected happens, a lot, in schools and classrooms. A parent may show up unexpectedly with a question or concern, or an administrator or colleague may need to speak with a teacher about a very legitimate issue (the bell schedule that day, an impending field trip or assembly, etc.). If a teacher cannot be at the door as all students arrive, or is there but is distracted by conversations with other adults, PGD is unlikely to work, and should probably be scuttled for that day. Thus, in addition to the planning for individualization described in the next section, a simple level of planning requires teachers to think through which day(s) of the week PGD is most feasible.

Once at the door, the remainder of the strategy (both steps 2 and 3) involves simple verbal (or gestural, for some greetings, like fist bumps) interactions. First, the teacher greets the student by name ("Good morning, Kennedy!" or "Hi, Dalton"), and *may* include a gesture as well (fist bump, high five). Second, the teacher provides a prompt or precorrection designed to enhance the odds the student will begin class successfully. A generic prompt about what's happening that day or class period is needed for all students (e.g., "first just copy down the challenge problem," "after you put your things away all you'll need is a pencil and your notebook").

Recall that we have been describing Step 3 in the process of PGD as involving a prompt *or* precorrection (see Chapter 8). In fact, the opportunity to use a precorrection is one of the most valuable and potentially impactful aspects of PGD. A precorrection is what the name implies and is described in detail in Chapter 8. In sum, a teacher can essentially "correct" a behavior before an error occurs; that is, *before* a failure to meet a given expectation. In other words, instead of waiting to react (probably in a negative way) after a student fails to meet a particular expectation or engages in some type of inappropriate behavior, a teacher can significantly increase the odds of a student engaging in behavior that meets expectations by providing a specific prompt, one which is unique to this student and context, right before the expected behavior should occur. In fact, PGD provides the perfect framework and opportunity to offer precorrection.

The notion of a precorrect also implies that the teacher has seen firsthand how certain students are struggling with specific behaviors and expectations. This is usually not a problem!

Most teachers can say fairly easily which students experience the greatest struggles – and thus create the greatest or most frequent classroom management challenges. If the teacher has seen a student consistently struggle to find their place upon entering the classroom, fail to put their belongings or homework in the proper place at the start of class, or simply take a long time to settle in and focus on the tasks at hand, any of these would be excellent targets for a precorrective statement. In truth, a precorrect is really just a prompt about what the student needs to do to be successful; the main difference is that a precorrect is individually designed for a particular student, based on observations of specific contexts in which there are consistent breakdowns in meeting expectations. The precorrect is designed to circumvent that breakdown. As we describe below, this idea – designing a specific precorrection for a given student – is one of the main reasons that a little pre-planning is necessary. As we hope is clear, however, this planning is simple and is not time-consuming, making PGD one of the easier management strategies to plan and implement in classrooms.

What Do I Need to Begin Using Positive Greetings at the Door?

While one of the reasons PGD is highly recommended is because it requires very little in the way of advanced preparation, and no materials whatsoever, we do encourage teachers to think through a few things as they consider the use of PGD and plan for its implementation. We provide a simple planning template (see Figure 4.2 for a blank template and Figure 4.1 for a completed example), guiding questions (see Figure 4.3) for teachers to use as they think through how they can use and individualize PGD, and a self-assessment checklist (Figure 4.4).

As can be seen in Figure 4.2, the advanced preparation consists mainly of the teacher thinking through and perhaps making a few notes about how the steps in implementing PGD might be implemented just a bit differently for each student. First, the teacher may need to consider the types of greeting students may prefer or respond to better, and of course, this may vary according to the age or grade level of students. For example, some students may prefer a more overt or demonstrative greeting (e.g., "Good morning, Carlos! It's so great to see you today!" along with a pat on the back) while others may respond well to subtle greetings (a simple fist bump and nod). We think it's a good idea to also think through topics that might be good to avoid for certain students. For example, if a student tends to have conflicts on the bus, it's probably not a great idea to ask about the ride to school as the student is entering the classroom.

Second, a teacher needs to think through the ways reinforcement can be provided in Step 2 of the procedure. For many students, this can simply be a generic praise statement (but one that is still *behavior-specific* – see Chapter 10) about something simple like showing up for class on time, or remembering materials (e.g., "thanks for being on time!" or "good job remembering your notebook/textbook"). This is also a good time to think about those students whose attendance or other behavior is inconsistent; those who struggle to be on time, or those who often fail to bring the right materials to class. Many of these students may benefit especially from specific acknowledgment and reinforcement when they *do* meet these expectations. That said, it's also important to think about what obstacles may be preventing a student from making it to class, or to school at the start of the day, on time. For example, a young student who is frequently late to school because he or she relies on an adult for transportation is a very different scenario than a student who is late to class because he or she stops to talk to friends along the way. Therefore, we encourage teachers to focus on reinforcing behaviors that are within the student's control.

Finally, and perhaps most importantly, the third step of the procedure may be especially important to think through in advance so that it can be individualized as necessary. The research we referred to earlier has demonstrated that PGD can help almost any student engage in their work more quickly, stay on task longer, and disrupt lessons less. But because this step is meant to include both a prompt and a precorrection as necessary, it is designed very intentionally to support those students who are known to struggle with these transitions as they enter the classroom. Thus, it is a good idea for the teacher to at least think through the specific precorrections that will be provided to individual students. Note that we are not suggesting *each* prompt and precorrection needs to be individualized for *every* student – many students will benefit and be successful with a general reminder of the expectation for a given day (e.g., "the schedule's on the smart board; remember to copy down your assignments for today in your planner"). But think about those students – hopefully a small number – who really struggle with transitioning, entering the classroom, and settling into their work. What are the specific trouble spots that prevent them from meeting expectations? Do they successfully find their place, put away backpacks or things they've brought with them, turn in homework or assignments according to an expected routine? Whatever the trouble spot – wherever the breakdowns most often occur – a specific precorrection can be beneficial. As one example, we have known students who complete a good majority of their assignments, but then often simply fail to turn many of them in on time and in the right place – completed assignments are found days later tucked into a binder, or stuffed into a backpack. In such cases, a specific precorrect is clearly warranted. And note that it is not a negative – not a *correction* – but a *precorrection*, all embedded in a positive interaction:

> [James, who is missing nearly 50% of homework assignments this grading period, arrives to class on time, with his backpack. His teacher greets him at the door]
>
> *Teacher:* "Good morning James! Great to see you on time and with your backpack. Remember to get your homework out on your way to your desk, so you can drop it in the homework basket on my desk."

What Does Positive Greetings at the Door look Like in a Classroom?

Below, we provide two examples of what the use of PGD might look like in a classroom. First, to highlight its key components, we provide a simple example of how PGD can be used in an elementary classroom where the teacher, Ms. Cardigan, has few serious behavioral concerns, but still wants to make sure students learn and can successfully navigate classroom routines. Note that she is also aware that building positive relationships with her students is important in increasing their odds of success in school. In a subsequent example, we describe a middle school classroom where the teacher, Mr. Argyle, has several students who struggle to meet even basic expectations. Nonetheless, he too sees the potential of PGD as a simple strategy to lay the groundwork for success for all his students.

Elementary Example

Ms. Cardigan teaches a diverse class of third-graders who vary considerably in their backgrounds, strengths, and skill levels both in academics and in meeting the behavioral expectations that will allow them to be successful in school. Her class includes multiple students who receive special education supports based on identified disabilities, several students who are multilingual, and two students with formal 504 plans that detail some simple accommodations she provides due to attention deficit hyperactivity disorder. While she consistently reports that she has "zero" behavioral concerns in regard to conflict or aggression of any type among her students, she reports that these two students are "constantly in motion" or always seem to be needing attention. With the help of her consulting teacher, she had identified the start of class as one of her biggest hot spots – it seems to take *forever* for the kids to settle in and get started with their day. They have decided to try PGD to see if that will help them get students off on the right foot in a positive way.

Knowing that PGD involves simple steps and that she has very few serious concerns or trouble spots, Ms. Cardigan's preparation is simple. She does spend a few minutes thinking through the differences among her students in terms of their preferences and interaction styles. For example, she decides that Kaitlin will receive a cheerful greeting ("Hello, Kaitlin, so nice to see you today!") and a glowing comment, either about her materials or effort ("and you've got your backpack – good job!"), or even a simple observation ("and look what color bow you have in your hair today – I like it!"). For Terrance, however, she knows a subdued "morning Terrance" and a simple fist-bump will be much better received and ultimately effective; he prefers not to have attention focused on him publicly. Her only other preparation is to make sure she has a consistent prompt ready, which in her case is the same for all students, as they are still not at 100% with their morning routines. She simply says, following her greeting and positive statement, some version of "backpacks in your cubby, homework goes in the basket on my desk, then please make sure you have a pencil out for our warm-up." After only one day of implementing PGD, Ms. Cardigan feels very good about the start to her day. She discusses with her consulting teacher how they both perceive a more positive tone and "vibe" in the classroom, and they decide to meet to discuss their continued use of PGD. First, they realize that while they both believe things went very well, they need to figure out whether they can collect data (e.g., assignments completed) or look at some existing data (e.g., points earned in their existing school-wide system) to see if these validate their perceptions. Second, they want to discuss how frequently they can and should use PGD. While in their excitement they're tempted to use it every day, they realize that might not be practical given their varying schedules (e.g., some days they have P.E. first thing), and in fact may be more beneficial to apply it to the times they've had the most difficulty getting kids started and engaged. They decide to consider trying it out two to three times a week, targeting "gold days" on which they have language arts during their first block of the morning.

Secondary Example

Unlike Ms. Cardigan above, Mr. Argyle teaches middle school science, and he describes two of his classes as "impossible to manage." In discussions with his seventh grade team colleagues, he has noted that each of these two classes just seems to have a mix of students that creates tons of activity and lots of noise, and he describes in particular that he often takes nearly half a class period just trying to get students in the classroom, in their places, and settled into work. Upon further discussions with a consulting teacher, they decide that fourth period seems to be his most challenging class, but he also realizes that there are really only a small number of students who seem to be most active, and they often distract other students, pull them into conversations, or encourage them to gather in the back of the classroom to socialize as they enter the classroom, instead of taking their seats. They decide that PGD might be a great strategy to try at the start of 4th period, and they further discuss two students in particular. One of the students, Devon, is just very distractible and gregarious. He is a capable student, but just needs frequent reminders to stay focused. He also knows Devon is very into sports – both playing and watching sports on TV. Another is Angelo, who is similar to Devon in distractibility and activity level, but also struggles academically, including that he seldom keeps up with assignments or remembers his homework or other materials, and typically needs explicit support to stay engaged in any academic task. He knows that Angelo lives with a large extended family of relatives, and that there are several pets in their house. Mr. Argyle takes these into account as he thinks about how he will greet students as they enter his 4th period class.

As he initiates PGD for the first time on a Monday morning, Mr. Argyle makes sure to position himself at the doorway early. This works well as he has a lunch break immediately prior (which is another reason he thought it would be most practical to try PGD for the first time with this class). He greets each student by name as they arrive, with a simple "hello" or "welcome." He adds a fist bump for those he believes are comfortable with that (this is something that is common for him and many of his students to do). For most students, he adds a positive comment as well: "great to see you on time," "looks like you remembered all your materials; great job"). For Devon, he adds two things after the greeting itself. First, he says, "wow, did you see that playoff game last night?" Devon reacts excitedly, saying, "oh, I know! and did you see…?") relating his favorite moments. Mr. Argyle reacts with a smile, but then pivots because it's not the time for a lengthy conversation. "Yep. It was amazing. We can talk more about it at lunch." He gestures toward his desk and says to Devon, "Head over to my desk so you can drop your homework in the basket before you sit down. Then all you need to do is copy down today's homework from the board. OK?" He watches Devon head toward his desk, cautiously optimistic. Next, he greets Angelo. "Angelo! Great to see you!" He sees that Angelo has his backpack (which he sometimes forgets or leaves in his locker after lunch), so adds, "if your homework's in that backpack, fish it out and drop it in the basket on your way to your seat." After these two simple greetings, Mr. Argyle sees that both Devon and Angelo are, in fact, headed toward his desk, Devon with his homework already in his hand, and Angelo rifling through his backpack searching for his. While he sees this as a possible improvement already, he also notes that neither Devon nor Angelo is talking to or distracting other students at all, so is very hopeful that PGD has, in fact, helped him get this class started off on a better foot.

A quick note about PGD, especially as we just described in Mr. Argyle's classroom: PGD will not solve all the challenges a teacher faces or result in a "perfect" classroom. Recall the research we cited earlier; PGD did not result in 100% engagement, or zero disruptions. It did, however, move engagement from around 45% to over 70% almost immediately. And that is Mr. Argyle's goal – to make his class, especially this fourth period class, more manageable. If most of his students will engage more quickly, as they appeared to do with his first use of PGD, they're less likely to be distracted by Devon and Angelo. And, if Devon and Angelo can be engaged more readily or directed toward their expected activities, they become far less likely to *try* to distract others.

A second note relates back to a theme of this book, which is that these positive, mostly antecedent (i.e., preventive) strategies also are beneficial in that they can help build and maintain positive relationships. We know that Mr. Argyle had described his class as "unmanageable." How do you suppose he and his students would have perceived the climate in that classroom, or the relationships between teacher and students? It would seem highly likely that the environment might have been described as chaotic at best, or maybe characterized by frequent conflict (i.e., Mr. Argyle correcting or admonishing kids for being out of their place or too loud; students not getting to work). In contrast, with PGD each day begins with a series of positive statements from

Positive Greetings at the Door Planning Template

General Considerations – What behavioral expectations have generally been difficult for your class as a whole?

Noise level; students distracting each other. Lots of movement but not getting to seats and starting to work. Takes a long time to get everyone started.

Greeting Components

Describe all components in specific detail and how they will be introduced to the student.

		GREETING IDEAS & PREFERENCES	TOPICS		REINFORCEMENT	PROMPTS & PRECORRECTIONS
			REMEMBER	AVOID		
ALL STUDENTS		My usual (hello/welcome) Fist bump for some	General things I learn about each student	None	Positive comments about things I want to see: on time, brought materials, went straight to seat	Prompt to follow voice level and go right to area
SPECIFIC STUDENT CONSIDERATIONS		DEVON Warm, positive greeting	Plays/watches sports	None	Check in about recent games (playoff coming up)	Drop homework in basket; copy down new homework
		ANGELO Warm, positive greeting	Big extended family Pets	None		Get backpack; turn in homework. Go right to seat.

Data Collection Plan

Describe the specific behavior targeted for improvement: Entry routine –
Two students go directly to seat within 30 seconds of entering class, following the voice level
Describe the metric (e.g., % of time on-task) and method for data collection:
Percentage of days students go to seats within 30 seconds with no more than 1 reminder; keep weekly chart for both students

FIGURE 4.1 Completed Example of Positive Greetings at the Door Planning Template

Mr. Argyle (20 or more positive, individualized statements), and an increased likelihood that many – maybe most – students engage in their expected tasks. Note that this in turn provides Mr. Argyle with additional opportunities to acknowledge students meeting expectations ("good job getting to work, Devon;" "Thanks for getting that homework into the basket, Angelo!"), hopefully shifting the balance of his own interactions from an over reliance on redirects or corrections, toward much more frequent positive acknowledgment. We see great potential here for such a shift to contribute positively to the overall climate or tone of the classroom, as well as the perceptions of both students and teachers regarding the relationships between them.

Final Thoughts

In this chapter, we described the key elements of PGD, which is a highly recommended strategy for getting students engaged at the start of a day or class period. As we described, the use of PGD has been associated with better engagement (students get to work faster), more sustained engagement (they persist longer in the tasks at hand), and fewer disruptions and less off-task behavior. This last part is a logical outcome of the first two; if students are more engaged in their work, they will by default be less off-task or disruptive. The procedure is simple, consisting of three basic steps: (1) greet students at the door, individually, as they enter the classroom; (2) provide a positive or reinforcing statement; and (3) provide a prompt or precorrection regarding how they can successfully meet expectations for that day or class period.

PGD comes highly recommended for several reasons. First, it's *very* easy to plan for and implement, and in fact requires no additional materials and just a few moments of thought to consider a few questions about how it will be implemented, and especially how it can be individualized as needed. Using the template provided, teachers can consider first how they will greet students, individualizing based on student preferences and interaction styles (e.g., a demonstrative verbal greeting; a subtle greeting along with a gesture, like a fist bump or high five). They also consider how to reinforce or interact positively with students, choosing at times to simply offer a positive interaction (e.g., "I see y'all won the basketball game last night") or in some cases to reinforce specific behavior (e.g., "thanks for being on time" or "good job remembering your notebook"). Finally, the teacher should consider whether a general prompt is all that's needed (e.g., "all you need to do is copy the first problem for the board before we get started"), or, in cases where a student has struggled in this context to meet expectations, whether a more specific precorrect is warranted. For example, if a student has tended to wander the classroom and forget to turn in assignments, the teacher might add "remember to drop your homework in the basket on your way to your desk."

A second reason we recommend PGD is because of the consistency of some of its key elements with the ideas of building and maintaining positive relationships with students. A positive greeting at the door surely enhances a sense of belonging and warmth – key elements of positive teacher-student relationships. Further, individualizing greetings to meet student preferences, adding positive statements – personalized as much as possible – and then using preemptive prompts to encourage behavior that meets expectations, all contribute to that positive climate, and given what research tells us about the effects of PGD, ultimately limits the extent to which teachers will need to implement corrective, and potentially negative consequences.

References

Allday, R. A., & Pakurar, K. (2007). Effects of teacher greetings on student on-task behavior. *Journal of Applied Behavior Analysis, 40,* 317–320.

Cook, C. R., Fiat, A., Larson, M., Daikos, C., Slemrod, T., Holland, E. A., Thayer, A. J., & Renshaw, T. (2018). Positive greetings at the door: Evaluation of a low-cost, high-yield proactive classroom management strategy. *Journal of Positive Behavior Interventions, 20,* 149–159.

Positive Greetings at the Door Planning Template

General Considerations – What behavioral expectations have generally been difficult for your class as a whole?

Greeting Components
Describe all components in specific detail and how they will be introduced to the student.

	GREETING IDEAS & PREFERENCES	TOPICS		REINFORCEMENT	PROMPTS & PRECORRECTIONS
		REMEMBER	AVOID		
ALL STUDENTS					
SPECIFIC STUDENT CONSIDERATIONS					

Data Collection Plan
Describe the specific behavior targeted for improvement:

Describe the metric (e.g., % of time on-task) and method for data collection:

FIGURE 4.2 Positive Greetings at the Door Planning Template

STEPS	QUESTIONS	NOTES
Positive Greetings at the Door Guiding Questions		
GREET STUDENTS	For all students: • What *verbal* greetings do students prefer? • What *nonverbal* greetings do students prefer? (fist bump, high five, simple nod, etc.) • Remember to use students' names, even if just one word (e.g., "Carlos" (*offers fist bump*))	
PROVIDE POSITIVE STATEMENTS/ REINFORCEMENT	For all students: • What will you reinforce? (e.g., being on time, remembering materials) • What are other positive statements you can make? (e.g., comment about an achievement or preferred activity, based on student interests (e.g., 'how's that new puppy?' 'did you win your game last night?' • Are there any topics to avoid? (problem areas or triggers that might be perceived negatively or create conflict)	
PROVIDE PROMPT/ PRECORRECTION	For all students: • What is the generic prompt for the day (e.g., "all you need is a pencil; we'll take our quiz as soon as the bell rings" "take a seat quickly so we can get to the assembly") For students who struggle to meet basic expectations: • What are the hotspots or where breakdowns occur? (e.g., failing to put belongings away, not taking a seat) • What specific precorrections can be used for these students? (e.g., "remember, backpack in your cubby before you take a seat."	

FIGURE 4.3 Positive Greetings at the Door Guiding Questions

Positive Greetings at the Door Steps & Self-Assessment			
0→Not in Place 1→Partially in Place 2→Fully in Place			
STEPS	How Did I do?		
1. Stand at the doorway before students arrive and remain until they all enter the classroom.	☐ 0	☐ 1	☐ 2
2. Greet students individually, including using their names and an optional gesture.	☐ 0	☐ 1	☐ 2
3. Provide positive statement or reinforcement.	☐ 0	☐ 1	☐ 2
4. Provide prompts and/or precorrections.	☐ 0	☐ 1	☐ 2
Notes & Reflection:			

FIGURE 4.4 Positive Greetings at the Implementation and Self-Assessment Checklist

5

Behavioral Momentum

In this chapter, we explain how and why behavioral momentum can be used to improve student behavior. We begin by providing a definition and description of this strategy, followed by a brief overview of the research that supports the use of this strategy. Next, we explain how behavioral momentum can build positive relationships with students, particularly those who demonstrate challenging behaviors. Finally, we describe how to implement this strategy and provide two examples of what this practice might look like in a classroom. The supplemental resources for this chapter include a planning template (one blank for your use and one completed as an example) and a self-assessment checklist to support implementation fidelity.

What Is Behavioral Momentum?

Behavioral momentum is an approach based upon fundamental principles of physics that teachers can use proactively and methodically to ease a student toward compliance with directions and engagement in tasks, especially when the student has a pattern of predictable struggles with these behaviors. Implementing behavioral momentum involves delivering a short series of directions (sometimes called high-probability request sequences) starting with simple things a student is very likely to do (e.g., "push in

DOI: 10.4324/9781003469599-8

your chair," "take out your pencil," "give me a fist bump") before giving a difficult direction (e.g., "solve these word problems," "time to come in from recess"). It turns out we can build a momentum of compliance, even with our students who seem like immovable forces when it comes to doing difficult tasks or following any of our directions.

The concept behind behavioral momentum is built on a borrowed principle of Newtonian physics (Nevin et al., 1983). Specifically, the first law of motion states that bodies at rest stay at rest, and those in motion stay in motion. This fits very well with what many teachers have experienced from students. Namely, those students who are compliant tend to keep on complying, whereas certain students seem absolutely stuck in a state of noncompliance that is predictably unlikely to change. Teachers can benefit from imagining these stuck students like a boulder resting on top of a hill – full of potential energy that can be unlocked and turned kinetic with just the right nudge. Fortunately, teachers can harness this potential energy of stuck students by applying behavioral momentum with a small sequence of nudges that build a snowball effect of compliance.

Even students with chronic, challenging, noncompliant behavior do comply with certain directions and tasks some of the time. When teachers identify these directions, students are likely to follow (high-probability requests), they can deliver a few of them to get the student on a roll of compliance before introducing a direction that tends to meet noncompliance (a low-probability request). Proactive teachers employing this strategy sidestep unwinnable power struggles that could lead to further challenges. Instead, with this strategy, teachers are essentially greasing the wheels of compliance, which sets students up to follow directions they rarely would have complied with before.

How Do I Know Behavioral Momentum Works?

Behavioral momentum research confirms the good news that students who exhibit noncompliant behaviors are not simply stuck and that this relatively simple strategy can help teachers foster student success. Researchers have examined the impact of developing behavioral momentum through high-probability request sequences across a range of student populations and school levels. For example, Axelrod and Zank (2012) employed behavioral momentum to support students with behavior disorders who exhibited high rates of noncompliant and escalated behavior. The students were very unlikely to follow certain classroom expectations and directions, such as remaining quiet, staying in their seats, working on tasks, and putting away inappropriate materials (e.g., toys). During the intervention, their teachers would provide them with three high-probability requests (e.g., "pick up your pencil," "give me a high five," "stand up"). The students significantly improved their rates of compliance, at least doubling (and in some cases quintupling) them, and maintained the improvement even once the high-probability requests were faded out.

Reviews of the evidence base suggest that behavioral momentum can have a significant impact on a range of important student behaviors, such as increasing compliance, improving engagement, decreasing latency to begin tasks, improving transitions, reducing prompts needed, and even improving academics (e.g., spelling mastery, writing output; Common et al., 2019). One component of behavioral momentum that seems to be a key ingredient driving success across these outcomes is contingent reinforcement delivered after each instance of student compliance, creating repeated experiences of success for students. These students may have experienced repeated failures and challenges in school, in essence digging in their heels to avoid difficult and undesirable tasks and expectations. By delivering doses of incremental success and reinforcement, teachers set these students up to see that success and reinforcement are available to them even in the face of low-probability requests.

How Does Behavioral Momentum Build Positive Relationships with My Students?

Students who engage in a pattern of noncompliance may have a long history of repeatedly engaging in power struggles with teachers and other adults in their lives, often leading to negative interactions, reprimands, and other punitive consequences. Rather than waiting for a student to fail again through noncompliance, teachers implementing behavioral momentum are focused on preventing this negative cycle from taking place. Instead, they do what good teachers do with academics: they proactively provide strong instruction and scaffolded supports to help students successfully learn new skills without waiting for them to practice errors. Behavioral momentum involves setting students up to be more likely to successfully engage in appropriate behavior, providing more opportunities for positive interactions between teacher and student. Students may begin to feel differently about themselves as they experience repeated behavioral success and the positive outcomes that come with it. Moreover, by design teachers provide much higher rates of reinforcement, including positive feedback, when implementing behavioral momentum. Whereas constant power struggles may destroy relationships, these repeated positive teacher-student interactions forge them.

Imagine the seventh grade student who has a long history of noncompliant and challenging behavior in school. Teachers know of his reputation and hope not to see him on their roster at the start of the school year because there can be so much stress in teaching students like him on top of all the other responsibilities of the education profession. A typical interaction with this student might involve asking him to get out his workbook for a simple independent assignment, followed by him crossing his arms or putting his head down and just plain not doing it. This can easily and often lead to a series of interactions between teacher and student that are increasingly tense and negative, and at times, erupt into the student being sent out of the classroom. The assignment, the teacher, the classroom – these can all become aversive to the student and actually fuel further noncompliance. On the other hand, imagine the teacher equipped with a positive and proactive mindset and the strategies in this book who initiates a different series of interactions. The teacher asks the student for a fist bump, and thanks him with a smile when he gives one. The teacher follows this up by asking for one word to describe the student's weekend and gives positive feedback when the student is able to muster up that word, no matter what it is. Then the teacher asks him to take out that workbook. Will he do it? The evidence suggests he is substantially more likely to comply than had the teacher skipped these easy interactions. And if he does do it, the teacher gets to provide behavior-specific praise (see Chapter 10), and engage in even more positive interactions, such as distributing tangible reinforcement (see Chapter 11). How could this not build a positive relationship?

How Do I Implement Behavioral Momentum in My Classroom?

Although behavioral momentum is a strategy a savvy teacher can keep in their back pocket to implement on the fly when it occurs to her that a student may struggle to comply with a particular request, it is more likely to foster student compliance through some degree of planning and preparation. This is especially important because, in principle, the strategy is built upon building and maintaining momentum, which requires high-probability requests that actually work. A worst-case scenario for the strategy involves the student complying with one or more easy requests but then *not* complying with an easy request before the low-probability request is even given. Momentum is lost in that case, so teachers are best served by preparing ahead to ensure a greater likelihood of repeated student compliance. Behavioral momentum can be broken down into six steps, which we describe briefly in the next subsections.

Step 1: Identify the Low-Probability Request(s) to Prioritize for Intervention

The first step in implementing behavioral momentum is to identify when the strategy will be of greatest benefit for improving student behavior. Consider when the student is least likely to follow directions or comply with requests or show some form of resistance, which could include times when the student does comply but seems to take forever to do so. This might be during certain activities (e.g., when asked to work on independent writing prompts), instructional contexts (e.g., when asked to engage in a cooperative learning strategy with peers), or settings (e.g., when with a certain teacher or adult). Focus on noncompliant behavior and contexts or activities that are a high priority for change. As you experience success with behavioral momentum for prioritized behaviors and situations, you can apply it to others that are of less concern.

Step 2: Brainstorm Possible High-Probability Requests

Once low-probability requests have been identified, the next step involves coming up with a list of potential brief, high-probability requests you think the student would likely comply with willingly. It may be helpful to observe what the student tends to go along with as well as asking others who know the student well (e.g., parents/guardians, other teachers). These easy requests can be academically related (e.g., "take out your pencil and paper," "write your name at the top"), but they can also be completely unrelated to instruction (e.g., "tell me about what you had for dinner last night"). You can also look for things that naturally occur that the student does (e.g., will she give you a high-five on the way through the door if you hold your hand up?). For certain students (e.g., younger students, students with particular disabilities), simple, brief requests (e.g., "touch your nose," "show me ten fingers") may be both appropriate and ideal. Ideal requests are those that can be completed rapidly and strung one after the next. A long list of possible requests is ideal, so you can find the ones that work and vary them in practice. Aim to identify at least eight to ten options.

Step 3: Test Out the High-Probability Requests

The third step involves taking a scientific approach to maximize the likelihood that you will actually build and maintain momentum when implementing this strategy; it is the key reason why this strategy works best when planned in advance. For this step, it is important to try out each of the options listed in Step 2 to see if they actually work. Test each one out a few times across one or more school days to ensure they tend to lead to compliance, and remove any from the list that do not work most of the time, as those are obstacles to momentum. It may be necessary to brainstorm additional possible high-probability requests if your list becomes too short after testing.

Step 4: Deliver a Brief Series of High-Probability Requests, Following Each One with Reinforcement Once the Student Complies

Step 4 involves actual implementation of the behavioral momentum sequence. When it is time to deliver a low-probability request to the student, first provide the student with two to four of the high-probability requests from your final list. For each request, provide a brief wait time for the student to comply, then provide some form of reinforcement after each instance of compliance (see Chapter 13). One of the most practical, yet powerful ways to quickly reinforce student behavior is to provide behavior-specific praise (see Chapter 10). Then, immediately follow up by providing the next high-probability request to maintain the momentum. As you implement this strategy over time, it is best to vary the high-probability requests used and the sequence in which you use them, which is part of why a longer list is beneficial.

Step 5: Deliver the Low-Probability Request

Now that you have built up momentum through a series of successful high-probability requests, it is time to provide the low-probability request. It is best to do so as soon as possible after the final high-probability request to ride the wave of momentum, ensuring the greatest likelihood of success. Once you have provided the difficult request, provide a wait time for the student to begin complying. When the student complies, provide another round of reinforcement either in the form of specific praise or by giving something that is even more meaningful to the student, such as a token or ticket that can be traded in for a something else at a later time (see Chapter 11).

Step 6: Monitor the Impact of the Intervention and Adjust Requests as Needed

As with all behavior strategies, collecting data on the impact of the intervention is critical – it can tell us whether and how well an intervention is working, and when to stick with it, modify it, or – in some cases – scrap it altogether. With behavioral momentum, there's another wrinkle: you need to see if the "easy" requests you decided on up front are, in fact, holding up as high-probability requests. Thus, for Step 6, you will want to monitor student compliance over time with both low-probability and high-probability requests. We've tried to make this easy to do at a glance with the template provided in Figure 5.2. Compliance with high-probability requests will help you know if you need to discard and replace any of them to improve the effectiveness of this strategy. And of course, compliance rates with the targeted low-probability requests will show you pretty clearly whether behavioral momentum is working. As a ballpark, we'd recommend reviewing data weekly, but of course, this can vary based on how frequently you use the strategy (e.g., 2× per week, 3× per week). There is no magic number here, but it is important to plan how you will record data about the student's behavior (using our template or your own) and how often you will analyze it to guide your efforts going forward. Again, hopefully this template puts the data across several sessions in one place, where simple review can be accomplished easily and patterns will be obvious.

What Do I Need to Begin Implementing Behavioral Momentum?

Implementing behavioral momentum requires little more than a solid plan to implement well (and even can be implemented on the fly with certain students who require less intentional strategizing). The strategy rarely requires any particular materials unless you identify high-probability requests that rely on certain items (e.g., "please pass out these papers") or plan to implement a token economy (see Chapter 11) as part of your reinforcement strategy. It may be most helpful simply to think through your roster of students to identify those for whom following directions and expectations is a substantial challenge. Then, you might start just by observing these students for a few days to note the many ways they do, in fact, comply. It can feel like such students *never* follow directions or expectations, especially because it is often only their misbehavior that draws or even forces our attention, but careful observation will reveal a surprising number of things these students will gladly do.

Once you see that some forms of compliance are possible from all students, you will be more equipped to implement this strategy successfully. To support your efforts, we have provided a behavioral momentum planning template (see Figure 5.2) to help think through prioritizing low-probability requests, brainstorming and testing high-probability requests, identifying a reinforcement method, and collecting data. We encourage teachers to begin by completing this plan for one student to practice building skill with this strategy; it may even be helpful to invite a colleague or two to help with brainstorming easy requests. An example of a completed planning template (see Figure 5.1) is also included. Finally, we have included a self-assessment checklist (see Figure 5.3) that includes a checklist of each step for behavioral momentum to support full implementation of the strategy and maximize your likelihood of success with your students.

What Does Behavioral Momentum look Like in a Classroom?

We provide two examples below to illustrate implementing behavioral momentum with students in the classroom. In the first example, you will read about Mr. Hughes, a kindergarten teacher who uses behavioral momentum with a student who refuses to transition to carpet time instruction, which often leads to a power struggle that escalates into bigger problems. In the second example, you will read about Ms. Mandeel, a ninth grade special education teacher in a resource classroom, who implements behavioral momentum with a student who simply will not even get started on independent writing tasks.

Elementary Example

Mr. Hughes teaches a class of kindergartners with a wide array of needs. Although nearly all his students occasionally need additional support learning to follow classroom expectations and routines, Mr. Hughes has one particular student who requires a lot more of his attention. Arya loves engaging in different centers with other students, especially when the stations involve activities that allow her to be creative and make art. Unfortunately, when it's time to transition to the carpet for whole group instruction, Arya simply will not budge. She stays seated at whichever center she's currently engaged in and won't even look up, avoiding eye contact with Mr. Hughes. When he comes over to gently remind her to come over to her square on the carpet, she pretends she cannot hear him. If he keeps talking to her about needing to come over to the carpet, Arya will cross her arms and put her head down and eventually crawl under the table, refusing to come out. Trying to manage a full class of kindergartners and maintain instruction, Mr. Hughes can become understandably frustrated with Arya, at which point he has sometimes used a sharper tone of voice than he would like to reprimand her, which does not help him to get Arya moving. There have been days when it could take Arya half an hour or more to get back on track, and others where Mr. Hughes has just given up and left her at her center so he can maintain instruction with his other students.

Despite the challenges they have around transitioning to carpet time, Mr. Hughes has worked on building a strong, positive relationship with Arya (and all his students) by getting to know her and implementing simple universal strategies like positive greetings at the door (see Chapter 4). Arya enjoys these greetings and has a special fist bump she created to use with Mr. Hughes. When he greets her, Mr. Hughes often asks her to give him one word to describe her morning, and she likes coming up with different words to use like it's a game. There are, in fact, many things Arya enjoys doing, including helping Mr. Hughes with different things. When Mr. Hughes shared his concerns about Arya's transition behavior with the school instructional coach, the coach shared about the benefits of behavioral momentum, and Mr. Hughes agreed to give it a shot.

Later that week, when center time was coming to an end and carpet time was about to begin, Mr. Hughes was prepared with the knowledge that he could predict the likely problem he would face with Arya. And he knew that if you can predict a problem, you can often prevent it with some proactivity. He had spent some time noting the requests Arya already consistently followed and even tested out a few new ones that he had a hunch would work. Even though he had already greeted Arya that morning at the door, he joined her at her center and held out his fist, saying with a smile, "Give me one of those special fist bumps, Arya!" When she did, he said, "Thanks! You give great greetings! Give me a word to describe how centers have been today." Arya replied, "Outstanding!" Mr. Hughes said, "You have the best words, Arya! Now, can you please put our colored pencil bin away in its cubby?" Arya was happy to do this for him and took the colored pencils over to the cubby, which happened to be very close to the carpet. Then Mr. Hughes said, "Thanks for putting those away, Arya; you're so responsible! All right, please head to your square on the carpet." The whole sequence had been going so well, but Mr. Hughes was still a little nervous as he gave the low-probability request. But he was soon cheering inside as Arya kept being on a roll and went to her square, so he gave her one last dose of behavior-specific praise paired with a ticket from their classroom token economy system and gave directions to the rest of the class to begin transitioning to the carpet.

Secondary Example

Ms. Mandeel teaches resource language arts for ninth grade students with disabilities. All of her students need specially designed instruction and other supports to help them successfully learn the content in her class. Some students need more than just academic supports as well. For example, her student Devon has wonderful ideas when engaged in collaborative dialogue with Ms. Mandeel or his peers during pre-writing activities.

He likes brainstorming and discussing new ideas in response to various writing prompts. However, when it comes time to work independently and actually write, Devon will not even try to start. He will not even reach for his backpack to start getting out his notebook and pens, often just staring out the window instead or putting his head down on his desk. If Ms. Mandeel stays right by his side supporting him and guiding him step-by-step, he will get out his materials and write some, but as soon as she leaves to help another student, he closes his notebook and his head goes down. All of her students need her support, and Ms. Mandeel knows Devon is capable and also needs to learn to at least attempt some of this work without her.

She decides to implement behavioral momentum and meets with her colleague, Mr. Liedtke, who teaches ninth grade social studies and has a strong relationship with Devon. Together, Ms. Mandeel and Mr. Liedtke brainstorm a variety of possible high-probability requests they think Devon is likely to comply with as they fill out the planning template (see Figure 5.1 for a completed sample). They've seen him do many of these things, but they are not certain which are the most reliable, so they test each one out. Nearly all of the easy requests they identified work consistently. However, getting out a writing utensil or cleaning off his desk were not effective, so they decide not to include these when implementing the strategy.

The next time independent writing is scheduled, Ms. Mandeel implements a sequence of high-probability requests. On Monday, she asks Devon to erase the board, pass out graded papers, and copy a few directions for her onto her smartboard. Devon willingly follows all these directions, and Ms. Mandeel reinforces his compliance with behavior-specific praise each time immediately after he complies. When she asks him to get out his materials and start writing, the moment feels magical to her because Devon actually does it and completes several paragraphs before she comes around to check on him. She decides to continue using behavioral momentum and varies her easy requests. She has success with the strategy throughout most of the week and uses her simple data collection chart to make decisions about what to do going forward. In reviewing her data, Ms. Mandeel realizes

Behavioral Momentum ◆ 81

Behavioral Momentum Planning Template

Student:	Context (class, time of day, activity):	Low-probability request (what the student refuses to do):
Devon	Writing/language arts	Get out materials; begin independent writing

High-Probability Requests
(check requests that work consistently)

Possible Requests	Tests (+ worked, - failed)	Possible Requests	Tests (+ worked, - failed)
☒ 1. erases board	+ + +	☒ 7. works independently on computer	+ + +
☒ 2. passes out papers & materials	+ + +	☒ 8. gives high fives/fist bumps	+ + +
☐ 3. takes out a pen or pencil	- + -	☒ 9. runs errands	+ + +
☒ 4. files papers for teacher	+ + +	☐ 10. clears off desk	- - -
☒ 5. copy problems onto the board	+ + +	☐ 11.	
☒ 6. works independently on puzzles, word finds, etc.	+ + +	☐ 12.	

Data Collection Chart

✓ = complied with request   X = did not

	M	T	W	Th	F
High-probability requests					
Erase board	✓	✓	✓	X	
Pass out papers/materials	✓		X		
Copy problems/sentences on smartboard	✓	✓	✓	X	✓
Run errand to office		X		X	X
File homework papers					✓
Low-probability request					
Get out materials and begin independent writing task	✓	X	✓	X	✓

FIGURE 5.1 Completed Example of Behavioral Momentum Planning Template

that asking Devon to run an errand to the office is consistently not working anymore, so she removes it from her list of options. She also notices that on Thursday, none of her requests worked at all and decides to check in with Mr. Liedtke as well as Devon to see if something different might have been going on that day.

Final Thoughts

In this chapter, we described how to apply behavioral momentum, which is a powerful strategy that can transform classroom dynamics, particularly for students who struggle with compliance. By understanding and leveraging the principles of behavioral momentum, teachers can create a positive cycle of success and reinforcement that encourages even the most resistant students to engage with challenging tasks. This approach not only improves student behavior but also enhances teacher-student relationships, building trust and a more supportive classroom environment. Behavioral momentum is not just about getting students to follow directions – it involves fostering a sense of achievement and belonging in students who may often feel disconnected or discouraged. When students experience repeated success, they begin to see themselves as capable learners, which can lead to increased motivation and a more positive attitude toward school as well as improvement in a variety of desirable student behaviors.

As you begin to implement this strategy in your classroom, remember that consistency and patience are key. Behavioral momentum requires thoughtful planning and observation and is best implemented using a more systematic approach, testing out potential high-probability requests before implementation. Though it requires some work on the front end, the rewards – more engaged students, fewer power struggles, and a more harmonious classroom – are well worth the effort. By investing time in understanding your students' strengths and using them to build momentum, you set the stage for a more productive and positive learning experience for everyone.

References

Axelrod, M. I., & Zank, A. J. (2012). Increasing classroom compliance: Using a high-probability command sequence with noncompliant students. *Journal of Behavioral Education, 21*, 119–133.

Common, E. A., Bross, L. A., Oakes, W. P., Cantwell, E. D., Lane, K. L., & Germer, K. A. (2019). Systematic review of high probability requests in K-12 settings: Examining the evidence base. *Behavioral Disorders, 45*(1), 3–21.

Nevin, J. A., Mandell, C., & Atak, J. R. (1983). The analysis of behavioral momentum. *Journal of the Experimental Analysis of Behavior, 39*(1), 49–59.

Behavioral Momentum Planning Template

Student:	Context (class, time of day, activity):	Low-probability request (what the student refuses to do):

High-Probability Requests
(check requests that work consistently)

Possible Requests	Tests (+ worked, - failed)	Possible Requests	Tests (+ worked, - failed)
☐ 1.	―― ―― ――	☐ 7.	―― ―― ――
☐ 2.	―― ―― ――	☐ 8.	―― ―― ――
☐ 3.	―― ―― ――	☐ 9.	―― ―― ――
☐ 4.	―― ―― ――	☐ 10.	―― ―― ――
☐ 5.	―― ―― ――	☐ 11.	―― ―― ――
☐ 6.	―― ―― ――	☐ 12.	―― ―― ――

Data Collection Chart

✓ = complied with request   X = did not

	M	T	W	Th	F
High-probability requests					
Low-probability request					

FIGURE 5.2 Behavioral Momentum Planning Template

Behavioral Momentum Steps & Self-Assessment	
0→Not in Place 1→Partially in Place 2→Fully in Place	
STEPS	How Did I do?
1. Identify the low probability request(s) to prioritize for intervention.	☐ 0 ☐ 1 ☐ 2
2. Brainstorm possible high-probability requests.	☐ 0 ☐ 1 ☐ 2
3. Test out the high-probability requests.	☐ 0 ☐ 1 ☐ 2
4. Deliver a brief series of high-probability requests, following each one with reinforcement once the student complies.	☐ 0 ☐ 1 ☐ 2
5. Deliver the low-probability request.	☐ 0 ☐ 1 ☐ 2
6. Monitor the impact of the intervention, using data to guide your decision making.	☐ 0 ☐ 1 ☐ 2
Notes & Reflection:	

FIGURE 5.3 Behavioral Momentum Implementation and Self-Assessment Checklist

6

Instructional Choice

In this chapter, we explain how and why instructional choice can be used to improve student behavior. We begin by providing a definition and description of this strategy, followed by a brief overview of the research that supports the use of this strategy. Next, we explain how instructional choice can build positive relationships with students, particularly those who demonstrate challenging behaviors. Finally, we describe how to implement this strategy and provide three examples of what this practice might look like in a classroom. The supplemental resources for this chapter include a planning template (one blank for your use and one completed as an example) and a self-assessment checklist to support implementation fidelity.

What Is Instructional Choice?

Instructional choice – sometimes referred to simply as "choice" – is a strategy teachers can use in advance of an activity or lesson, especially if they anticipate problems with behavior or academic performance, to prevent these problems from occurring in the first place. Using choice can increase students' compliance, task initiation, and the amount of time spent on task. Implementing instructional choice is as simple as giving students a few options for how to engage in a task or follow directions. Usually, just two or three options that don't get in the way of learning goals are best. There are several ways to offer instructional choice, but some of the most common approaches include giving students options for the materials they will use, the location of where they will work on the task, the order of tasks, and the way in which assignments are completed (e.g., independently or with a partner).

This strategy has been shown to be useful for improving student outcomes in many areas, including behavior, social interactions, and academic engagement and success. Choice can also be a powerful way to build positive relationships with students. Choice is especially effective when implemented preventively, with teachers pre-planning two or more options for students, and then using choice in potential trouble spots throughout the day. For example, teachers may plan to use choice specifically in classes or content areas where many of their students have a hard time engaging in their work, sustaining attention, or complying with teacher directions. In other words, teachers can use choice specifically to prevent problems from occurring in those classes or times of day that are their most challenging. Choice can also be pre-planned, reactionary, or used "on the fly" (we describe each in the next sections) and teachers can provide choice to all students in a classroom, or on an individual basis for students who may have difficulty meeting specific behavioral expectations or academic tasks.

Pre-Planned Choice

Sometimes, teachers know challenging behavior has become a pattern or is more likely to occur with certain students. In these cases, just winging it – continuing to use the same instruction or management strategies – but hoping for a positive outcome isn't likely to work. In such cases, pre-planning instructional choices to head off misbehavior becomes important. One way teachers can pre-plan choice is by considering more than one option for the output of the learning task: are there multiple ways a student might demonstrate their mastery of content or a specific skill? This is a strategy many teachers are likely aware of and already use in their daily practice. For example, if students are completing a research project, a teacher may create an assignment that gives students an option of writing a report, preparing a video, or creating an infographic. Or, teachers may provide students a choice of activities to engage in when they have completed their assignments, such as writing in a journal, drawing a picture, or reading a book of choice.

While the examples above describe ways teachers can use pre-planned choice to structure assignments, this type of choice can also be used in relatively simple ways throughout the day. For example, a teacher may pre-plan to use instructional choice by copying a graphic organizer on two different colors of paper. Then, when handing out the graphic organizers before instruction begins, the teacher can ask each student to choose which color of paper they would like to use. Because the color of the paper does not interfere with the learning objective, this is an excellent way to give students at least a little control over their learning and, according to research, even this simple use of choice can increase the likelihood of students starting and finishing their work.

Reactionary Choice

Sometimes, a teacher may realize "after the fact" that it would have been a good idea to offer a choice to a student. We call this use of choice "reactionary choice" and we suggest using it when a student is hesitant to engage in a specific behavior or learning task. However, we have also found that some teachers may be reluctant to use reactionary choice because they feel like providing a student with choice after a student refuses to begin a task allows a student to "win" in a power struggle (in other words, to be reinforced for not starting their work). We view this differently. If teachers can carefully implement a reasonable choice at the moment they see a student just beginning to struggle, or clearly starting to fade, disengage, or simply shut down, they may prevent a serious escalation of resistance and even greater behavioral concerns. In these situations, a teacher can move the needle from what would have likely been *no* engagement or task completion, to at least *some* engagement or task completion, which we think ultimately results in a "win" for everyone.

If we consider the graphic organizer example from above, there may be occasions when a teacher runs out of time to copy the graphic organizer on two different colors of paper or – based on our own classroom experience – the copier jams during their planning period. After passing out the graphic organizer, a teacher may notice that one student in particular has not responded to the directions for the learning task, so the teacher repeats the directions and asks the student to restate them. Although the student responds by restating the directions, she places her head on her desk instead of beginning the assignment. At this point, the teacher realizes that he forgot to offer instructional choice to the student, a strategy that usually works very well for her. Therefore, the teacher decides to offer reactionary choice by giving the student the option to work on the assignment at her own desk, at a small table near the teacher's desk, or on a cushion in the classroom library (e.g., "Seems like you're having a hard time getting started; do you think you could work better at the table up front, or maybe on a cushion in our library? You pick."). In this scenario, the teacher's use of reactionary choice increases the likelihood that the student will now engage in the assignment and decreases the likelihood of the non-compliant behavior escalating.

"On the Fly" Choice

As with all instruction, there are decisions teachers make at the moment, or "on the fly" as they are teaching. Although we encourage teachers to pre-plan for their use of instructional choice as much as possible, the great news is that even if they forget to pre-plan, they can still use this strategy at the moment by offering simple choices that don't require any extra preparation. Examples of this include offering students the choice to complete an assignment using pen or pencil (or marker; often a popular choice) or giving the option to complete an assignment with a partner or independently. Again, consider a teacher who is using graphic organizers. A few moments before distributing the graphic organizer, the teacher considers that one of his students is having a rough day – she's just been kind of "off" and has hesitated to do independent work. As the day continued, the student's behavior became more challenging. After giving directions to the whole class and passing out the materials, the teacher quietly offers a choice to the student: "It seems like you're having a tough day today. Instead of completing this entire graphic organizer now, why don't you choose two of the sections that you would like to work on now, and then we can work on finishing the last section tomorrow. If you want to finish the last section after you do the two that you choose, great. If you're not up for it, that's okay. You can read quietly or listen to an audiobook after you finish." Although the choice in this scenario was offered "on the fly," the teacher was still able to use the strategy to show empathy and support for the student, prevent possible challenging behaviors, and increase the likelihood of task completion.

How Do I Know Instructional Choice Works?

Researchers have examined many ways teachers can implement choice or include choice in their everyday instructional and behavior management routines. The basic finding of this research: instructional choice has been shown to have positive impacts on both academic and behavioral outcomes for nearly all students (Royer et al., 2017). In addition, even very simple choices, like choosing to write with pen, pencil, or marker, or the example of choosing between two colors of paper, tend to increase students' motivation to engage in a given task. Maybe even more importantly, we have learned that the use of choice can be effective for students who exhibit some of the most challenging behaviors. For example, Jolivette et al. (2001) found that the use of choice was associated with an improvement in social and academic behaviors for students with emotional and behavioral disorders (EBD). In addition to leading to better outcomes for all students, including those with challenging behaviors, choice is viewed positively by both teachers and students. Teachers describe it as easy to use, and report that it usually fits into their routines quite easily. Students – not surprisingly – also say they like having choices about their work or school day (e.g., Ennis et al., 2021).

Our sense is that one reason the use of instructional choice is likely effective is because when students are given choices and autonomy, it allows them to feel in control in an environment where they may often feel that they have little say in how their learning occurs.

How Does Instructional Choice Build Positive Relationships with My Students?

One element of building positive relationships with students involves making sure that their ideas and input are openly solicited and respected – that their voices are heard. In most versions of traditional schooling, students are told what to do, where to sit, when to line up, etc., virtually all day long. As we have suggested, a simple benefit of using instructional choice is that students are given control over some significant elements of their learning. We think this is even more true in certain types of choices. Consider examples of choice like choosing what color handout to work on, or what to write with to complete an assignment. Research certainly supports those as helpful in increasing the likelihood students will engage in a given task, and this conveys some level of autonomy in that students can express and choose a favorite (favorite color, favor writing implement). But compare that with what we view as even 'bigger' choices, sometimes referred to as between-activity choices, in which students gain control over how to approach the tasks they need to complete. The most common examples of between-activity choices are choosing the order of assignments, or even when to complete an assignment. Order of assignments means just what the name says; a teacher might say "During our literacy block today you need to read silently for 15 min, complete the vocabulary exercise on p. 47, and revise and turn in the introductory paragraph of the essays we started yesterday. You may pick which one you work on first." Of course, teachers may need to provide support (e.g., timers, verbal prompts) to help students monitor their time, but this type of choice demonstrates an entirely new level of respect and trust for students' autonomy.

A similar and possibly even more impactful choice might involve what time of day to complete assignments; for example, a special education teacher who is supporting a student over an extended period of time throughout the day might say, "OK, we have a spelling review and a math lesson to do today, and we can do one this morning and one this afternoon. When do you want to do math?" We think these may represent out-of-the-ordinary choices students are not typically offered, and simply allowing them to choose when to work on a given task conveys that we as educators recognize that they may feel tired or anxious, or that some days they may feel like tackling the 'harder' topics (for them) first, while other days they may wish to give themselves a break by taking on the 'easier' or more preferred assignment first. Another approach that empowers students to have a say in their learning experience involves offering a choice in the topic or content of an assignment or project. For example, a teacher could offer students choice in selecting which animal and habitat to research for a science project; or students may choose which novel they would like to read out of three pre-selected texts. While this type of choice is slightly different from offering day-to-day or moment-to-moment choices, the other types of choice described can be easily embedded. Consider the science project example. A student is given the choice of which animal and habitat and then, during science class, the student can choose where in the classroom to do his research (e.g., their desk, the classroom library) and the order in which to accomplish the tasks necessary to complete the project. Adults have control over these decisions for many, if not most, of their daily activities, but allowing students to have some control is a key element of respecting their perspective and empowering them in the learning process.

Finally, while the examples above highlight things like autonomy and respect for individual differences and preferences, we think using choice "on the fly" as we have described it may be the best example of all of how relationships can be strengthened with this strategy. Consider again the student who is struggling or shutting down during a lesson. Just acknowledging the struggles shows a level of empathy and awareness (e.g., "hey, it looks like you're really having a hard time getting into this today"). While acknowledging their state is important, acting upon that recognition may be even more powerful to building and maintaining a positive relationship (e.g., "maybe you could focus better and get started if you sat at the back table, or worked at my desk?" or "OK – I know this might look overwhelming, because there's 20 problems; how about you choose any 10 problems on the page to complete and then you can be done for today?"). Again, we think this can send a powerful and positive message to students that the teacher (a) recognizes when they are struggling (or distracted, tired, upset, etc.), and (b) is willing to act upon that by making things better or more manageable for them.

How Do I Implement Instructional Choice in My Classroom?

Instructional choice can be implemented in two primary ways in the classroom: between-task and within-task (sometimes called *between-activity* choices and *within-activity* choices). To offer between-task choice, teachers simply let students pick the order of their tasks. For example, students in a language arts class may be required to complete a reading comprehension assignment, vocabulary activity, and a written entry into a journal. To offer between-task choice, a teacher would allow students to choose the order of completion. Whereas one student may choose to complete the comprehension assignment first, another may opt to complete the journal entry before moving on to other assignments.

Within-task choice is provided when a teacher offers a student options for completing a specific task, such as:

- *where* to complete the task (e.g., at the student's own desk or at another location in the classroom),
- *how* to complete the task (e.g., creating a written report or producing a graphic representation),
- *with whom* to complete the task (e.g., independently or with a partner), or
- *with what materials* to complete the task (e.g., handwritten or using a computer).

Another option for within-task choice may be provided by allowing students to select a certain number of problems to complete in a given task. For example, a student may choose seven out of ten items on a worksheet to complete. Teachers may also provide students with the choice of topic for assignments, such as writing prompts or projects (i.e., the assignment is the same – a paragraph, story, or essay – but the choice of topic is left to the student).

The first step in implementing instructional choice is to identify the problem behavior or activity that needs to be addressed. We'd like to point out that although choice has a strong evidence base, teachers do not need to provide choice all day, every day, or in every content area. Rather, we recommend choice as a targeted intervention that may be most useful in contexts in which struggles, failure, or non-compliance have become predictable for one or more students. Next, the teacher should generate a list of acceptable choices to offer to students. During this step, it is also important for the teacher to determine if there are choices that are not acceptable or appropriate to offer. For example, if offering the choice of working with a partner, are there certain pairs of students who should not work together? Similarly, will students be allowed to choose their own partner, or will the teacher assign a partner once the student decides if he or she wants to work independently or with a classmate? A variation here is that teachers can provide the choices available by identifying only acceptable options (e.g., "you may partner up with anyone at your table or work independently"). Other considerations for choice include assessing whether or not there are certain areas (e.g., working at the teacher's desk), topics, or materials that are not appropriate for a particular assignment. When planning to use instructional choice between tasks, teachers should also ensure that the order of task completion is not a critical element for student learning. It is important that a choice should not be given regarding order of completion if the successful completion of one task depends on the previous successful completion of another.

After determining which choices will be offered and making specific considerations for the task, the next step is for the teacher to prepare any materials needed or make any adjustments to the learning environment that may be required to implement choice. For example, a graphic organizer may need to be copied on two different colors of paper. Or a space in the classroom library may need to be prepared if students will be given an option for where to work. Once preparations are made, the teacher then provides the student with the pre-planned options prior to the activity or situation where behavior improvement is needed. Just like with academic questions, it is essential to provide the student with wait time after offering options. Then, the teacher simply lets the student select and engage in whichever option they prefer. Note that the student engaging in their choice is a sign of success to be celebrated (e.g., "great choice, thanks for getting started on your work!"). Finally, the last step is to monitor the impact of choice on the student's behavior and make changes as needed.

What Do I Need to Begin Implementing Instructional Choice?

Teachers can approach planning to use instructional choice in two ways. First, teachers should consider what choices may be offered to the entire class. Second, teachers should consider whether any individual students may benefit from having additional options. The instructional choice planning template (see Figure 6.2) offers options for planning for the whole class and for individual students. We encourage teachers to begin by completing this planning guide for one activity or period in their classroom and then gradually increasing the ways choice is offered to their students.

In the supplemental resources for this chapter, we have included a planning template (Figure 6.2) that can be used to help you think through how you might use instructional choice in your own classroom. The template includes examples of target behaviors that can be improved through the use of choice and examples of between-task and within-task choice options with an area for you to make your own notes about specific details and preparations. At the bottom of the planning template, there is an area to describe your data collection plan so that you can monitor the use of choice and determine whether the behaviors targeted are improving. An example of a completed planning template (see Figure 6.1) is also included. Finally, we have included a checklist of the steps needed to use instructional choice and a self-assessment checklist (see Figure 6.3), which will support accurate implementation as you are using instructional choice in your classroom.

What Does Instructional Choice look Like in a Classroom?

A clear benefit of instructional choice is that it can be easily used with students of all ages, grades, and abilities. Below, we provide three examples of instructional choice being used in a classroom. In the first example, you will read about Mr. Sullivan, a first grade teacher, who uses pre-planned instructional choice to encourage the on-task behavior of a first grade student during independent work time. In the second example, you will read about Mrs. Lopez, a seventh grade math teacher who uses reactionary choice to support a student in completing a challenging assignment. Finally, you will read about Ms. Hedrick, a tenth grade English teacher who offers "on the fly" choice to her entire class as she announces a new assignment.

Elementary Example (Pre-Planned Choice)

Adrian is a first grade student who often has a difficult time staying at his desk and being on-task during independent work time. Mr. Sullivan has noticed that most of the time, Adrian wanders to the classroom library or to the front carpet area, so he decides to offer Adrian a choice of where he will sit while completing an independent phonics sorting task after small group instruction is over. After Mr. Sullivan explains the sorting task to the group, he asks Adrian if he would prefer to complete his sorting task while sitting in the classroom library or on the front carpet. Adrian is excited and quickly selects the option of completing his work in the classroom library. Mr. Sullivan asks Adrian to repeat the directions back to him and reminds him of the expectations for independent work time before Adrian heads to the classroom library to complete his task. Adrian remained on task until his assignment was completed and then, rather than wandering around the classroom, he stayed in the classroom library and explored the newest books that Mr. Sullivan had recently added to the shelves.

Instructional Choice Planning Template		
Focus for Choice: ☐ Whole Class ☒ Individual Student: _Adrian_	**Behavior to Improve** ☒ Task Engagement ☐ Work Completion ☐ Disruptions ☐ Following Directions ☒ Other: _Staying in assigned area_	**Context** (class, time of day, activity where problem behavior is likely): _Independent work (especially phonics) – will focus on independent sorting task after small group time_
Possible Choices Select all possible appropriate/acceptable choices for the student(s) in this context		**Details & Preparation Needed**
Between-Tasks ☐ Order of tasks/content areas/activities ☐ Activity Menu/Choice Board (e.g., choose 3 tasks in a row on Tic-Tac-Toe Board)		

Within-Tasks
☐ Items to Complete Within a Task/Activity
  ☐ Odds/Evens
  ☐ Pick ___ problems/items to do
  ☐ Other
☐ Product Format
  ☐ Paper/Report ☐ Presentation/Speech
  ☐ Video ☐ Dialogue with teacher
  ☐ Audio recording ☐ Other
☒ Where to Work
  ☒ Desk ☐ Table
  ☐ Teacher Desk ☐ Flexible Seating Area
  ☒ Carpet/Floor ☒ Other
☒ With Whom to Work
  ☒ Independent ☐ Preferred Adult
  ☐ Peer ☐ Small Group
  ☒ Teacher ☐ Other
☒ Materials to Use
  ☐ Pencil ☐ Pen ☐ Marker
  ☐ Specific Paper ☒ Device ☒ Other
☐ Reinforcer/reward to work for
☐ Other: _____
		Easiest for me is giving him choice to work at his desk, on the front carpet, or in our classroom library (Adrian likes it there). Need to have his phonics sorting materials travel-ready (keep in small tub) and space available on carpet & in our classroom library.
		
		Could give choice to work by himself or with me, but only on days where the rest of class can be more independent.
		
		Could give different sorting materials to work with: words to cut out on paper & sort, phonics sorting app, have words and sorting organizer on a google slide on his chromebook. (More prep needed)

Data Collection Plan Describe the specific behavior targeted for improvement: _Time where Adrian is in his assigned area actively working on his sorting task or doing an approved activity (e.g., reading) after completing the task_ Describe the metric (e.g., % of time on-task) and method for data collection: _% of time on task with momentary time sampling (every 2 min I'll record if he's currently in his area and on-task)_		

FIGURE 6.1 Completed Example of Instructional Choice Planning Template

Secondary Example (Reactionary Choice)

At the end of her direct instruction lesson about chance and probability, Mrs. Lopez distributes a worksheet with 10 word-problems for students to solve. A few minutes later, she notices that Jana has not started the assignment and is sitting at her desk with her head down. Mrs. Lopez quietly asks Jana if everything is okay, and Jana responds by telling her that she hates math, and she doesn't feel like doing this "stupid assignment." Mrs. Lopez asks Jana a few questions to assess her understanding of the content. After determining that Jana understands the content and the assignment directions, she decides to offer a choice to Jana. Mrs. Lopez acknowledges that Jana is having a rough day and tells her that she understands she is not feeling up to completing the assignment, so instead, she can choose to complete either the odd-numbered problems or the even-numbered problems. Jana perks up and seems surprised by this choice; she opts for the odd-numbered problems and upon completion, Mrs. Lopez praises her for her effort (see Chapter 7).

Secondary Example ("On the Fly" Choice)

Ms. Hedrick's tenth grade English class has been learning about how authors made choices regarding the structure of text, ordering of events, and manipulation of time to create suspense or surprise in literature. The class has just finished reading *Fahrenheit 451* by Ray Bradbury, and Ms. Hedrick is announcing an assignment for students to identify three ways that Bradbury creates suspense in the novel. Originally, Ms. Hedrick was going to assign this as an essay. However, as she is announcing the assignment, she realizes that this assignment can be completed in a variety of ways. She decides to offer students options for how they will complete the assignment, and she provides the following choices: a traditional essay, a drawing or graphic, or a multimedia presentation. She also asks students if they have other ideas for how they might complete the assignment. One student suggests writing a song or rap, and another student suggests an oral presentation. Although Ms. Hedrick will not have time for oral presentations in class, she offers students the option of recording their oral presentation on a platform such as

Zoom, Canvas, or Flipgrid that she will be able to view at a later time. Without any additional planning, Ms. Hedrick was able to provide five additional options for completing this assignment than what she had originally planned, and all students seemed interested and motivated to begin work on these projects.

Final Thoughts

We hope this chapter has made it clear that instructional choice is a powerful, easy-to-implement strategy that is well-supported by research, and that there are several ways to use choice in classrooms to support improved behavior, better academic outcomes, and more positive relationships with students. We described how choice can be implemented (a) proactively, in contexts where predictable failures are anticipated; (b) reactively, when resistance in students is encountered; or (c) "on the fly," as teachers encounter unexpected opportunities to offer students a choice, even when no specific choice was pre-planned. We described several ways that choices can be offered, including within-activity choices (e.g., where to sit, how to complete an assignment) and between-activity choices (e.g., order of assignments, or when to complete a given assignment). We also tried to convey that choice is among the easiest strategies teachers can use; while some pre-planning is necessary (and we provided templates for this planning, and examples of the use of choice in classrooms), in the vast majority of cases the planning and preparation needed are minimal. In short, instructional choice is a strategy all teachers should have in their repertoire!

An important benefit – and another argument for all teachers to be prepared to use choice in a variety of contexts – is the potential of choice to positively influence teacher-student relationships. The effects of instructional choice on getting students engaged in their academic work and improving behavioral outcomes are well-documented (e.g., Royer et al., 2017), but choice can also be important to building and maintaining relationships with students. Specifically, we described how providing choice in itself conveys teacher support for students' autonomy and preferences, and we provided examples that illustrate how the use of choice can increase positive interactions between students and teachers. Acknowledging when students are struggling and supporting them with a choice (i.e., reactionary choice) may send the particularly valuable message that not only are students' needs recognized, but that teachers are ready to respond to those needs with empathy, and with a positive, supportive response.

References

Ennis, R. P., Lane, K. L., & Flemming, S. C. (2021). Empowering teachers with low-intensity strategies: Supporting students at-risk for EBD with instructional choice during reading. *Exceptionality, 29*(1), 61–79.

Jolivette, K., Wehby, J. H., Canale, J., & Massey, N. G. (2001). Effect of choice-making opportunities on the behavior of students with emotional and behavioral disorders. *Behavioral Disorders, 26*, 131–145.

Royer, D. J., Lane, K. L., Cantwell, E. D., & Messenger, M. L. (2017). A systematic review of the evidence base for instructional choice in K–12 settings. *Behavioral Disorders, 42*(3), 89–107.

Instructional Choice Planning Template		
Focus for Choice: ☐ Whole Class ☐ Individual Student: _____	**Behavior to Improve** ☐ Task Engagement ☐ Work Completion ☐ Disruptions ☐ Following Directions ☐ Other: _____	**Context** (class, time of day, activity where problem behavior is likely):
Possible Choices *Select all possible appropriate/acceptable choices for the student(s) in this context*		**Details & Preparation Needed**
Between-Tasks	☐ Order of tasks/content areas/activities ☐ Activity Menu/Choice Board (e.g., choose 3 tasks in a row on Tic-Tac-Toe Board)	

Within-Tasks	☐ Items to Complete Within a Task/Activity
	  ☐ Odds/Evens
	  ☐ Pick ___ problems/items to do
	  ☐ Other
	☐ Product Format
	  ☐ Paper/Report ☐ Presentation/Speech
	  ☐ Video ☐ Dialogue with teacher
	  ☐ Audio recording ☐ Other
	☐ Where to Work
	  ☐ Desk ☐ Table
	  ☐ Teacher Desk ☐ Flexible Seating Area
	  ☐ Carpet/Floor ☐ Other
	☐ With Whom to Work
	  ☐ Independent ☐ Preferred Adult
	  ☐ Peer ☐ Small Group
	  ☐ Teacher ☐ Other
	☐ Materials to Use
	  ☐ Pencil ☐ Pen ☐ Marker
	  ☐ Specific Paper ☐ Device ☐ Other
	☐ Reinforcer/reward to work for
	☐ Other: _____	

Data Collection Plan *Describe the specific behavior targeted for improvement:* *Describe the metric (e.g., % of time on-task) and method for data collection:*		

FIGURE 6.2 Instructional Choice Planning Template

Instructional Choice Steps & Self-Assessment

0→Not in Place 1→Partially in Place 2→Fully in Place

STEPS	How Did I do?		
1. Identify the problem behavior or activity that needs to be addressed	☐ 0	☐ 1	☐ 2
2. Generate a list of acceptable & appropriate choices to offer to students.	☐ 0	☐ 1	☐ 2
3. Prepare any materials needed or make any adjustments to the learning environment that may be required to implement choice.	☐ 0	☐ 1	☐ 2
4. Provide the student with the pre-planned options prior to the activity or situation where behavior improvement is needed.	☐ 0	☐ 1	☐ 2
5. Provide wait time.	☐ 0	☐ 1	☐ 2
6. Allow the student to select and engage in whichever option they prefer.	☐ 0	☐ 1	☐ 2
7. Monitor the impact of choice on the student's behavior and make changes as needed.	☐ 0	☐ 1	☐ 2

Notes & Reflection:

FIGURE 6.3 Instructional Choice Implementation and Self-Assessment Checklist

7

Increasing Opportunities to Respond

In this chapter, we explain how and why increasing opportunities to respond can be used to improve student behavior. We begin by providing a definition and description of this strategy, followed by a brief overview of the research that supports the use of this strategy. Next, we explain how increasing opportunities to respond can build positive relationships with students, particularly those who demonstrate challenging behaviors. Finally, we describe how to implement this strategy and provide two examples of what this practice might look like in a classroom. The supplemental resources for this chapter include a planning template (one blank for your use and one completed as an example) and a self-assessment checklist to support implementation fidelity.

What Is Meant by Opportunities to Respond?

This chapter focuses on Opportunities to Respond, commonly abbreviated as OTRs, which comes as a recommended strategy because research has consistently shown that students do better – in several different ways (more on that in a moment) – when they are actively responding to instruction, rather than just being passive learners (e.g., listening to a teacher talk or lecture). OTRs are important to think about for another reason, too: students with disabilities, or those who are at risk for other academic or behavioral challenges, tend to receive fewer OTRs than their peers (when in fact they probably need them even more than their peers). This is easy to understand – it may be human nature for the teacher to call more often on those students the teacher believes are more likely to have the "right" answer, rather than call on those who may give incorrect (on unrelated) responses, or simply may not answer at all.

One way to think about OTRs is to consider a formal definition: an opportunity to respond is a teacher-initiated action that requires some verbal or motor response on the part of the student. While this may sound a bit formal or complex, the idea is really quite simple: during instruction, are students asked to respond in some way? Perhaps more importantly, how *frequently* does this occur? A lot of what teachers will hear or read about OTRs focuses not just on the message that OTRs are a good idea, but more often on ways to increase *rates* of OTRs in each instructional context or lesson. This last part is due to pretty consistent research over many years that shows that in most classrooms, OTRs occur at rates that are less than ideal for learning. A final note on definition is this: while an OTR itself is really just the opportunity for a student to respond, it should go without saying that when students do respond – as they will tend to do when appropriate OTRs are delivered – the teacher should always acknowledge the response in a positive way. Reinforcing responses, both for being correct and for the effort to actually offer a response, is a critical element to maximizing perhaps the most positive benefit of OTRs, which is to keep students engaged.

But what does an OTR actually look like in practice? Noting the definition says an OTR is a teacher-initiated action, it may be simpler to just recognize that in the vast majority of cases this is literally a verbal statement: the teacher makes a request or asks a question. But as we note below in our examples and guidelines for practice, the response the student makes can take many forms, and in fact it is best practice to vary these intentionally to target different needs and contexts. We highlight three ways OTRs may differ: (a) a teacher may ask for a group versus an individual response; (b) the form of the actual response – the behavior required – may vary (e.g., a verbal response, a written response, or some gesture, like a thumbs up); or (c) what we call the level of the OTR may vary – the teacher can ask for a simple parroting of a response ("we have to make sure the denominators are the same. What has to be the same, Carl?"), or ask a more complex content-related question (e.g., "who can name a branch of government? Raise your hand if you know one"). Both are OTRs, but require a different level of thought, effort, and skill or knowledge. We describe each of these dimensions in more detail below.

Group versus Individual OTRs

This distinction is both simple and practical. An individual OTR is directed at an individual student (e.g., "Joseph, what letter is this?"), whereas a group OTR is directed at a large group, or even the whole class ("OK, class, let's quickly review the state capitals we've learned. Everyone, the capital of Alabama is…" [waits for response]). While it might be ideal in some ways to elicit lots of individual responses from every student during instruction, this is only really practical or even possible during 1:1 instruction (or maybe very small group instruction), which can only happen in limited instances and brief times throughout the day. In contrast, consider the challenge of trying to give every one of 20, 25, or 30 kids even one opportunity to respond, let alone multiple opportunities, in a single lesson. One way to increase the number and rate at which any individual student receives an OTR is for the teacher to simply mix in group and individual OTRs. In a practical sense, using a mix of group and individual OTRs is good for engagement – the teacher is essentially calling on most or all students frequently (i.e., when a group OTR is delivered, every student in the class or in that instructional group is considered to have received an OTR). This can be especially useful in keeping kids engaged, and more specifically in re-engaging kids whose attention may be fading. If the teacher sees a student starting to daydream, for example, a quick OTR sequence can help bring him back (e.g., "Ok, for this next part everyone just needs a pencil. What do we need for this part, Freddy?").

Beyond the practicality of varying group and individual OTRs, this can also be directly beneficial instructionally. Suppose a teacher knows a particular student is just beginning to grasp some aspect of new content – and thus is not proficient and would be unlikely to be 100% accurate (or even 80%) in responding. The teacher could intentionally ask a group OTR, followed by an individual OTR to that specific student. Imagine this scenario, during a math review session:

Teacher: "Ok, everyone, what's 7 times 7?"
Group answers (with most, but not all, students chiming in): "49."
Teacher: "Right. 7 times 7 is 49. William, what's 7 times 7?"
William repeats: "49."
Teacher: "Great job, William; 7 times 7 is 49."

Note that several really good things happened in this simple interchange. First, because the teacher knew William is not firm in his multiplication facts, she did NOT call on him individually – putting him on the spot – with a challenging question. She knew the odds were high that he'd either (a) get the answer wrong, requiring her to engage in some correction and re-teaching; (b) shut down (e.g., "I don't know") or maybe not answer at all; or (c) respond inappropriately (e.g., "how would I know?"). But she also looped back to him immediately, right after he had just heard the correct answer from the group – she knew now that the odds of him responding correctly in that sequence were now really high. Thus, not only did she not put him on the spot and risk a negative or at least corrective instructional exchange, she was able to reinforce him for participating with a correct response. Finally, from a simple instructional standpoint – what did William, and in fact all students, hear in that brief exchange? They heard the correct answer (49) to that problem *four separate times* (either a student response, or the teacher repeating it). Further, they heard zero incorrect responses. Students – especially those who may have been struggling or simply just learning that content for the first time – will benefit tremendously from hearing, and giving, a high rate of correct responding. To reiterate this point, consider a possible alternative. Suppose a teacher asks simply, "who knows what 7 times 7 is?" Then suppose a student shouts out, "56!" Then another says, "no… I think it's 48." Even if the teacher now gives the correct response, students have already heard the wrong answer more often than the correct response. While some students can absorb this, those who struggle may now be at even greater risk of confusion – they don't know, and are now less likely to remember, which of the many different answers they just heard is actually correct. In short, using group and individual OTRs strategically makes sound instructional sense.

Nature of the Response in an OTR

We highlight that teachers administer nearly all OTRs with a verbal statement or request. But the student response can and should vary. Put simply, most teachers know that good instruction is much more than simple verbal exchanges. We list several examples of the type of OTRs a teacher may request in Table 7.1. Note that some are used simply to mix things up – to keep kids engaged and interested. For example, we have found consistently that when we demonstrate the use of individual dry-erase boards in our college level courses, our students are reluctant to give them up and ask if we can use them more regularly in our

TABLE 7.1 Forms of Opportunities to Respond

Response form	Application example
Thumbs up or down	"Tell me if this fraction has been reduced to lowest terms; thumbs up or down."
	"Japan was part of the Axis Powers in World War II. Agree or disagree – show me with a thumbs up or down."
Yes/no cards (each student has a set of cards; one with YES and one with NO)	"Look at the first sentence – any punctuation errors? Show me yes or no."
Dry-erase boards (individual)	"Ok – when I point to the problem, you have 30 seconds to write down your answer. Hold the board to your chest to show me you're ready, and then only turn it over when I say, 'show me your answer'.")

courses. Some response forms, however, are important because they are more than just a yes/no or a right/wrong response – they require the student to demonstrate the precise skill we may be working on (e.g., solving a math problem, including writing the response in the correct form and in the right place; spelling a word correctly).

Another reason several of these forms of group OTRs are recommended is that they provide the teacher with a simple means of monitoring how students are doing – whether they are getting the material during a given lesson. In the case of the thumbs up/thumbs down or response card methods, the teacher can do a quick scan of the room and see at least in a general sense whether most or all kids seem to be getting a concept. Note that we do NOT suggest that this is a precise method of individual assessment or progress monitoring but that it can be useful as a general guide for teachers at the moment as to whether they can move on with a lesson (if most or all kids seems to be responding correctly), whether they need to slow down, provide more examples, or re-teach a specific concept (if most or a large number of kids seem to be showing incorrect responses), and whether certain students would benefit from additional instruction in a small group.

And one final note about thumbs up specifically – we have heard at times that teachers might ask a student how they're doing on a particular assignment or task, or basically ask "are you getting this, Terry?" or "do you understand – let me know with a thumbs up." While we fully endorse the idea of checking in with students, a caution here is that some students who struggle academically may not be very skilled at this type of awareness. In other words, they don't always know whether or when they got lost on a problem or assignment, whether they're 'doing it right,' or whether or not they truly understand a concept. Thus, while this type of question might technically be considered an OTR, we caution against using this in most contexts. In contrast, a thumbs up is still appropriate for many specific content-related questions (e.g., "can we reduce this fraction further?"), as those are a true check of knowledge or understanding of a very specific skill or task.

Level of OTR

We use the term *level* here simply to note how the nature of questions that make up OTRs can vary. For example, when actively instructing students in academic content, it's perfectly reasonable to ask for responses to fairly complex or difficult questions about the content at hand (e.g., "so why do you think the Romans devoted so much attention to building aqueducts?"). But most OTRs are not deep or difficult questions – indeed OTRs should *not* be that difficult at all, and there should always be a high likelihood of correct responding. Content-specific questions can be basic recall and simple application questions, and can even be as simple as parroting a response just given. Teachers may also seek responses by just asking simple logistical questions about the day's task or assignment. For example, a teacher may explain an assignment by telling students to complete five problems of their choosing from a worksheet, to share with a partner and check their work, and then to turn in their completed sheets to the folder on her desk. She might then ask a series of questions ("how many problems do you need to do, Robert?" "and what do you need to do before you turn them in, Callie?" and finally, "everyone, where do you turn in your completed papers?" In the examples we provide in the final sections of this chapter, you can see the teachers varying these levels considerably.

How Do I Know OTRs Work?

Research on OTRs confirms exactly what you might expect. The overarching message from research is simple: higher rates of OTRs typically result in higher rates of engagement, which in turn is associated with improved academic performance and reductions in disruptive or off-task behavior. MacSuga-Gage and Simonsen (2015) summarized studies on teacher delivered OTRs in K-12 classrooms, and their general findings have been consistently confirmed by similar reviews (Common et al., 2020). Teachers who increase their rates of OTRs can expect to see things like increased active student responding (a no-brainer! Students will respond more given more opportunities to do so), more on-task behavior, and a greater percentage of academic engaged time.

Among the findings of these reviews is also the notion that varying types of OTRs, like we described above, may also be particularly beneficial. For example, specifically including group (or "choral response") OTRs may be beneficial, and at least one study showed specifically that the best outcomes were observed when teachers taught with a mix of both individual and group response OTRs. Interestingly, one of the most commonly researched types of OTR has been response cards, and these outcomes follow the pattern of improving both academic and behavioral outcomes. While we suspect the most effective teachers use a variety of OTRs, we speculate that response cards may be especially effective for some students because of the active nature of the response required – it's not just a verbal response. Response cards require, at minimum, raising or showing a preprepared response card (e.g., a yes/no card), or actually writing a response on a card and then raising it. Again, our experience is consistent with this research in that students of all ages (including our college students) really seem to enjoy engaging in this type of response activity; at minimum, they tend to persist and stay engaged when it is implemented.

Finally, Sutherland and Wehby (2001) provided one of the earliest reviews of research on the effects of OTRs when they focused specifically on the effects of OTRs on students with emotional and behavioral disorders (EBD). We find this especially valuable, as we might argue that students with EBD may be among those students most in need of supports that help them stay engaged in classrooms. In addition to confirming the positive academic and behavioral effects noted above for all students, the review by Sutherland and Wehby also found that rates of OTR were generally quite low in most classrooms. While the precise target rate for OTRs has been debated, these researchers found rates well below one OTR per minute in most classrooms, while most recommendations suggest a *minimum* of 3–5 OTRs per minute during periods of active instruction. In short – rates of OTRs do not appear high in most classrooms, and research consistently confirms the benefits of OTRs, including the specific benefits of increasing the rate at which they occur. We suppose it is theoretically possible to offer too many OTRs, or to offer them too quickly. One rule of thumb in this regard has been to simply make sure the OTRs do not come so fast or frequently that students don't have time to respond. Still, given all we have learned from the extensive research on this topic for at least two decades, we are very comfortable encouraging all teachers to use the strategies outlined in this chapter to increase their rates of using a variety of OTRs during instruction with all students.

And to be clear, our emphasis on the importance of OTRs is because engagement is what we're really after. This is because engagement itself is a really good predictor of both academic and social or behavioral success. The logic here is simple – if students are actively engaged in a lesson (e.g., listening to the teacher when appropriate, responding to questions verbally, producing written responses when asked or required), they are certainly more likely to learn content and acquire skills than when they are not engaged (e.g., not looking at or listening to the teacher but daydreaming, looking out the window, or putting their head down; refusing to respond to questions, or offering off-task comments). But as should be obvious, engagement also implies that students are on-task and working appropriately – and thus they cannot also be disruptive or off-task.

How Do OTRs Help Build Positive Relationships with My Students?

We have defined how OTRs can help students become more engaged and maintain that engagement, and how this leads to both academic and behavioral success. Indeed, the research on OTRs provides very strong evidence of these effects, which leads us to recommend it to all teachers. But we also stress the importance of positive relationships between students and teachers as key to students' success. How do OTRs contribute to this? A simple way to think of this is to remember what OTRs accomplish above all else – engagement. Moreover, this engagement is established by enhancing and increasing the reciprocal communications and positive interactions that occur between teachers and students. Recall that we noted research suggesting that rates of OTRs – the simple act of teachers getting responses from students – is woefully low in most classrooms. In other words, it is quite possible for many students to spend significant parts of their day, maybe even entire class periods, with little to no direct interaction with their teachers. They may be passive learners, of course, and may even be considered passively engaged if they sit still, listen, and do not disrupt the class. Indeed, many teachers might find this acceptable. But in the absence of any interaction, and positive interactions specifically, we cannot say that there is a positive relationship between student and teacher.

Note further the simple point we made when defining OTRs: they should be made up predominantly of questions or requests students can easily comply with, and the teacher should be sure to reinforce both correctness and the effort students put into responding. We do not suggest that OTRs alone are a fix-all for relationship building, but especially in classes where students experience few or no OTRs and the positive feedback that follows nearly all of them, enhancing these rates even a little is certain to contribute to an overall positive relationship between students and teacher. For this reason, we argue that increased rates of OTRs are surely a key ingredient, among many, that contribute to positive student-teacher relationships.

How Do I Implement OTRs in My Classroom?

We describe in the next section (What Do I Need to Begin) some key elements to planning for the specific use of OTRs – targeting specific times of day, content area classes, and students for whom increased rates of OTR are probably a good choice as a first effort at improving engagement. But for the moment we talk in this section about some simple strategies teachers can use, highlighting some of the distinctions we described earlier in defining OTRs and the ways they can vary. First, let's look at perhaps the simplest form of OTR – a simple verbal question – and how it can vary. Consider this example:

Teacher: "OK, remember that yesterday when we started adding fractions, the first thing we looked at was the denominators. What was the first thing we looked at, Charlie?
Charlie: "The denominators."
Teacher: "Right, denominators. Thank you, Charlie. And – everyone – we had to determine if the denominators were the… _____" (voice trails off as she gestures to the entire class to respond).
Several students chorally respond at the same time: "…same."
Teacher: "Exactly! Denominators need to be the same before we can add the fractions."

Notice that the teacher used an individual OTR for Charlie, and then a group OTR for the entire class. As the lesson progresses, she would continue to use a mix of group and individual OTRs. But notice too how she used these forms of OTR. She used a simple parroting or recall OTR for Charlie – all he needed to do was literally repeat what she had just said. Perhaps she knows he struggles with math, or his attention frequently wanders (or both), and she just wanted to engage him early on. Next, she asked a question that may have been slightly more difficult – what was it about the denominators students needed to focus on? And would they remember that from yesterday's lesson? Perhaps the teacher wasn't sure all students would remember, and didn't have confidence any one student she might call on would give the correct response. Thus, she chose to offer a group OTR, figuring that at least a critical mass of the students in the class would offer the correct response – which they did. This in turn gave her the chance to praise them for that correct response. Implementing these verbal OTRs and asking for a mix of individual and group responses are not difficult at all, and, as we note in the next section, require very little planning or preparation. Indeed, the primary prep work is in deciding when (during what instructional times or class periods) to use this type of OTR, and giving some thought to those students who would most likely benefit most from individual OTRs.

A very popular form of OTR involves response cards, which can either be prepared in advance, or can be some form of blank card or individual dry-erase board on which students write their responses. Common forms of prepared response cards include Yes/No cards, or A, B, and C (or 1, 2 and 3) cards. To use prepared response cards, the teacher asks questions throughout the lesson that can be answered with the cards (i.e., a yes/no question, or a multiple choice question). Yes/no cards may be the simplest to incorporate into instruction. To use these, the teacher simply pauses at any given moment to check for understanding by offering a yes/no question (e.g., "OK, look at problem #4. Can I add those fractions in their current form? Show me with your response card"). The use of multiple choice cards (A, B, C) requires a bit more preparation, but is not too complicated. Suppose, for example, in a government lesson the teacher displays on the board or screen that A = the executive branch, B = the legislative branch, and C = the judicial branch. She can then ask a series of questions during the lesson and ask students to hold up their cards to indicate which branch of government she is referring to (e.g., "Brown versus Board of Education struck down laws that allowed schools to be segregated – which branch of government was responsible for the Brown decision?"). An obvious benefit of prepared response cards is that they are re-usable – once a teacher has a set of yes/no cards, or A, B, and C cards, these can obviously be used again and again in almost any context where OTRs may be a useful strategy.

An equally popular alternative to prepared response cards is write-on or dry-erase response cards. While some schools or districts may have purchased sets of small, individual dry-erase boards for classroom use, an inexpensive alternative we've seen teachers commonly use is the homemade version – a sheet of heavy cardstock inserted into a clear sheet protector. Providing one of these to each student, along with a dry-erase marker and a tissue or paper towel to use as an eraser, provides students with their own individual dry-erase response card. While these are simple and largely self-explanatory to use, there are a few guidelines to keep in mind. First, the responses students are asked to write should be brief – the solution to a math problem, a vocabulary or spelling word, or even the letter or number of a correct response from among several choices. Response cards are not meant to be used for writing lengthy responses. Second, the precise procedure for using response cards should be taught and rehearsed (just like most other school-related skills). A common sequence taught to students is that they turn their response card over, face down, as soon as they have written their answer. Then, only on the teacher's signal do they lift their response cards so the teacher can see. Because it's important that the teacher can see all responses with a quick scan of the room and thus get an idea of what students are understanding versus struggling with, we stress the need to define for students exactly how response cards are used (we like to have then flip up their cards and hold them to the chests, or 'just under your chin'). As noted, we teach and practice this skill prior to using it during instruction to make sure students can quickly and easily use the cards as intended.

In addition to verbal OTRs and response cards, teachers can also have students use gestures, like a thumbs up or thumbs down (used just like a yes/no card), or even just a hand raise. For a hand raise, the teacher simply uses hand-raising as a 'vote' – for example, a teacher might say, "True or false: part of the cell is called the nucleus – raise your hand if you think this is true." Of course, there are several options for increasing OTRs that incorporate technology (e.g., Slido, Zoom polls, iClicker) and when available, these can be an excellent way to vary the types of OTRs. However, we think it is important to emphasize (hence our low-tech examples) that you do not *need* technology to increase OTRs in your classroom.

What Do I Need to Begin?

It should not be difficult at all for teachers to *implement* OTRs, given as we noted that the vast majority of these are simple verbal statements or requests. The more important parts, we think, are helping teachers focus on a few key aspects of their use of OTRs, namely (a) the frequency they are used (i.e., increasing rates of OTRs); (b) varying the types of OTRs that are offered (or more precisely the types of responses that are required); and (c) making sure that all students receive multiple OTRs. Toward this last point, while it is important that ALL students receive high rates of OTRs during instruction, this may be especially important for students who are prone to disengaging, losing attention, becoming disruptive, or just struggling academically. As we have suggested, when a student is just beginning to lose attention – to fade or check out – a simple OTR might be a good way to get them re-engaged, and we recommend particularly a very simple OTR (e.g., "Callie, look at problem number 3 – are those denominators the same?"). At the end of this chapter, we have included a planning template that includes a data collection tool (see Figure 7.2), a completed example of the template (see Figure 7.1), and a fidelity checklist (see Figure 7.3). The planning template we provide has a place to record any materials that might be needed for teachers who are hoping to use more than just verbal OTRs (e.g., dry-erase boards, yes/no cards, and clickers).

What Does It look Like in the Classroom?

In this chapter, we defined opportunities to respond (OTRs) and described the documented benefits of teachers increasing the rate at which they use OTRs during instruction. The following examples provide descriptions of what the use of OTRs might look like in an elementary classroom, with Mr. Vasquez, and in a secondary content class taught by Ms. Wingfield.

Elementary Example

Mr. Vasquez teaches a class of third-graders that includes several students with disabilities, and two others who have 504 plans due to attentional problems associated with ADHD. A special education teacher, Ms. Dunbar, consults with him and occasionally co-teaches certain lessons, but he is responsible for most academic instruction for his class. Ms. Dunbar suggested a few strategies for increasing OTRs, and demonstrated these during a couple of their co-taught lessons, after which Mr. Vasquez was hooked. Especially when he served as the support teacher during these lessons, he was amazed that he could easily see his students – including those who struggled most with inattention or disruption – staying engaged much more than he would have predicted and responding even better as Ms. Dunbar praised their responses and attention. He adjusts his own instruction in a couple of ways.

First, Mr. Vasquez is committed to simply adding in more verbal OTRs during his normal instruction. He keeps a 3x5 card on his clipboard with a column of dates listed on it, and simply records tally marks for OTRs he delivers during language arts each day. He has set an informal goal of 20 per lesson, though for now, he is really just trying to document and increase the rate at which he offers OTRs. He also has made notes on this card about four students he is most concerned about – they are the ones who most frequently lose attention during lessons, and often end up disrupting others with off-task comments. He watched Ms. Dunbar engage them with two strategies. One was to use simple, logistical OTRs (e.g., "Ok, guys – all you need for this next part is a pencil and one piece of paper. What do you need for this part, Jamal?"). The other was to use a group OTR on a content-related question, followed by an individual OTR for one of the target students:

Ms. Dunbar: Everyone, what's the capital of Ohio?
Whole class, in unison: Columbus.
Ms. Dunbar: Good. Steven – what's the capital of Ohio?
Steven (mumbling): Columbus.
Ms. Dunbar: Good job, Steven. Columbus is the capital of Ohio.

Mr. Vasquez lists his four target students on the card as well, to remind himself to make sure to give them each at least five individual OTRs during each lesson (in addition to the regular OTRs he will use for all students). The first noticeable change he makes is that now he begins each lesson with a statement of expectations, objectives, materials needed, etc., and uses a mix of groups and individual OTRs to confirm these with students. In doing this with every lesson, he notices that classes and lesson begin much more smoothly now, and he feels much more confident that he can keep most of his students engaged throughout most lessons now, and even when this fails he feels he has more time to work individually or in small groups when they begin to struggle or disengage.

Secondary Example

In contrast to Mr. Vasquez, Ms. Wingfield teaches 7th grade science, and one class period in particular seems to be her most challenging. There are a few students in this class with IEPs for their learning disabilities, but Ms. Wingfield describes the whole class as just being "super active" and difficult to settle down. Even when the students focus on the task at hand, she finds that they talk out constantly – sometimes with appropriate questions or shouting out answers, even though she has tried to stress hand-raising as an expectation – but just as often with random, off-task comments or conversations. She learned about OTRs from a colleague, and has read up on response cards in particular. She thinks her students will especially enjoy having a manipulative – a dry-erase board to write on – so decides to give this a try (see Figure 7.1 for her completed planning template). She explores purchasing individual dry-erase boards for the class, but in the short term decides to just make her own so she can try out using response cards. She inserts sheets of cardstock into individual clear sheet protectors, and at the start of each lesson passes out one of the homemade dry-erase cardstock response cards, a dry-erase marker, and a tissue to use as an eraser. She also prepares several simple PowerPoint slides that contain vocabulary words from the current unit. Each slide lists two or three vocabulary words identified with the letters A, B, or C (e.g., Slide 1: A = mitosis, B = meiosis; Slide 2: A = diffusion, B = diffraction; Slide 3: A = mass, B = volume, C = weight).

When the lesson begins, Ms. Wingfield makes sure each student has the needed materials and reminds them they only need their response card, their marker, and their tissue for this activity (she checks this with a group reminder, followed by

Increasing Opportunities to Respond ♦ 119

Opportunities to Respond Planning Template

Content Area: *Science*		Specific Students to Target: *Clarence – off-task and talking out*	
OTR Method (e.g., choral/group, whiteboards, response cards)	**Materials Needed**	**Steps to Introduce & Implement** (including any needed changes to current instruction)	**Sample OTRs**

Response Cards – dry erase boards	*Cardstock, sheet protectors, dry erase markers, tissue*	1. *Prepare vocab slides*
		2. *Provide OTR materials & remind students to only have them out*
		3. *Model & practice how to respond*
		   a. *Write response letter*
		   b. *Turn board face down*
		   c. *Hold up on signal*
		4. *Provide OTRs with wait time & feedback*
		5. *Ask one student to share their response*
			Mitosis vs. Meiosis – this involves one cell division

Goal: *(aim for a specific OTR rate) Start with 2/min during vocab warm up; build up to 3+/min*

Data Collection Directions: During instruction each time you provide an OTR, make a tally mark in the OTR data column below. Count the number of tallies and record in the total OTRs column. Record the length of the lesson in minutes. Then, divide the total number of OTRs by the length of the lesson to get the rate of OTRs per minute.

DAY	OTR Data	Total OTRs	Lesson Length (min)	OTR Rate
Monday	||||| ||||| ||||| |||||		21	10	2.1/min
Tuesday	||||| ||||| ||||| |||||	20	12	1.7/min
Wednesday	||||| ||||| ||||| ||||| |||||	25	11	2.3/min
Thursday				
Friday				

FIGURE 7.1 Completed Example of Opportunities to Respond Planning Template

some verbal OTRs: "you need your dry-erase sheet, one marker and a tissue, and that's all. What three things do we need?"). As the lesson begins, she displays Slide 1, which has A = mitosis and B = meiosis. She then asks a few questions about each, and asks students to write down A or B on their response card, but to keep the sheet flat on their desk, face down, until she signals for them to show their responses. For example, she first asks, "this involves one cell division; write down A or B"). She repeats the question once, allows about 15 sec for students to write down A or B, and after one last prompt ("everyone ready?"), says "show me your answer." The students raise their response cards so she can see them all, and she notices that virtually all students got this one correct. She first reinforces their responding and raising their cards correctly – "good job everyone; I can see everyone's answer, and I can read them all clearly." She calls on one student who got the correct answer, but is seated next to one of the few students who did not write the correct response. "You said A for mitosis, Angelique – why?" Angelique responds with a simple, "well, in mitosis the cell divides once, but in meiosis there are two cell divisions." Ms. Wingfield responds, "that's right – mitosis involves one cell division, while meiosis involves two." Turning to the student who answered this question incorrectly, Ms. Wingfield quickly adds, "which process has only one cell division, Clarence?" He begrudgingly says softly, "mitosis," and Ms. Wingfield reinforces him with a "yep – mitosis has one cell division" before moving right into the next questions: "OK, erase your boards and answer this: which process involves body cells?" She continues the process for only 10–15 min during most science classes, focusing on engaging students as well as orienting them to the vocabulary they will use in the lesson or assignment for that day.

Final Thoughts

In this chapter, we defined opportunities to respond (OTRs), and briefly described the extensive research that supports the use of OTRs. We highlighted especially the idea that when teachers increase their rates of OTRs, students tend to be more engaged, more successful academically, and less disruptive or off-task. We described several ways OTRs might vary, including how they are delivered (e.g., group versus individual OTRs) as well as the actual response teachers ask of students (a verbal response, a gesture like a thumbs up or down, or the use of response cards). Included in our discussion of the varying types of OTRs a teacher uses was a brief discussion of how this also makes instructional sense; a teacher could use a group OTR, for example, just prior to asking an individual student for a response as way to prompt that student toward the correct response, and avoid putting them on the spot unnecessarily in terms of content they have not mastered yet. We also pointed out that increasing OTRs – especially in classrooms where there are currently low rates of OTRs – may have indirect benefits for student-teacher relationships. By initiating a larger number of interactions in the form of OTRs, and with these designed specifically to lead to high rates of correct responding, teachers set up numerous additional opportunities for student success and teacher affirmation of that success in the form of verbal or other reinforcement. For all these reasons, the use of OTRs and particularly increasing the rates of OTRs teachers provide comes as a highly recommended practice.

References

Common, E. A., Lane, K. L., Cantwell, E. D., Brunsting, N. C., Oakes, W. P., Germer, K. A., & Bross, L. A. (2020). Teacher-delivered strategies to increase students' opportunities to respond: A systematic methodological review. *Behavioral Disorders*, 45(2), 67–84.

MacSuga-Gage, A. S., & Simonsen, B. (2015). Examining the effects of teacher-directed opportunities to respond on student outcomes: A systematic review of the literature. *Education and Treatment of Children*, 38(2), 211–239.

Sutherland, K. S., & Wehby, J. H. (2001). Exploring the relationship between increased opportunities to respond to academic requests and the academic and behavioral outcomes of students with EBD: A review. *Remedial and Special Education*, 22(2), 113–121.

Opportunities to Respond Planning Template

Content Area:

Specific Students to Target:

OTR Method (e.g., choral/group, whiteboards, response cards)	Materials Needed	Steps to Introduce & Implement (including any needed changes to current instruction)	Sample OTRs

Goal: *(aim for a specific OTR rate)*

Data Collection Directions: During instruction each time you provide an OTR, make a tally mark in the OTR data column below. Count the number of tallies and record in the total OTRs column. Record the length of the lesson in minutes. Then, divide the total number of OTRs by the length of the lesson to get the rate of OTRs per minute.

DAY	OTR Data	Total OTRs	Lesson Length (min)	OTR Rate
Monday				
Tuesday				
Wednesday				
Thursday				
Friday				

FIGURE 7.2 Opportunities to Respond Planning Template

Opportunities to Respond Steps & Self-Assessment	
0→Not in Place 1→Partially in Place 2→Fully in Place	
STEPS	**How Did I do?**
1. Increase rate of opportunities to respond.	☐ 0 ☐ 1 ☐ 2
2. Vary opportunities to respond by:	
☐ Group vs. individual opportunities to respond	☐ 0 ☐ 1 ☐ 2
☐ Form of responses	☐ 0 ☐ 1 ☐ 2
☐ Level of opportunities to respond	☐ 0 ☐ 1 ☐ 2
3. Ensure all students receive multiple opportunities to respond.	☐ 0 ☐ 1 ☐ 2
Notes & Reflection:	

FIGURE 7.3 Opportunities to Respond Implementation and Self-Assessment Checklist

8

Precorrection

In this chapter, we explain how and why precorrection can be used to improve student behavior. We begin by providing a definition and description of this strategy, followed by a brief overview of the research that supports the use of this strategy. Next, we explain how increasing precorrection can build positive relationships with students, particularly those who demonstrate challenging behaviors. Finally, we describe how to implement this strategy and provide two examples of what this practice might look like in a classroom. The supplemental resources for this chapter include a planning template (one blank for your use and one completed as an example) and a self-assessment checklist to support implementation fidelity.

What Is Meant by Precorrection?

This chapter focuses on precorrection, a simple strategy that serves exactly the purpose its name implies. Think for a minute about the term *precorrection*. In school, the word *correction* implies pretty clearly that something has gone wrong – a student has failed to display a behavior they needed to in order to meet expectations in some context, and perhaps even engaged in a negative behavior that created even bigger problems. When these breakdowns occur, the term *correction* is often used to describe what the teacher had to do next. Unfortunately, in practice, corrections that occur after a behavioral breakdown are too often negative, and do not include a teaching component – and therefore are generally not successful in helping students become more likely to meet expectations in the future. We acknowledge that corrections are certainly necessary at times, but what if the need for corrections could be reduced? How could problem behaviors be prevented before they occur? Even better – what if this preventive strategy actually helped teach students the behaviors they need to be most successful? That is exactly how the term and strategy known as precorrection evolved.

As we suggested, the definition of precorrection is as straightforward as its name. The basic definition is simple – a precorrection (sometimes just called a "precorrect") is *a specific prompt provided by the teacher about a behavior that will help a student to meet expectations*. Further, and importantly, *a precorrect is provided just prior to the context in which that behavior is needed*. There are several additional elements that make precorrection such a powerful and useful tool, and we elaborate on these in a later section when we describe the steps teachers use to develop and implement the precorrection strategy. For the moment, note that precorrection is intended to specifically target contexts in which the teacher has seen repeated difficulty meeting expectations. We think most teachers would have little trouble identifying those contexts (e.g., in what situations might you predict that Johnny most often experiences a breakdown in meeting expectations? Upon entering the classroom? Transitioning from the classroom to the lunchroom? Working with a partner during science class?). As with most behavior or classroom management strategies, it is critical that the teacher reinforce the student as immediately as possible after they display the behavior that meets expectations (e.g., with behavior-specific praise – see Chapter 10). Thus, in its simplest form, precorrection involves:

1. Identifying the context(s) in which behavioral breakdowns most often occur.
2. Identifying and defining specific behaviors that would allow the students to meet expectations.

3. Providing a specific prompt to the student regarding those expectations immediately prior to the context in which they are needed.
4. Reinforcing the student immediately when expected behaviors are displayed.

How Do I Know Precorrection Works?

The basic ideas that underlie precorrection – making expectations clear, prompting behavior that meets those expectations, and reinforcing those behaviors when they occur – are well-supported by years of research as foundational components of effective, explicit instruction. While these ideas definitely influenced early applications of systematic instruction in academic skills, especially for struggling learners, researchers soon realized that the same instructional principles that support academic success could and should be applied just as directly to behavioral concerns. Colvin and colleagues (1993) provided one of the earliest direct explanations about how these principles apply to teaching and supporting behavior in their description of precorrection. Since that time scores of research studies have confirmed that when teachers provide precorrection statements regarding specific behavioral expectations prior to a context in which failures have become predictable, students' rates of appropriate behavior or engagement increase, while rates of problem behavior decrease. In fact, reviews of this research (see Ennis et al., 2017; Sherod et al., 2023) not only support precorrection as effective but show that it has been successful across age and grade levels, including preschool, elementary, and secondary classrooms, and further that it has proven beneficial in a variety of contexts in those settings; entering classrooms, transitioning between classes or activities, and even playground behavior.

How Does Precorrection Help Build Positive Relationships with My Students?

Most of the interventions we have suggested in this book are positive and preventive in nature, and precorrection is among the strategies that best exemplify these priorities. By definition, precorrection is an antecedent strategy – it defines a step teachers take *before* a problem occurs, with a clear goal of not just preventing problem behavior but supporting students in engaging in the successful behaviors needed in a given context. We believe at least three characteristics of precorrection directly contribute to building and maintaining positive relationships between teachers and students. First is a fundamental reason: precorrection is based on the very premise that it is better to prevent problems than to react to them after the fact. Reacting to problem behavior often, unfortunately, creates very negative interactions between student and teacher. Even done well, such corrections draw attention to a behavioral breakdown or negative behavior rather than a success and contribute to the cycle experienced by too many students with challenging behavior: they get attention (negative attention, of course) from teachers or escape a task demand more often when they do something wrong than when they do something right.

Second, precorrection may demonstrate to the student that a teacher is aware of struggles in a given context, and more importantly conveys that the teacher is invested in helping the student succeed by offering words of encouragement. And note the key difference in tone with a precorrect as we have defined it. The teacher does NOT phrase the prompt in a negative way, mention what not to do (e.g., no running, no talking, no hitting others), and of course should especially avoid pointing out past failures (e.g., "I don't want to see you running in the hallway again today"), even though we are most likely targeting a context in which the student has experienced repeated difficulty meeting expectations. Instead, the teacher presents a simple positive statement about how the student can meet expectations in that activity or context (e.g., "remember to walk with your hands by your side as we head to lunch," or "make sure you're quiet as you copy down the homework, but be sure to raise your hand if you have any questions").

Finally, given that precorrection sets students up for a high rate, or at least a higher rate of success, the teacher now has additional opportunities to praise students for their positive effort in meeting expectations. Again, using behavior-specific praise when these positive behaviors occur will surely convey warmth and a sense of caring from the teacher (e.g., "I saw how quietly you walked to lunch with hands to yourself today; great job!" or "good job taking a seat right away, and getting the challenge problem done, Carlos. Thank you!"). We think that acknowledgments like this are not only consistent with a behavioral framework in that they are likely to lead to increases in those desired behaviors, but they also show students quite directly that the teacher is paying attention, and noticing the successes students have. We cannot emphasize enough how important this may be to relationships, especially for those students who have more often experienced teachers noticing and calling them out for behavioral breakdowns.

How Do I Implement Precorrection in My Classroom?

We described four steps in the 'simple' version of implementing precorrection in the beginning section of this chapter and emphasize again that the cornerstone in precorrection is simply this: providing a specific prompt toward the positive behavior(s) that will allow the students to meet expectations (Step 3 in our list below). In this section, however, we elaborate on some of the considerations necessary for teachers to most effectively plan and implement precorrection. We note that some authors address these considerations by describing a plan for precorrection that includes 6 or 7 steps; these include modifying the context when needed (which we include under Step 1), and actively teaching the behavior needed to meet expectations (included under Step 2). We hope that for ease of planning it may be simpler to think of precorrection as consisting of these four steps. We describe each very briefly in the next subsections.

Step 1. Identifying the Context

We note in Table 8.1 that precorrection is not meant to be used all day every day, or with every student. It is true that general prompts about behavioral expectations are probably a good thing and should be used frequently anyway. In fact, this is consistent

TABLE 8.1 Steps in Planning and Implementing Precorrection

Step	Considerations
1. Identifying the context(s) in which behavioral breakdowns most often occur.	♦ Identify target contexts in which predictable failures occur (trouble spots throughout the day) ♦ While prompts are generally a good idea ahead of most activities, tasks, and transitions, the formal use of precorrection is probably best targeted at a small number of problem areas ♦ Are there any modifications to the environment that might help? (e.g., reminders of expectations posted on the board or wall; a change in seating or partner pairs)
2. Identifying and defining specific behaviors that would allow the students to meet expectations.	♦ What *specific* behaviors are needed to meet expectations in the contexts identified? ♦ Does the student have the skills necessary (can they reliably display these behaviors)? If not, brief instruction (modeling, practice or rehearsal, feedback) is probably needed. ♦ Even if the student has the skills, brief practice, with feedback, is probably necessary.
3. Providing a specific prompt to the student regarding those expectations immediately prior to the context in which they are needed.	♦ Precorrective statements are brief, and positively stated, e.g., "head to your seat and copy down the challenge problem;" "remember to stay in a single line against the wall as we enter the cafeteria."
4. Reinforcing the student immediately when expected behaviors are displayed.	♦ Provide verbal praise as soon as possible when the prompted behavior is displayed ♦ Be sure to make the praise behavior specific (e.g., "great job, Dahlia – I saw you went straight to your seat and already copied down the problem for today!")

with most school-wide models of tiered support (e.g., PBIS). For example, before going out for recess, a teacher might quickly review expectations with the whole class – "Ok, we're heading out for recess. Who can remind me of one of our playground expectations?" Precorrection, however, is a bit more formal process that is generally intended for (a) a small number of students, and (b) in a small number of hotspots in which there have been repeated difficulties in meeting expectations. A simple way to think about this might be: in what contexts, instructional times, times of day, etc., is a teacher most frustrated that kids are failing pretty consistently to meet expectations? As with most tiered models (e.g., PBIS), one way these are referred to is the contexts in which there are 'predictable failures.' As we suggested earlier, we don't imagine many teachers will have any trouble at all with Step 1 – in our experience, it is very easy for teachers to name those times of day or contexts in which they are most frustrated with high rates of challenging behavior (e.g., "my fourth period class right after lunch," "any transition!" and "science class, when they have to work with partners on an experiment").

Step 2. Identifying and Defining Behaviors that Will Meet Expectations

If it's easy to identify the contexts in which problems occur, it should be relatively easy to follow that up with a definition of the behaviors that the teacher would like to see in those contexts. What should students be doing? Or more accurately, what specific behaviors do students need to display in order to be successful in meeting expectations? As we note in Table 8.1 and in the planning template (see Figure 8.2) at the end of this chapter, this is a really important step, and not one that can be glossed over. After all, the behavior that is expected will form the heart of the precorrect itself – it has to be very clear because that is precisely the behavior that will be prompted. We encourage teachers to think carefully about concrete, observable behaviors (or operationally defined behaviors, in behavioral terminology). In other words, it's not enough to say students need to 'follow the rules,' or 'be responsible,' or conversely to 'not be disruptive.'

We also note in Table 8.1 that a direct teaching component is often needed when it is not clear whether the student is capable of displaying the desired behavior – or maybe just not able to do so consistently. This need not be elaborate for most students. Such teaching might involve only a couple of sessions in which the desired behavior is first defined and modeled ("here's what it would look like to head to your seat quietly and copy down the challenge problem; watch me"). After the teacher models the behavior, the student might be asked to demonstrate the behavior briefly in a role play situation. The teacher would provide feedback (corrective feedback if needed, but hopefully behavior-specific praise, e.g., "great job, you showed me *exactly* how to head to your seat quietly and copy down the assignment"). Following only a few very brief sessions, students should be ready for the teacher to use precorrection in real contexts. And a quick note about this teaching and rehearsal – we stress that for most students, this can be very brief (a few minutes) and should only take a session or two. This is because the primary goal here is to make sure the student and teacher are on the same page about exactly what the expectation is, and what it looks like in practice. We are well aware that for some students with serious or chronic challenging behavior, a few brief sessions are surely not enough to gain entirely new skills, and then to expect them to be displayed at a high rate of success. But note – when used in isolation, precorrection is *not* intended as an intensive intervention for serious challenging behavior that occurs at a high rate or at high intensity. Rather, it is a positive, antecedent strategy that is useful for nearly all students who simply experience repeated challenges to meet expectations in a given context, and for whom the addition of these specific and planned reminders, as well as the reinforcement that follows them, can be predicted to make a difference.

Step 3. Providing the Precorrective Prompt Just Prior to the Context in Which It Is Needed

Once the contexts and behaviors that will meet expectations in those contexts have been identified and carefully defined, implementing the precorrection is easy. In fact, the hard part may simply be remembering to do so consistently at the outset of each activity or context the precorrection has been designed to address. As the activity begins, typically signaled by some sort of generic prompt and transition (e.g., a school bell; the teacher saying, "ok, time to line up for lunch," or the simple physical transition of entering a classroom), the teacher adds the precorrection. We provide descriptions of what precorrection looks like when implemented in the classroom in the last section of this chapter, but also offer a few simple examples of the form a precorrect might take in Table 8.2.

TABLE 8.2 Sample Precorrection Statements

Context	Precorrect
Entering Ms. Jones' fourth period math class (students have a hard time settling down after lunch, and often do not even go to their seats, instead just chatting with friends in the back of the classroom).	Teacher: *"good afternoon. As you head to your seat, remember to grab your math folder and copy down the challenge problem on the screen."*
Preschool playground during free play time (there have been lots of pushing and shoving around playground equipment, and several kids struggle to wait their turn).	Teacher: "OK, we can play outside for 15 minutes. Remember how we practiced taking turns, so let's show each other our best job and standing in line with our hands to ourselves if we're waiting at the slide."

Step 4. Reinforcing the Expected Behavior

This step should be the simplest of all, but again the hard part in reinforcing the expected behavior may be simply remembering to do so. Hopefully, the planning template at the end of this chapter helps you first to think through how you will convey behavior-specific praise – the words you will use – and then also serves as a prompt to do so. Consistently reinforcing the behavior the student needs to display, especially given that we're tackling a context in which there have been consistent failures, will be critical to the impact and ultimate success of precorrection.

What Do I Need to Begin Implementing Precorrection?

It should be quite easy for most teachers to use precorrection, and to do so with just a little preparation. As we alluded to in the introduction to this chapter and the definition of precorrection, in one sense precorrection is not very different from what good teachers probably already do in explicit academic instruction (e.g., provide prompts as needed toward correct responding), or in implementing tiered models of behavioral support (e.g., frequently reviewing and reminding students of behavioral expectations). But we also hope we highlighted a few ways that the use of precorrection as a specific strategy differs from these basic instructional uses. At the end of this chapter, we provide a simple planning template (see Figure 8.2) you can use to think through these issues, and plan for the specific use of precorrection in a given context. Here are a few of the things to think through as you plan. First, think for a few moments about a small number of contexts that seem to be your biggest trouble spots – the places where challenges in meeting expectations seem to occur most often. One way to think of it – what are the most frustrating or anxiety-producing times of your school day, when kids just don't seem to be able to do what they need to do? Second – and as we said earlier, if you can identify the contexts, this part should be easy – what are the specific behaviors students are *supposed* to do in these contexts, but are routinely failing to do? The important part here is to operationally define these behaviors – remember, you can't just use 'follow the rules' or 'be respectful' as the behaviors here. Name the exact behaviors students would need to engage in to be successful in this context: walk quietly with hands to yourself; put backpacks in your cubby, walk to your seat, and copy down the homework assignment. These behaviors form the basis for the actual prompt you will use when you implement precorrection. Third – implement the strategy! It's really as simple as stating the prompt you planned in the previous step, and to state that prompt immediately before the context or activity in which that behavior is expected. Finally, it's critical to make certain to reinforce – in an obvious and positive way – just as soon as you can when the student engages in the behavior you just prompted. We try to make these steps even more clear in the examples (see Figure 8.1) in the next section, and we elaborate more on reinforcement strategies that pair well with precorrection in Chapters 10 (token economies) and 11 (behavior-specific praise). We have provided a self-assessment checklist to support implementation of precorrection at the end of this chapter (see Figure 8.3).

What Does It look Like in the Classroom?

We have defined the key elements of precorrection, and described how teachers can plan and implement precorrection in the classroom. In this section, two examples – one from an elementary classroom and one from a high school context, highlight what these elements look like in practice.

Mr. Cardoza teaches a diverse class of active and capable second-graders in an urban context. His students are not only diverse in terms of ethnicity and first language, but in terms of academic strengths and mastery of basic school survival skills. While Mr. Cardoza frequently says that he "loves their energy," his class is described by other teachers – mostly positively – as the 'loudest' classroom on the hallway. While he maintains a very positive attitude, as the year has worn on, even Mr. Cardoza realizes he needs to help his students master some additional skills that will set them up for success as they navigate other classes and teachers in subsequent school years. He has become concerned in particular that it takes a long time for his class to 'settle down' upon entering the classroom at the start of the day. In discussions and informal observations with other teachers on his grade team, he has realized that his students tend to run or stumble into class – mostly happily – but then congregate at the window or back tables for several minutes every day to just chat with their friends. While he was fine with this at first as the kids seemed happy and there were few conflicts, he has realized that he is losing lots of instructional time as he struggles to get students into their seats and settled into the day's instruction. Moreover, this happens in the morning when students first enter the classroom, and again after lunch when they return to class.

Mr. Cardoza heard about precorrection in a professional development session, and in the examples the speaker described, he could totally see his own classroom. Students were consistently failing to meet expectations at predictable times nearly every day, always in the same contexts. He decides to try precorrection and plans out his prompt carefully. His plan is shown in Figure 8.1. As students enter the classroom in the morning, Mr. Carodza will remind them to put away their things and take a seat, and that all they will need is a pencil to start the challenge problem on the board. The students do a challenge problem every morning, which they enjoy; but, his students have had a hard time starting this simple activity – they will read the problem aloud casually

Precorrection Planning Template		
Specific Students or Situations to Address: All students during transitions Three students especially (CT, DC, and KS)	**Predictable Trouble Spots Throughout the Day:** Transitioning into the classroom at start of day and after lunch	**Challenging Behavior to Improve:** Students hanging out at back tables, talking, not going to seats or getting started – lost instructional time
Precorrection Components *Describe all components in specific detail and how they will be introduced to the student.*		
Expectations	Describe the concrete, observable behaviors you want to see from students: Enter classroom quietly Put their things away in cubby or desk Take a seat (in their assigned place) Take out materials needed for their first assignment/activity (e.g., a pencil, notebook)	
Prompt(s)	List possible positively stated, precorrective statements: Remember to put things away; go to desk quietly, keep out a pencil for the challenge of the day.	
Reinforcement	Describe how desired behavior will be reinforced: Behavior specific praise (e.g., great job putting your things away; thank you for going right to your seat)	
Special Considerations	☐ Environmental Changes to Support Behavior ☐ Instruction on Skills Needed by Student(s) ☐ General Prompts about Expectations for All Students ☒ Other Describe any necessary considerations to address: Combine precorrections with positive greetings at the door as students enter the classroom first thing in the morning	
Data Collection Plan Describe the specific behavior targeted for improvement: How long it takes students to go to seats and start the challenge problem Describe the metric (e.g., % of time on-task) and method for data collection: Duration it takes all students to begin working on challenge problem		

FIGURE 8.1 Completed Example of Precorrection Planning Template

from the back of the room before even taking a seat, and then just shout out comments – some at least oriented to the task (e.g., "hey – does anyone know how to do this?"), but just as many are completely off task or inappropriate (e.g., "uh, can we just X out of that challenge problem and watch some YouTube videos?"). Mr. Cardoza decides he will implement precorrection by using a simple prompt students as they enter the classroom: "Good morning, everyone. Please remember to put your things away as you head quietly to your desk but keep a pencil out to start on our challenge problem." Of course, he makes a note to be sure to quickly reinforce any and all students who meet this expectation.

In a secondary classroom context, while we know that older students can be different in many ways from younger students, the concept of precorrection is the same. One point we stress when talking to teachers is that we sometimes think there is a belief that older kids don't need reminders about basic expectations (i.e., "they should know how to follow the rules by now!"). But again, both our own experience and research suggest that even high school students meet expectations better when prompts are provided, and the targeted nature of precorrection can be especially impactful. Consider a simple example. We think most students at a secondary level would understand the basic expectation that devices (phones) are to be put away during certain instructional times. But, because this is a hotspot – a predictable failure – we have encountered often, we highly recommend that teachers use a simple precorrect that includes a prompt about devices before those instructional times when this is a requirement. Again, it can be very simple: "OK, guys, thanks for taking a seat. Now, for our book discussion, you only need your copy of the novel and any notes you've taken. And remember, please put devices away so I can't see them, and you can't see them." The teacher was positive (thanks for taking a seat), made clear how students can meet expectations (have your book and notes out), and noted the trouble spot (having devices out) by stating specifically, in positive terms, what students need to do to avoid that problem.

Final Thoughts

In this chapter we defined and described how to apply precorrection in classroom and school contexts (including hallways, cafeteria, playground, etc.). We emphasized that while the basic elements that make up precorrection (e.g., prompting students in advance about the expectations in a given context) sound a lot like simply good teaching, the structured way we recommend teachers use precorrection makes it ideal for tackling those difficult contexts where teachers encounter repeated and predictable challenges. In this way, we think precorrection can be a go-to tool for teachers to tackle some of the more frustrating contexts they experience throughout the day – such as a particular class period or a transition time.

We noted that the elements in planning and implementing precorrection are also simple, and with only a few minutes of thought, teachers can be ready to use precorrection in a structured way. The basic steps are to (1) identify the contexts(s) in which predictable failures to meet expectation seem to occur most often; (2) identify and define the specific behaviors students need to display to meet expectations in those contexts; (3) implement precorrection by offering a detailed prompt about expected behaviors immediately prior to the context in which they are needed; and (4) strongly reinforce (most often with behavior-specific praise) the expected behaviors as soon as they occur. We emphasized that research has pretty consistently supported that this simple process can result in observable improvement in behavior that meets expectations, and corresponding reductions in problem behavior. In short, we believe precorrection is a tool that all teachers should know and be able to use with relative ease to address some of their more frustrating classroom management challenges.

References

Colvin, G., Sugai, G., & Patching, W. (1993). Precorrection: An instructional approach for managing predictable problem behaviors. *Intervention in School and Clinic, 28,* 143–150.

Ennis, R. P., Royer, D. J., Lane, K. L., & Griffith, C. E. (2017). A systematic review of precorrection in PK-12 settings. *Education and Treatment of Children, 40,* 465–495.

Sherod, R. L., Jones, J. S., Perry, H., & Oakes, W. P. (2023). Precorrection: Empowering teachers and families to support students in varied learning contexts. *Preventing School Failure: Alternative Education for Children and Youth, 67*(2), 91–97.

Precorrection Planning Template		
Specific Students or Situations to Address:	Predictable Trouble Spots Throughout the Day:	Challenging Behavior to Improve:
Precorrection Components *Describe all components in specific detail and how they will be introduced to the student.*		
Expectations	Describe the concrete, observable behaviors you want to see from students:	
Prompt(s)	List possible positively stated, precorrective statements:	
Reinforcement	Describe how desired behavior will be reinforced:	
Special Considerations	☐ Environmental Changes to Support Behavior ☐ Instruction on Skills Needed by Student(s) ☐ General Prompts about Expectations for All Students ☐ Other Describe any necessary considerations to address:	
Data Collection Plan *Describe the specific behavior targeted for improvement:* *Describe the metric (e.g., % of time on-task) and method for data collection:*		

FIGURE 8.2 Precorrection Planning Template

| **Precorrection Steps & Self-Assessment** | | | |
| 0→Not in Place 1→Partially in Place 2→Fully in Place | | | |
STEPS	How Did I do?		
1. Identify the context(s) in which behavioral breakdowns most often occur.	☐ 0	☐ 1	☐ 2
2. Identify and define specific behaviors that would allow the students to meet expectations.	☐ 0	☐ 1	☐ 2
3. Deliver a specific prompt to the student regarding those expectations immediately prior to the context in which they are needed.	☐ 0	☐ 1	☐ 2
4. Reinforce the student immediately when expected behaviors are displayed.	☐ 0	☐ 1	☐ 2
Notes & Reflection:			

FIGURE 8.3 Precorrection Implementation and Self-Assessment Checklist

9

Precision Requests

In this chapter, we explain how and why precision requests can be used to improve student behavior. We begin by providing a definition and description of this strategy, followed by a brief overview of the research that supports the use of this strategy. Next, we explain how increasing precision requests can build positive relationships with students, particularly those who demonstrate challenging behaviors. Finally, we describe how to implement this strategy and provide two examples of what this practice might look like in a classroom. The supplemental resources for this chapter include a planning template (one blank for your use and one completed as an example) and a self-assessment checklist to support implementation fidelity.

What Is Meant by Precision Requests?

In its simplest form, the strategy known as precision requests has been described as a structured way to give directions in order to enhance compliance. Like all the strategies in this book, we include precision requests in our list of recommended practices for two reasons: (a) it works (there's good evidence to support the positive effects of precision requests in helping students meet expectations), and (b) we believe many of its key elements can help build and maintain positive relationships with students. We offer a few thoughts, however, before describing its implementation. First, we sometimes worry that teachers might be turned off to a strategy like precision requests if they hear it described as a way to "increase compliance," which was the language used in many early descriptions and studies of precision requests. As we assure teachers we work with, however, "compliance with a request" is a good thing, and many times each day it is simply what a student needs to do to meet basic expectations. It is NOT a teacher bossing kids around, or ruling with an iron fist, and it's not just "training" kids to be compliant. Rather, it's as simple as this: if a teacher says, "OK, readers, it's time for reading. I need Kelley, MacKenzie, and Gregory to join me at the reading table," that's a request. We really hope Kelley, MacKenzie, and Gregory *comply*. (And by default, that they do not engage in defiance, disruption, or other behavior that fails to meet expectations). Again, as we describe in this chapter, precision requests provide a structured way to give a direction – a request – in a way that increases the likelihood that students will indeed comply.

A second thought, before we dive into the details, is that the original form of precision requests provided a very detailed and structured format for the delivery of the request, and that format included not only reinforcement for meeting expectations, but a *response cost* component as well. Those familiar with the language of behavior analysis will recognize response cost as a punitive procedure that involves taking away some reinforcer, like taking away a point. In truth, however, we have often taught precision requests without this punitive element, as a general strategy for all teachers. We emphasize only those critical characteristics and elements of the request or direction itself – how to deliver requests – and then, of course, the need to swiftly acknowledge and reinforce compliance. In other words, we think that nearly all teachers can use these positive parts of precision requests to enhance their teaching and management routines without actually using the response cost element. To be clear, the data on precision requests (including the full routine in which response cost is used) suggest that it can be very effective in increasing compliance and reducing disruptions and other problem behavior. In that sense, we fully endorse its use for targeted intervention for individual students experiencing particular challenges in specific contexts (perhaps thought of as a Tier II intervention). But in this chapter, we describe primarily those basic positive elements that make it more likely a request will be followed, even in the absence of the response cost element. We note that some researchers have begun to explore this idea, too, examining whether a precision request routine can operate just as efficiently without punishment (Sabey et al., 2021; more on this in the section, "How Do I Know Precision Requests Works?").

So, what exactly is a precision request? Again, precision requests are a structured way to give directions that incorporate variables that are likely to increase the chances students will comply with the request. The characteristics, or variables, that make up a precision request are presented in Table 9.1. We elaborate on each component or characteristic in the sections that follow.

How Do I Know Precision Requests Works?

Precision requests in the form we describe here evolved from initial work by Neville and Jensen (1984), which was then elaborated upon by many scholars; one of the earliest descriptions we refer to often was presented in the *Tough Kid Book* (Rhode et al., 1993; we refer teachers often to the *Tough Kid Book* and series of resources, as we find these to be among the most practical, user-friendly, and evidence-based resources around). Since that time, a number of researchers have continued to examine precision requests, or its various components, including using precision requests alone or in combination with other strategies to increase compliance and to reduce challenging behavior (e.g., Martini-Scully et al., 2000). While some scholars will point out that relatively few studies have tested precision requests specifically as a standalone strategy, we are nonetheless confident in recommending this strategy for several reasons. First, there are indeed several studies that have shown it to have positive

TABLE 9.1 Components and Characteristics of Precision Requests

Component or characteristic	Notes on What the Teacher Does
1. Non-question format	Present a direction as a statement of what is needed to meet expectations, rather than a question.
	"Kelley, please come to the reading table," instead of "Kelley, would you like to come to the reading table?"
2. Specific	Use specific behavioral terms that describe exactly what the student is expected to do.
	"For science you'll need to take out your textbook, your notes, and something to write with," instead of "It's time for science; make sure you're prepared."
3. Given in close proximity	Position yourself as near to the student as possible; part of this simply means you can communicate a direction in a conversational volume and tone of voice, rather than calling out across a sometimes noisy classroom.
4. Eye contact	You should attempt to gain the student's attention, ensured by eye contact; this is, of course, much easier if you're positioned near the student as noted above.
5. Provides time to comply	Research recommends that teachers provide at least 5 seconds for a student to *begin* compliance (in other words, it's only after at least 5–10 seconds of literally no reaction at all by the student that a teacher might consider that the student is being noncompliant).
6. One request at a time	Students often need to complete complex multistep tasks, but when compliance is the issue, one request at a time should be delivered (and hopefully reinforced, followed by the next direction).
	"Carli, please put your things in your cubby, and take a seat." [Carli complies]. "Great job taking a seat and being ready, Carli! Now, take out your planner and write down today's homework assignments" instead of "Carli, please put your things in your cubby, then take a seat, take out your planner and write down today's homework assignment."
7. Compliance is reinforced	Reinforce the student immediately upon compliance! This is as simple a behavior-specific praise statement (see Chapter 10).

(Continued)

TABLE 9.1 (Continued)

Component or characteristic	Notes on What the Teacher Does

8. Procedure is taught	The procedure for using precision requests involves providing the initial request with a "Please."
	
	For example:
	
	1. "James, please push in your chair and line up for P.E."
	   - If student complies, reinforce with behavior-specific praise.
	   - If student does not comply after 5–10 seconds, teacher issues a more direct request, using *I need you to*, and, if using the response cost element, adds the potential for a reductive technique:
	2. "James, I need you to push in your chair, and line up for P. E., or you will lose one of your points* for the morning."
	   - If student complies, reinforce with behavior-specific praise.
	   - If student does not comply with the second request after 5–10 seconds, the teacher implements the consequence and repeats the original request in Step 1. ("James, you have lost one point; now please push in your chair and line up for P. E.")

*Consequence should be small but relevant, such as a single point as part of a larger system, or one minute of recess.

effects, either alone or in combination with other strategies, in both general education and special education classrooms (e.g., Musser et al., 2001). Second, and perhaps more practically, the core *components* of precision requests (e.g., stating how students can meet expectations clearly and in positive terms, reinforcing behavior that meets those expectations with behavior-specific praise) are well-supported by extensive research. Moreover, the key variables recommended as part of a precision request itself (e.g., eye contact) have separately been validated as important contributors to helping students meet expectations. In short, precision requests and the structured delivery and reinforcement that accompany them are highly recommended.

How Does Precision Requests Help Build Positive Relationships with My Students?

We don't presume that precision requests were developed for the specific reason of building positive relationships with students. But as we hope has become clear in this volume, we have emphasized strategies that are proactive, positive, and have characteristics that at minimum contribute to the development and maintenance of such positive relationships. We chose to include precision requests not only for its evidence base and ease of implementation, but because we also see several obvious ways we think it meets that relationship-building criterion. Consider some of the key elements of precision requests. For example, the strategy emphasizes giving a request or direction in close proximity to a student. While this may seem like a no-brainer, we can easily see the opposite– the teacher who shouts across the room ("James, you need to take a seat and get your science book out") – as being problematic for multiple reasons. First, it draws attention to James, and does so in a way that indicates he is already being noncompliant, or at least that the teacher believes he will have trouble being compliant. Compare that to the teacher who walks over to James and quietly says, "I need you to take a seat and take out your science book." And note that in this case she is not berating James or even suggesting he is or might soon be noncompliant (i.e., she did NOT say "why aren't you in your seat?"). We think a quiet, supportive but firm reminder about how to be successful, delivered essentially 1:1, conveys considerably more respect. We think the same can be said for adding eye contact to that proximity. Of course, teachers should also consider students' backgrounds. If eye contact from the student to teacher is not culturally appropriate, it would be okay to omit this step. The same goes for disabilities, as some students with disabilities may not consistently make eye contact.

A perhaps obvious way we think precision requests can help with relationships lies in the reinforcement it calls for – as soon as a student complies with a request, the teacher praising that behavior specifically (e.g., "thanks for sitting down quietly with your book out") conveys that behavior is noticed and appreciated. While we advocate for frequent and specific praise anyway, we find that precision requests provides both a structured reminder for teachers to actually *use* behavior-specific praise, and maybe more importantly sets students up to receive more – the teacher using precision requests by definition will be providing very specific requests, which the student is now more likely to comply with, thus creating a cycle of more frequent, positively reinforcing interactions. This is particularly important for students who are prone to demonstrating challenging behavior, as these are the students who benefit from praise the most, but typically receive it the least.

How Do I Implement Precision Requests in My Classroom?

We described eight steps in the classic version of precision requests as it was originally designed (presented in Table 9.1). We elaborate briefly on each step in this section and include a planning template (see Figure 9.2 for a blank template and Figure 9.1 for a completed example) and a self-assessment checklist at the end of this chapter that will help teachers plan and implement precision requests.

1. Non-question Format

We have seen teachers (good teachers, including ourselves) default to phrasing lots of directions or requests for students as questions. Sometimes, we think this is completely inadvertent. Imagine yourself saying to an individual student, "Kami, would you like to join me at the reading table?" or even saying excitedly and in a positive tone to your entire class, "OK, who's ready for math time?!" While we can accept and acknowledge that a skilled teacher could probably work these phrasings into lessons once in a while with few problems, in truth these carry at least the potential for conflicts or breakdowns. As we say to our students, if you ask a question (e.g., "James, are you ready to start your math assignment?") you need to be prepared for the answer to be "no."

2. Specific

If you've taken any behaviorally oriented behavior or classroom management course, you know well the idea of operationally defining behaviors; it really just means to be specific about exactly what the student should be *doing*. For example, "respecting the teacher" is not a behavior, but "raising your hand and waiting to be called on before speaking" is a behavior. Operationally defining behaviors is a foundational component of tiered systems of behavioral support, such as Positive Behavioral Interventions and Supports, in which broad expectations (e.g., "be respectful") are translated into specific behaviors that show how one demonstrates being respectful (e.g., "being quiet while others are speaking"). With precision requests, that same logic is really important. If we're going to ask a student to do something, it's way more likely he'll comply if we state precisely what it is we want him to do (thus the name *precision* requests!).

A further note here on a concern we sometimes encounter is this: it is quite reasonable that teachers want to eventually reach a point where they can say something very broad (e.g., "time for math, everyone") and students both *know* what to do (put away materials from a previous activity, get out math book, workbook, etc.), and successfully *comply* with that request fully. That said, both our experience and research tend to confirm that while that's an excellent goal, not all students are there yet, and the likelihood of compliance for all students can be greatly enhanced when a detailed precision request is used.

3. Given in Close Proximity

We hope this element is obvious, but we also know even this simple idea can be challenging in a busy classroom with 20, 25, or more students. And we have seen the hurried and harried teacher essentially shouting from across the room, not in a harsh or negative tone, but shouting only to be heard (e.g., "Jason and Jeffrey, you need to take a seat and get out your math homework"). We can only reiterate that whenever feasible or possible, moving within closer proximity to a student before delivering a request is associated with a better chance of compliance. Accepting that it's not always easy to do, we nonetheless encourage teachers to take the extra few seconds to walk nearer to the student before issuing a request. Taking those few seconds now may end up saving the teacher considerable time compared to the effort that might be needed when noncompliance escalates.

4. Eye Contact

We view eye contact simply as a means of ensuring that the teacher had the student's attention, and can have at least some confidence that the request was heard and understood. In practice, this typically means that the teacher would approach a student, call them by name, look them in the eye and wait for them to establish eye contact before delivering a request. But a couple of notes are important about this element, too. First, as we've mentioned, eye contact may be challenging for students with disabilities and it also carries implications for cultural awareness. Therefore, it is critical that teachers do not insist on eye contact from students for whom eye contact with teachers is not culturally normative or for whom demonstrating eye contact is a challenge. In our view, eye contact can simply be set aside in these contexts, and the other elements of precision requests should still result in enhanced compliance. A second potential issue has to do with sustained eye contact. In a precision request, eye contact is established only for the few seconds it takes to deliver the request. Sustained eye contact can be perceived as a threat, which a precision request clearly is not meant to be. Nor is a precision request meant to be a stare-down, as the teacher awaits compliance. As we describe it to teachers, "move into closer proximity, establish eye contact if appropriate, make the request, and get out of there."

5. Provides Time to Comply

Based on our experience teaching kids with significant behavioral challenges, we think one particular aspect of this "time to comply" element is critical. That is, that teachers should provide time for students to *begin complying* with a given request. If students do at least begin to comply with 5–10 seconds, that is a win – basically, it is compliance. Think for a moment about what this might look like for a given student, especially one who struggles even a little with routines and meeting basic expectations. At the end of a given activity, suppose the teacher says, "OK, Charlie, almost time for math; please put your art materials away and take out your math book, workbook, and a pencil." We have seen many students almost flustered by this, as they rush to try to finish up some part of the previous activity, put one set of materials away, and find the right materials for the next activity or class. Indeed, it may take several minutes for even the most organized and efficient of students to complete all these things. What we encourage here would be reinforcement for *beginning* to comply, and maybe a prompt to ensure that the remainder of the task is completed. In the example just mentioned, suppose Charlie says, "Ok – but I need to write my name on the back," and after carefully (and slowly) doing so, he puts his art project away at the back of the room. The teacher could now say simply, "Great job putting that away, Charlie. Now, remember to get your math materials ready back at your desk." Contrast that with what a teacher might say if frustrated with how long it's taking Charlie to comply (e.g., "Hurry up, Charlie. We're all waiting on you so we can start Math"). Again, we encourage the first response – reinforcement in the form of specific praise, and a further prompt – as we consider Charlie's behavior to reflect at least the beginning of compliance, whereas the second possible teacher response ("Hurry up, Charlie") seems to imply pretty clearly that the teacher is frustrated and likely considers Charlie noncompliant.

6. One Request at a Time

As we noted above, while it's probably a goal for students at all levels to follow multistep directions, the fact is, this expectation is sometimes simply too much for some students. What's more, we think that the nature of learning and behavior is such that the person who knows the routine and expectation (typically the teacher in our context, but think of how this also applies to parents, or significant others) almost always overestimates the ability of the learner (or other person) to remember all parts of a requested routine. Consider some extreme – but maybe not too unlikely – examples.

- "OK, class, before you pack up your things, remember to turn all homework into the green homework folder, place your signed test on my desk in the orange folder, return all your math supplies – any protractors and compasses – to the math bin at the back table, and make sure there are two sharpened pencils at your desk for tomorrow's test."
- "Julian, there's a lot you need to do before dismissal if you don't want to miss your bus. You need to finish up what you're working on, clean up your desk, stack your chair in the back of the classroom, and pack up your backpack."

7. Compliance Reinforced (and Noncompliance Redirected)

This element should be far and away the simplest, as it literally just builds directly off the request just delivered. If you've asked a student to push in their chair, say "good job pushing in your chair" as soon as possible when they complete that task. You can certainly elaborate or modify slightly for different students, particularly those of different ages and grade levels: an enthusiastic "great job pushing in your chair, Annie!" or "nice job passing those out for me, Stevie. I appreciate that." The reason it's included as a separate step is merely to remind teachers to do it, and to highlight not only the need to reinforce every instance of compliance, but to do so with behavior-specific praise. When we teach about precision requests, we frequently remind teachers that if they've decided to implement precision requests, it's likely because they have experienced at least some students pretty consistently failing to meet expectations. Thus, when students do comply, it's doubly important that they are reinforced quickly, consistently, and in behavior-specific ways.

In the event that students do not comply with the request, we suggest that teachers simply restate the request, perhaps with a reminder of the reinforcement. For example, if Patrice does not comply with her teacher's request to take out her science notebook, her teacher may say "Patrice, you won't be able to earn two points since you didn't follow directions when I asked, but you can still earn one point, so let's try again. Take out your science notebook and place it on your desk." Note here that the teacher did not take away any *previously* earned points, but rather, reduced the number of points available to earn. You may also notice that Patrice's teacher did not set the stage for a power struggle or argument, but rather, calmly and unemotionally restated the request. As we mentioned at the beginning of this chapter, some versions of precision requests include a response cost component if the student does not comply. In general, we try to avoid this component, but in some cases it is warranted and helpful. We describe that component in a moment.

8. Procedure Is Taught

The "procedure" in precision requests is often depicted as a flow chart (see https://limened.com/precision-requests/). This just helps teachers see the process where a request is issued, then either reinforced (in the case of compliance) or the teacher issues a second request with more direct phrasing and the addition of a reminder that failure to comply results in a consequence. The procedure itself is outlined in Table 9.1, and when we say here that the procedure is taught, we mean only that it is explained to students before it is implemented for the first time (see our examples below); for some students (young students, those with disabilities), a teacher may wish to walk through the procedure with their students once or twice in a role play situation, but in our experience lengthy instruction or explanation is usually not necessary.

What Do I Need to Begin?

Precision requests should be very easy to implement for most teachers with just a few minutes of planning in advance. We think of four simple steps or ideas a teacher may need to think through, aided by the planning template (see Figure 9.2) we provide at the end of this chapter. Briefly, to implement precision requests, a teacher must decide on:

1. **Directions that predict noncompliance.** In what contexts have you found students to be most often failing to meet expectations by not following simple requests or

directions? In other words – what are the requests they just don't seem to follow very successfully? We recommend identifying only one or a small number of these contexts at first.

2. **The exact precision request to be used.** This part should be obvious if Step 1 above was easy – what is the request that students are not following successfully? The one wrinkle here is that you should think through whether you have a very clearly stated behavioral expectation (e.g., rather than "time to get ready for math," something like "please have only your math workbook and one pencil on your desk" would be better).

3. **Reinforcement method.** This too is simple – behavior-specific praise is the goal here, so if you have identified clearly stated behaviors in Step 2, behavior-specific praise just names those behaviors when students engage in them (e.g., "good job getting out your workbook and pencil").

4. **Reductive technique (if used).** Part of this step is deciding if this is a context in which the reductive technique makes sense. There are at least two key considerations here. First, is there some reinforcer in place such that a small amount can be taken away by a response cost element? This can work if there is a point system already in place, for example, where a loss of one point might be meaningful, but not overly harsh. A related consideration involves the specific students involved. Even though the value of the reinforcer that might be taken away should be small, some students may not be able to handle any loss of a point or even a minute of recess – even when they retain most of their points or minutes. In our experience, we simply chose not to implement a response cost system if we believed it may lead to outsized reactions or meltdowns. Another intervention altogether would be a better choice. If a teacher decides to use this technique, we also suggest that removal of the reinforcer is done respectfully, so as not to call out or embarrass the student.

A final reminder is this – make sure that the student who loses any amount of reinforcement still has additional opportunities to earn reinforcers.

In addition to the planning template, we have also included an example of completed planning template (see Figure 9.1) and a self-assessment checklist to support your implementation of precision requests (see Figure 9.3).

What Does It look Like in the Classroom?

As we have described, the basic elements of precision requests are really quite simple. We hope these serve mostly as reminders to teachers about how to maximize the odds students will respond positively to basic requests from teachers around instructional, behavioral, or even just logistical matters throughout the school day. We also noted that precision requests as originally designed included a response cost (punitive) element. We recommend that teachers use the response cost element when they think it will help; most students will respond well to this, and again research tells us for those students, we may see both increased compliance and reductions in things like disruptive behavior. However, we also cautioned that there will be students whose behavior may worsen if a response cost is added. Of course, previous behavioral data can help teachers make this decision, but the reality is that most teachers probably know which students in their class are more likely to have a difficult time with response cost. If teachers believe a response cost could simply make matters worse (e.g., for the students you predict may react strongly at the thought of losing points), we suggest omitting that element and simply withholding the reinforcer (e.g., "Amelia, I need you to take out your math book if you want to earn a point" rather than "Amelia, I need you to take out your math book or you will lose a point."). Regardless of whether or not the response cost element is included, we encourage virtually all teachers to use the basic elements or characteristics of an effective direction or request in most of their instructional or management routines (e.g., in the hallway, walk over to Zach, make eye contact, and say softly, "I need you to walk on the right side with hands to yourself and voice at zero"). In the examples below, we first describe how Mr. Jordan uses these basic elements without the response cost. In a second example, we describe how Ms. Jimenez has decided the response cost element may help her students be more successful.

Elementary Example

Mr. Jordan is in his very first year of teaching and has taken a job teaching fourth grade in a suburban elementary school very near to where he grew up and went to school himself. He (perhaps naively) thought this would be an "easy" school for him to work in as a brand-new teacher. He has a laid back, calm demeanor, and hoped to be the type of teacher who developed a relaxed but respectful style with his kids. He often begins his day, and each class or lesson, with a very informal "ok, who's ready for some math?" or "why don't we read some more of our novel, guys?" While many of his students seemed to appreciate and respond to this style, he realized a few weeks into the school year that several students were simply not responding well; they would linger out of their seats, and take a long time to get settled into work with their materials out. He remembered an instructor in his behavior management class had raved about precision requests as an effective and "really easy to implement" strategy, so he decided to revisit this. He was able to find some simple summaries online (e.g., interventioncentral.org;) that listed the basic characteristics of a good precision request. He prints off the list (as shown previously in Table 9.1) and tries these out informally at the start of his day. After giving the general direction to the class that it's time for reading, he walks to the back of the room (proximity), and approaches first Kyle and then Javon, neither of whom are even in their seats. He makes eye contact with Kyle first, and says in a positive tone, "Kyle, please take a seat and get your reading book out." He moves on to Javon, and repeats the same. While Javon heads immediately to his seat, Mr. Jordan notices that Kyle has not even moved toward his desk 10 seconds later. Mr. Jordan quickly says "Thanks, Javon, for being seated and getting started," as he heads back closer to Kyle, makes eye contact again, and says "Kyle, I need you to take a seat now and get your reading book out." Even though it took two requests, Kyle slowly saunters toward his desk, after which Mr. Jordan simply says, "Thanks, Kyle. Good job heading to your seat to get started."

Secondary Example

In another example, Ms. Jimenez' teaches eighth grade math and science. A small number of students cause her headaches nearly every day in fourth period – they never seem to get started on their work, and at the start of nearly every assignment ask some version of the age-old questions: *Why do we even need to learn this?* or *When are we ever going to use this?* Ms. Jimenez heard about precision requests from the special education consulting teacher she sometimes works with, and wonders whether this might be a useful strategy. After a conversation, the two of them not only decide it might be worth a try but discuss the response cost element as well (see Figure 9.1 for their completed planning template). Because her school uses a school-wide system that awards Tiger Bucks to students for meeting expectations, Ms. Jimenez has built in a companion version in her class where students earn points for meeting various academic and behavioral expectations – every five points earns an additional Tiger Buck. At first, she didn't think points would even work with her eighth graders, but partly because bucks can be exchanged for things like homework passes, she learned that points have become valuable to her students – in fact, they talk all the time about how many points they have accumulated. Further, because they can earn multiple points each class period, she believes that losing a single point, while valuable, would not cause too much stress or a meltdown.

Ms. Jimenez tries out precision requests on the Monday after Fall break. She reminds students of the expectation about getting started on their work after she's finished her lesson (an expectation they know well by now), and also reminds them that they earn points when they meet that expectation. But she adds this time that if students have trouble meeting that expectation

156 ◆ Improving Student Behavior and Cultivating Meaningful Relationships

Precision Requests Planning Template

Specific Students to Support:
Alexandra
Kenya

Context with Predictable Challenges:
Math/Science co-teaching when starting assignments

Directions

Precision Request(s)

Describe requests students struggle to follow:
Begin independent work

Plan the exact precision request(s) to be used:
I need you to begin working. I need you to open your laptop/book and begin working on your problems.

Reinforcement Method

Reductive Technique

Describe how student compliance will be reinforced:
Behavior specific praise; can earn a point (5 pts gets a Tiger Buck)

Describe the response method (only if applicable):
Lose 1 previously earned point

Data Collection

(Each day, mark a + for student compliance with a request and a – for noncompliance, then calculate the percentage of compliance)

STUDENT	PRECISION REQUEST DATA									
	M	%	T	%	W	%	Th	%	F	%
Alexandra	+++	100	+++–+	80	++++	100				
Kenya	+–+	67	+–++	75	–+++	75				

FIGURE 9.1 Completed Example of Precision Requests Planning Template

even with reminders, they can lose a point. She implements the plan that very day. After a group instructional segment in which she's demonstrated, reviewed, and practiced with them some basic problems involving exponents, she asks them to complete five problems on their laptop. Most students dive right in, but Alexandra doesn't even open the laptop that's sitting on her desk. Ms. Jimenez walks over to her desk and says softly, "Alexandra, please open your laptop and start on these first five problems," but then keeps walking around to circulate around the room. When she notices after 10 seconds that Alexandra is doodling on a pad and has not even opened the laptop, Ms. Jimenez circles back and says a little more directly, "Alexandra, I need you to open your laptop and start on these five problems, or you will lose one of your points for today." Ms. Jimenez does not linger this time either, but when she notices Alexandra opening her laptop, she quickly says, "thanks, Alexandra, for getting started on the problems."

A quick note about the examples above – especially Ms. Jimenez. First, note that Alexandra did comply after the possible negative consequence was mentioned. Had she NOT complied, Ms. Jimenez would have said, "Alexandra, you've lost one point for today. Now, I need you to open up your laptop and start on these five problems." Ms. Jimenez was comfortable using this strategy with Alexandra because she felt confident that the point was a valuable motivator for Alexandra, but also that a single point was not SO valuable that taking it away would lead to a greater conflict or confrontation. We have certainly taught students – and imagine most teachers know some as well – who would NOT handle losing a point, or even the prospect of losing one, very well. If you predict that a given student would not handle this well at all, and in fact it would just make the situation worse for both student and teacher – we simply recommend not using this element of precision requests.

A final note about both these examples on a point we mentioned earlier: in both cases, Mr. Jordan and Ms. Jimenez had to offer more than one request or reminder before students complied. We recognize this can be frustrating for teachers, and we have heard teachers ask us sincerely, "why should I have to ask them over and over to comply with a simple request?" It's a valid point! But here's our response. First, we're using precision requests in this context because students have demonstrated predictable difficulties; in other words, something is clearly not working. Second, precision requests are not intended to be a non-stop series of repeated requests. If that happens – if the data shows that a given student is not improving in meeting a given expectation after multiple days or classes with precision requests in place – we recommend simply stopping the use of precision requests and trying something else. Finally, note again what these teachers did NOT do after students complied with a second or even third request. They did not point this out with a negative comment (e.g., "Next time, I'd appreciate it if you'd respond the first time I ask you"). Rather, when students complied and met an expectation, even with multiple reminders and even if a negative consequence had been used, teachers simply followed compliance with behavior-specific praise (e.g., "good job taking a seat and getting started"). Research tells us that behavior-specific praise in these moments, rather than any sort of correction or lecture about how to respond better next time, is the best way to help students more consistently be successful in meeting expectations.

Final Thoughts

In this chapter, we described the key elements of precision requests, and included the framework that has been recommended for delivering them. This included a listing of the key features of precision requests: the request is not stated in a question format; it is delivered in close proximity, with eye contact; one request is delivered at a time; and each successful response is reinforced. We also described the recommended framework for precision requests, which includes delivering the first request as a "Please..." statement. The next step if a student does not comply is phrased as "I need you to..." and may include a punitive element (e.g., "... or you will lose a point today"). While we fully endorse precision requests, we also noted that we encourage all teachers to review and use the key features of a precision request, even if they do not use the punitive component. In addition to general concerns about the possible overuse of negative or punitive procedures, we encourage individual teachers to think about students for whom a judicious use of the response cost element might be effective, compared to those students for whom this element may only make things worse. Whichever the case, we believe precision requests provide an efficient, easy-to-use tool to help all students meet basic expectations.

References

Martini-Scully, D. D., Bray, M. A., & Kehle, T. J. (2000). A packaged intervention to reduce disruptive behaviors in general education students. *Psychology in the Schools, 37*(2), 149–156.

Musser, E. H., Bray, M. A., Kehle, T. J., & Jenson, W. R. (2001). Reducing disruptive behaviors in students with serious emotional disturbance. *School Psychology Review, 30*(2), 294–304.

Neville, M. H., & Jensen, W. R. (1984). Precision command and the "Sure I will" program: A quick and efficient compliance training sequence. *Child & Family Behavior Therapy, 6*, 61–65.

Rhode, G., Jenson, W. R., & Reavis, H. K. (1993). *The tough kid book: Practical classroom management strategies*. Sopris West Inc.

Sabey, C. V., Calder, M. C., & Caldarella, P. (2021). Precision request: A secondary analysis of the use of praise, response cost, and reprimand. *Education and Treatment of Children, 44*(3), 185–198.

Precision Requests Planning Template

Specific Students to Support:	Context with Predictable Challenges:
Directions	**Precision Request(s)**
Describe requests students struggle to follow:	Plan the exact precision request(s) to be used:
Reinforcement Method	**Reductive Technique**
Describe how student compliance will be reinforced:	Describe the response method (only if applicable):

Data Collection
(Each day, mark a + for student compliance with a request and a − for noncompliance, then calculate the percentage of compliance)

	PRECISION REQUEST DATA									
STUDENT	M	%	T	%	W	%	Th	%	F	%

FIGURE 9.2 Precision Requests Planning Template

Precision Requests Components & Self-Assessment	
0→Not in Place 1→Partially in Place 2→Fully in Place	
COMPONENTS	**How Did I do?**
1. Use a non-question format.	☐ 0 ☐ 1 ☐ 2
2. Be specific about desired behavior.	☐ 0 ☐ 1 ☐ 2
3. Give requests in close proximity.	☐ 0 ☐ 1 ☐ 2
4. Establish brief eye contact, when appropriate.	☐ 0 ☐ 1 ☐ 2
5. Provide time to comply.	☐ 0 ☐ 1 ☐ 2
6. Make one request at a time.	☐ 0 ☐ 1 ☐ 2
7. Reinforce compliance, or redirect noncompliance.	☐ 0 ☐ 1 ☐ 2
8. Teach the procedure.	☐ 0 ☐ 1 ☐ 2
Notes & Reflection:	

FIGURE 9.3 Precision Requests Implementation and Self-Assessment Checklist

Part IV
Maintaining Appropriate Behavior

10

Behavior-Specific Praise

In this chapter, we explain how and why behavior-specific praise can be used to improve student behavior. We begin by providing a definition and description of this strategy, followed by a brief overview of the research that supports the use of this strategy. Next, we explain how increasing behavior-specific praise can build positive relationships with students, particularly those who demonstrate challenging behaviors. Finally, we describe how to implement this strategy and provide two examples of what this practice might look like in a classroom. The supplemental resources for this chapter include a planning template (one blank for your use and one completed as an example) and a self-assessment checklist to support implementation fidelity.

What Is Behavior-Specific Praise?

Behavior-specific praise (BSP) is a type of verbal reinforcement that is actually as simple as the name suggests. While it is a praise statement, it is not *just* a praise statement; it has to include mention of a specific behavior. So, although it is simple, there is an important difference between *behavior-specific* praise and generic praise. When delivering BSP, the desirable behavior is explicitly named and paired with verbal, positive reinforcement. Rather than simply saying "good job," a teacher would tell the student exactly what they did that was positive, such as "good job keeping your hands to yourself." At first glance, it may seem that there is not much difference between the two statements and you might wonder if adding the specific behavior to the praise really makes a difference. As we note later, research does tell us that BSP can be more impactful than a generic "good job" or "way to go" statement. Practically speaking, the simple addition of "keeping your hands to yourself" turns a general praise statement into an instructional statement.

To continue the example, consider students who are seated at their desks and then told to line up at the door because it is time for lunch. This activity – moving from the desk to the line at the door – requires that students engage in several specific behaviors in order to transition successfully. Students need to push in their chair, walk without running through the classroom, find their place in line, and wait (usually quietly) until it is time to exit the classroom. Now consider a student who is also known to push other students to get to their place in line, or who bothers other students by poking them on the shoulder or messing with their hair. If this student has made it to the line and is seen keeping their hands to themselves on a given day and hears "good job," they might wonder what exactly they did that led to this extra praise. In these situations, using BSP would help to clarify and reinforce that there was an improvement in the specific behavior of keeping their hands to themselves. Without the specific connection, a student might not realize that they are being praised for keeping their hands to themselves, and could think "yes, I pushed in my chair, walked to the line, and waited quietly." It may seem obvious to adults what the praise is for, but it is not always so obvious for young children, students with chronically challenging behavior, or those who have difficulty navigating the hidden curriculum.

Several definitions of what makes a praise statement "behavior specific" have been proposed (Madsen et al., 1968; O'Leary & O'Leary, 1977), but in 1981 one of the most well-known praise researchers, Jere Brophy, identified 11 guidelines for delivering effective praise. These characteristics and guidelines can be summarized into five main characteristics (Collins & Cook, 2016). In order to be considered BSP, the statement should be: (1) positive and nonjudgmental; (2) specific and corrective with details; (3) intentional, credible, and sincere; (4) immediately delivered in proximity to the student; and (5) varied in content and across students.

How Do I Know Behavior-Specific Praise Works?

The use of BSP to improve student outcomes is supported by more than five decades of empirical research (Ennis et al., 2020). In 1968, Madsen and colleagues examined the impact of a teachers' use of rules, praise, and ignoring on student behavior. Although the type of praise used by teachers in this study was not always specific, they found that when teachers praised their students, it helped with two main things. First, and most importantly, student behavior improved – there were improvements in work completion, attention, and even academic skills. Second, the teachers liked it. Specifically, they reported that they used praise more effectively when they focused on the demonstration of appropriate behaviors and that the overall classroom environment improved. As a result of these findings, Madsen and colleagues made recommendations for the characteristics of effective praise (e.g., praise specific, prosocial behavior; stay away from sarcasm; walk around the room to ensure that the praise and attention is evenly distributed among students) which has come to be referred to as BSP.

Despite decades of research supporting the use of BSP, some people nonetheless criticize the use of external reinforcement, specifically cautioning adults against using praise with children. One of the most notable critics was Alfie Kohn, who suggested that using praise is a way to manipulate kids, rob them of pleasure, and reduce their achievement. He argued that the use of praise can create "praise junkies" and lead to children losing interest in tasks because their attention is redirected and refocused on receiving praise. However, as we have pointed out, the data-based research on this topic suggests the opposite. We think many of the criticisms of the use of praise that have been suggested by researchers or the popular press stem from either a misinterpretation of the research, or maybe more often a misrepresentation of the recommended ways that praise can be most effectively delivered (Collins & Cook, 2016). There is no doubt, for example, that when praise is not used effectively (i.e., when it does not have the characteristics outlined above), it is less effective, or in fact may have no effect at all. When used incorrectly, such as constantly praising for routine or mundane tasks that students do not struggle with, students may actually be turned off by the use of praise (Brophy, 1981). However, when praise is used correctly – when individual student needs are considered, when it is *behavior-specific* and when it follows the guidelines for effective praise, the research is resoundingly clear: it works!

The importance and effectiveness of BSP is also evident when we consider executive function and self-regulation, both of which are mental processes that have been described by the Center on the Developing Child at Harvard University as being the air traffic control of the brain. These skills support us in planning and carrying out tasks, including changing our behavior or actions along the way if we are not on-track for the desired outcome. For all people, executive functions are not fully developed until early adulthood (i.e., early to mid-twenties), and for individuals with disabilities, there are often additional delays in the development of these skills. One of the reasons that BSP is so effective is that it communicates to students that they are on the right track. This is helpful in all areas that support success in and out of school, including academics, behavior, communication, and other functional skills. Indeed, research evidence suggests that the use of BSP can impact individual students and the class as a whole, decrease disruption and inappropriate behavior and improve time spent on task, rule-following, and overall compliance (Moore et al., 2019; Royer et al., 2019).

How Does Behavior-Specific Praise Build Positive Relationships with My Students?

Much like the other strategies we've described in this book, using BSP increases the number of positive interactions between students and teachers. One way that using BSP helps improve student-teacher relationships is that it improves the overall atmosphere in the classroom. Generally, when students are in an environment where there are more positive statements than negative ones, the overall mood in the classroom improves and naturally, the classroom is more likely to feel like a welcoming and safe place. More specifically, using BSP aligns with several characteristics of high-quality student-teacher relationships by increasing verbal engagement with students, demonstrating warmth, and increasing communication.

When we think about using BSP for students who have learning or behavior challenges, the connection to building positive student-teacher relationships becomes even more clear. Unfortunately, we know that students with or at risk for disabilities are more likely to receive negative or critical feedback than positive statements. Making a concentrated effort to use BSP with these students can drastically improve the negative to positive statement ratio. Consider the previous example of a student who is walking to line up at the door. Imagine a student who runs to their spot in line, chatting with friends along the way. It can be easy for teachers to fall into the cycle of saying "stop talking" or "you know you shouldn't be running in class." But a simple shift to first acknowledge what the student did correctly, and then offer corrective feedback, can make a huge difference. Now, instead of only hearing negative feedback, a student hears something along the lines of "You did a great job pushing in your chair. Next time, remember to walk quietly to line up." The same shift can be applied to academic feedback. Consider a student who struggles with writing complete sentences. Rather than jumping straight to telling the student what they need to correct, the teacher can preface the feedback with BSP praise – even if it is something as simple as "You did a great job using periods at the end of your sentences." These simple statements go a long way in fostering a supportive and positive relationship between teachers and their students.

How Do I Implement Behavior-Specific Praise in My Classroom?

The implementation of BSP is easy and straightforward. In fact, we think it is probably the simplest strategy to implement out of all the strategies presented in this entire volume. That said, there are some things you will want to do to make sure that you are implementing praise effectively and that it is, in fact, *behavior specific*. As we mentioned, the effective use of BSP can be summarized into five characteristics.

The first three characteristics are related to the content and tone of the statement. First, the statement should be positive and should not cast judgment. One of the most common mistakes we see in the implementation of BSP is related to this characteristic. Often, teachers will offer a BSP statement, but they will follow it with something related to the student's challenging behavior, such as "Excellent job lining up today; I'm glad you finally remembered to walk and not run." Although teachers very likely do not mean harm by this type of statement, it can come off as judgmental, and should be avoided. Rather, just tell the student what they did that's leading to your praise, such as "Excellent job walking to the door to line up." Next, the statement should specifically reinforce a behavior or skill and, if needed, should provide corrective feedback. We described this above with the sentence writing example. Next, the statement should be intentional and sincere. Students know when a teacher is just trying to make them feel good, or exaggerating an accomplishment, and those types of statements can actually be counterproductive. For example, there is no need to tell a student who is struggling in math that they are "the best problem solver around" or "the smartest kid you've ever known" if there is a chance that the student may interpret that as being insincere. Also related to sincerity is the tone of voice. Calmly telling a student who is struggling with their confidence in math "I know this was tough for you but I want you to know that you did a great job solving problems 3, 9, and 10; that shows me you're capable so let's look at how we can improve on the other problems so you're ready for next time" has a genuine tone. A statement like this lets the student know that you see the challenge but you also see their successes and their skills.

The remaining two characteristics of effective BSP are related to the delivery. To be most effective, BSP statements should be delivered as immediately following the demonstration of a behavior as possible. Of course, there will be times when this is not possible or, when delivery needs to be delayed based on student preference (we talk more about this below). That said, the general rule of thumb is to deliver praise immediately and in proximity to the student when possible. Finally, BSP statements should be delivered with variety. There are two main ways to vary the use of BSP. First, the actual phrases (e.g., "nice job turning in your work" or "I like that you remembered to put your backpack in your cubby") should be varied. Second, variation can be achieved by pairing gestures with statements (e.g., a thumbs up, fist bump, or high-five). Both of these approaches are simple and easy ways to help BSP from sounding robotic or meaningless to students.

What Do I Need to Begin Implementing Behavior-Specific Praise?

One of the biggest benefits of BSP is that it is completely free. You will not need to buy anything or prepare any additional materials – you already have everything you need to make a positive statement! Although BSP is very easy to implement, we suggest thinking through a few important things. First, think about the students who might not be receiving a lot of positive feedback from teachers and consider how you might identify their strengths more often. Related to this, be sure to consider individual students' skill sets. We mentioned that some students might find praise for routine tasks to be aversive or off-putting, but for students who struggle with routine tasks, it is perfectly appropriate to use BSP to reinforce their behavior. Second, be sure to think about any students who might not appreciate being singled out in front of their peers, even if it is positive, and identify some ways that you can deliver their BSP more discreetly. Perhaps for these students, you hold-off on delivering praise until you can do so quietly so that only they can hear you. Next, it's a good idea to think about how you might vary your praise statements. Think about your "go-to" praise phrases (e.g., "good job..." or "I like the way...") and brainstorm a few different ways that you could offer BSP. Finally, determine how you will keep track of your BSP statements, particularly if you have a goal to increase your statements in general, or to a few certain students. Some teachers ask a paraprofessional to help them track, while others might keep a few loose coins in one pants pocket, and then move them to the other pocket every time they deliver a BSP statement. At the end of this chapter, we have provided a planning template (Figure 10.2) to help you think through these considerations and collect self-monitoring data on your use of BSP (Figure 10.3).

What Does Behavior-Specific Praise look Like in a Classroom?

In addition to being easy to implement, an obvious benefit of BSP is that it can be used for students across all grade levels to reinforce a wide variety of skills. We have provided several brief examples of what BSP praise statements sound like, but in this section, we offer examples of how teachers can use BSP statements with specific consideration of academic and behavioral needs.

Elementary Example

Ms. Barton is a fourth grade teacher who has three students who have been struggling to follow expectations during recess (see Figure 10.1 for Ms. Barton's completed planning template). Darius has had a hard time waiting in line to use different playground equipment, Michelle has struggled to show good

Behavior Specific Praise Planning Template

General Considerations – What desired behaviors would you like to see more of from your class as a whole?
I would like to see students follow expectations at lunch and recess better, especially things like taking turns, sharing, and treating each other respectfully.

Behavior Specific Praise Components
Describe all components in specific detail and how they will be introduced to the student.

	STUDENTS TO SUPPORT	DESIRED BEHAVIOR	STUDENT STRENGTHS	STUDENT PREFERENCES	VARIED PRAISE STATEMENTS
1	Darius	Wait his turn in line	Responds well to precorrections	No specific needs	Great job___ I like how you___ Nice job___ Thank you for___
2	Michelle	Show sportsmanship by saying/doing something kind to the winner	Enjoys competing in different games and sports	High fives & fist bumps to celebrate and connect	Great job___ I like how you___ Nice job___ Thank you for___
3	Elliot	Share balls when other kids want to play too	Great knowledge of how to play football	Brief, more low-key interactions in front of peers	Great job___ I like how you___ Nice job___ Thank you for___
4					

Tracking Method & Data Collection Plan

Describe how you will track your use of behavior specific praise:
I'll use a handheld tally counter to keep count of how often I deliver BSP, and record it in a spreadsheet each day to make a graph of how I do over time.
Identify the specific behavior targeted for improvement and the metric (e.g., % of time on-task) & method for data collection:
I'll rate each student's behavior at the end of recess on a 10-point Direct Behavior Rating scale to keep track of how well they do engaging in appropriate behavior (e.g., waiting turns, sharing) across each week.

FIGURE 10.1 Completed Example of Behavior-Specific Praise Planning Template

sportsmanship when she doesn't win the jump rope contests, and Jax has been reluctant to share the football with the other kids in the class. Before recess, Ms. Barton reviews the expectations with the whole class and makes it a point to discreetly check-in with reminders for Darius, Michelle, and Jax before they run off to play. During recess, Ms. Barton pays close attention to these students and offers precorrection (see Chapter 8) to help remind them of the expectations. As soon as the students exhibit the behavioral expectation, she follows up with BSP (e.g., "great job waiting your turn, Darius," "Michelle, I like that you high-fived the winner of the jump rope contest today," and "nice sharing, Jax"). After recess is over, Ms. Barton also uses BSP to reinforce the entire class on their demonstration of the school-wide expectations by saying, "We had a great day at recess. You all did a fantastic job playing responsibly, safely, and respectfully."

Secondary Example
Mr. Cook is a tenth grade Advanced Placement history teacher who is fluent in both English and Spanish. This is helpful for Mr. Cook because the majority of his students are English Learners, whose first language is Spanish. One student in his class, Gabriella, has been struggling with the weekly essays. From what Mr. Cook has observed, Gabriella has a solid understanding of the content, but she struggles to convey that understanding in writing. Mr. Cook has been working with Gabriella to use graphic organizers to help her organize her thoughts and the main points she wants to make in her essays. This approach has helped Gabriella tremendously, but she has expressed that she is self-conscious because it feels like everyone else in the class "just gets it" and doesn't have to put as much effort into planning their writing. As a result, Gabriella is reluctant to use graphic organizers before starting her writing assignments, so Mr. Cook typically has to remind Gabriella to utilize this tool before she begins writing. Then, one day in class, before he has time to offer her a prompt, Gabriella begins the writing period by using a graphic organizer. Although Mr. Cook doesn't have time to assess the content (and, that is not one of his concerns anyway, as Gabriella consistently demonstrates content understanding),

he can still use this opportunity to reinforce her use of the graphic organizer. Since Spanish is Gabriella's first language and Mr. Cook knows that Gabriella is self-conscious about the way she perceives her pre-writing needs, Mr. Cook walks over to Gabriella's desk, kneels down, and very quietly says, "¡Excelente trabajo usando ese organizador gráfico, Gabriella!" (Excellent job using that graphic organizer, Gabriella). Mr. Cook's use of BSP creates a moment of connection – his use of Gabriella's first language shows respect and warmth, and his BSP statement communicates that Gabriella is on the right path.

Final Thoughts

In this chapter, we discussed the use of BSP, which we suggest is one of the easiest strategies to implement to help improve behavior and build better relationships with students. We gave special attention to the characteristics of what makes a praise statement effective because, as we noted, if used incorrectly, praise may have the opposite of the desired effect. As a reminder, BSP should be (1) positive and nonjudgmental; (2) specific and paired with corrective feedback if needed; (3) intentional in targeting specific behaviors and sincere by avoiding sarcasm or condescension; (4) immediately delivered and delivered in close proximity when possible; and (5) varied in phrasing and use of gestures.

In our experience, managing classroom behavior can quickly start to feel overwhelming, which can create a feeling of not knowing where to even start. We think that BSP is an excellent strategy to start with if you are feeling overwhelmed because it is easy to implement and it is completely free. Once you are comfortable using BSP, we encourage you to consider pairing this strategy with some of the other strategies described in this book, specifically behavioral momentum (Chapter 5) and precorrection (Chapter 8). Pairing these strategies is beneficial in a few ways. First, this combination sets students up for success and then reinforces them once they have demonstrated a particular behavior or skill. Additionally, it is an excellent way to foster positive student-teacher relationships. Imagine a situation where a teacher uses behavioral momentum before asking the student to complete a few math problems. Leading up to the request, there are a series of requests (at least three) that the teacher knows the student is likely to do. After each request and demonstration of student behavior, the teacher uses BSP. Then, the teacher can ask the student to complete a few math problems; hopefully, the student will comply by at least starting work on these problems, at which point the teacher can offer still another BSP statement. In this scenario, there is the potential for a minimum of four reciprocal and positive student-teacher interactions. Now, consider the alternative (the teacher simply asks the student to complete math problems). Even if the student engages and the teacher uses BSP, this is only one interaction. Of course, this is better than not using BSP at all, and for many students a single use of BSP is likely enough in many contexts. But for students who need more support, we think that pairing BSP with other strategies is the most ideal approach. The goal is to use whatever strategies work best for a particular student to help that student meet behavioral and academic expectations, and then to use BSP as we have outlined to reinforce those specific behaviors.

References

Brophy, J. (1981). Teacher praise: A functional analysis. *Review of Educational Research, 51*, 5–32.

Collins, L. W., & Cook, L. (2016). Never say never: The appropriate and inappropriate use of praise and feedback for students with learning and behavioral disabilities. In B. G. Cook, M. Tankersley, & T. J. Landrum (Eds.), *Instructional practices with and without empirical validity* (Vol. 29, pp. 153–173). Emerald Group Publishing Limited.

Ennis, R. P., Royer, D. J., Lane, K. L., & Dunlap, K. D. (2020). Behavior-specific praise in pre-K–12 settings: Mapping the 50-year knowledge base. *Behavioral Disorders, 45*(3), 131–147.

Madsen, C. H. Jr, Becker, W. C., & Thomas, D. R. (1968). Rules, praise, and ignoring: Elements of elementary classroom control. *Journal of Applied Behavior Analysis, 1*, 139–150.

Moore, T. C., Maggin, D. M., Thompson, K. M., Gordon, J. R., Daniels, S., & Lang, L. E. (2019). Evidence review for teacher praise to improve students' classroom behavior. *Journal of Positive Behavior Interventions*, *21*(1), 3–18.

O'Leary, K. D., & O'Leary, S. G. (1977). *Classroom management: The successful use of behavior modification.* Oxford, UK: Pergamon.

Royer, D. J., Lane, K. L., Dunlap, K. D., & Ennis, R. P. (2019). A systematic review of teacher-delivered behavior-specific praise on K–12 student performance. *Remedial and Special Education*, *40*(2), 112–128.

Behavior Specific Praise Planning Template

General Considerations – What desired behaviors would you like to see more of from your class as a whole?

Behavior Specific Praise Components

Describe all components in specific detail and how they will be introduced to the student.

STUDENTS TO SUPPORT	DESIRED BEHAVIOR	STUDENT STRENGTHS	STUDENT PREFERENCES	VARIED PRAISE STATEMENTS
1				
2				
3				
4				

Tracking Method & Data Collection Plan

Describe how you will track your use of behavior specific praise:

Identify the specific behavior targeted for improvement and the metric (e.g., % of time on-task) & method for data collection:

FIGURE 10.2 Behavior-Specific Praise Planning Template

Behavior Specific Praise Characteristics & Self-Assessment	
0→Not in Place 1→Partially in Place 2→Fully in Place	
CHARACTERISTICS	**How Did I do?**
1. Statement is positive and nonjudgmental.	☐ 0 ☐ 1 ☐ 2
2. Statement provides reinforcement for a specific behavior and, if needed, corrective feedback.	☐ 0 ☐ 1 ☐ 2
3. Statement is intentional and sincere.	☐ 0 ☐ 1 ☐ 2
4. Statement is delivered immediately after demonstration of the student's behavior.	☐ 0 ☐ 1 ☐ 2
5. Statement is varied from previous behavior specific praise statements.	☐ 0 ☐ 1 ☐ 2
Notes & Reflection:	

FIGURE 10.3 Behavior-Specific Praise Implementation and Self-Assessment Checklist

11

Token Economies

In this chapter, we explain how and why token economies can be used to improve student behavior. We begin by providing a definition and description of this strategy, followed by a brief overview of the research that supports the use of this strategy. Next, we explain how token economies can build positive relationships with students, particularly those who demonstrate challenging behaviors. Finally, we describe how to implement this strategy and provide two examples of what this practice might look like in a classroom. The supplemental resources for this chapter include a planning template (one blank for your use and one completed as an example) and a self-assessment checklist to support implementation fidelity.

What Is a Token Economy?

Token economies are used in many parts of our lives and if you have spent any time at all in schools, you have very likely seen some form of a token economy in action in classrooms. A token economy is a system in which a person (a student for our context here) receives some type of token (a literal token, a ticket, a fake dollar, etc.) for demonstrating a desired behavior. Then, at some point in time (daily, weekly, monthly), the tokens can then be exchanged for what is known as a backup reinforcer, which is simply a tangible item or activity that is valued by the individual. In a sense, our lives are driven by one big token economy. If you work, you receive a "token" in the form of a paycheck. The paycheck itself (once just a slip of paper; now more likely a simple electronic notice that money has been deposited in your account) is not actually worth anything itself – the value lies in what that token represents. You exchange that "token" for other things that you really do value – a house, a car, new clothes – the list goes on and on. In classrooms that use token economies, the time period between the demonstration of the behavior and the distribution of the token is typically much more frequent than in the paycheck example, but the idea is the same. When students exhibit a particular behavior, they can receive a token immediately that they can trade in at a later time for a backup reinforcer.

In classrooms, the use of token economies can vary greatly depending on the needs of the students and can be used on a class-wide and individual level. At the class-wide level, teachers who use token economies typically provide all students with the opportunity to earn tokens throughout the entire period or day, and earning tokens is usually connected to the class-wide expectations. Of course, many teachers will also use tokens to reinforce students who exhibit behavior that stands out in an extraordinary way – perhaps they offer help to a student who seems to be struggling, clean up more than their fair share of materials after an activity, or are overhead trying to cheer up a classmate who is down about something. Class-wide tokens are typically exchanged after larger periods of time, either the end of the week, month, or even the quarter. On an individual level, teachers can use a token economy to support students who have more intensive behavioral needs. In these situations, teachers would distribute tokens to students when they exhibit behaviors that align with their individual goals in addition to those that reflect classroom expectations. These tokens can be aligned with the class-wide system, or they can be used in their own "mini" token economy system, which allows for tokens to be traded-in more frequently than what occurs in the class-wide system. This is important for students who have or are at risk for disabilities that impact their behavior because they benefit from more frequent schedules of reinforcement (see Chapter 13). In either case, teachers should be sure to tell students why they are receiving the tokens and we suggest doing this through the use of behavior-specific praise (see Chapter 10).

How Do I Know Token Economies Work?

The use of token economies to improve behavioral outcomes has been supported by specific research for more than six decades, and the theory that supports this type of intervention has been around even longer (Kazdin & Bootzin, 1972). Token economies are a form of operant conditioning, which is central to the behavioral theory of B.F. Skinner, described as early as 1938. According to both theory and research, one reason token economies may be effective is because the novelty of reinforcers may not wear off as quickly as if students were being reinforced with the backup reinforcer every time (Ferster & DeMyer, 1962).

Consider a student who receives a small piece of candy every time they are seen demonstrating academic engagement. And note that we don't advocate the use of candy as a first choice or go-to reinforcer, though we DO acknowledge that food items can be powerful reinforcers for some students and contexts. Teachers may certainly wish to choose granola bars, fruit snacks, popcorn, etc., as more healthy options! For the sake of our example, perhaps the teacher has learned that candy is far and away the most desirable item this student consistently seeks and asks for. But how practical is it to provide candy, even a tiny piece, after every positive response? Instead, compare this to the student receiving a token every time they are seen demonstrating academic engagement, with the knowledge that they can exchange their tokens for a small piece of candy once they have earned 20 tokens. Not only is this a healthier approach, but it helps prevent students from becoming satiated – or unimpressed by the backup reinforcers. With any reinforcer, there is always the likelihood that the student may become bored with it – unmotivated by it – after repeatedly earning it (think of even your favorite food – after eating a large quantity of it, you find yourself "over it").

Other reasons that token economies are ideal is that they can easily be carried around by a teacher or paraprofessional and there is not a limit to the maximum number of tokens a student can earn (Ayllon & Azrin, 1968). Tokens also allow immediacy – it is very easy to give a student a token for assignment completion as soon as they complete each individual assignment, but very difficult to allow them access to a preferred activity (e.g., basketball in the gym) after *every* completed assignment.

Token economies have been used for supporting behavior change in a variety of settings, including both general and special education classrooms across all grade levels. The use of token economies is also effective for students of all ages, including preschool, but research indicates that they are more impactful for students ages 6 to 15 (Soares et al., 2016). Much of the research in schools has focused on increasing academic engagement and/or decreasing disruptive behavior by using token economies that allow students to exchange tokens for tangible reinforcers and/or preferred activities (Maggin et al., 2011).

Although token economies are effective for improving both academic and behavioral outcomes, they tend to have more of an impact on behavioral skills (Soares et al., 2016). This is likely because token economies cannot help bridge the gap when students don't have basic mastery of the skills we want to see increased. Consider a skill for which you have not had any training, such as performing an open-heart surgery. No amount of reinforcement will help you successfully complete that task if you have not had the appropriate instruction and opportunities to practice. The same applies to academic skills; no amount of reinforcement will increase reading skills, for example, without explicit instruction in those skills. This is probably why most of the research related to token economies for academics is focused on academic engagement, which we know is a strong predictor of academic success. In either case (academics or behavior) it is always important to consider whether students need additional instruction in the skill and if so, to provide that instruction before implementing a token economy system.

How Do Token Economies Build Positive Relationships with My Students?

Using token economies is an excellent way to build positive relationships with your students for a few reasons. First, distributing tokens, and pairing them with specific feedback for why the student is receiving them, provides more frequent opportunities for teachers to acknowledge when students are demonstrating behavior that is aligned with classroom and school-wide expectations. The same applies for students who have individualized goals.

Another way that token economies can build positive relationships with students is through the backup reinforcers. Selecting backup reinforcers that align with your students' likes, interests, and preferences is a way to communicate that you see and value their individuality. In some cases, teachers may choose to provide students with choices regarding the backup reinforcers. For example, a student may be able to choose between three preferred activities (e.g., time on an iPad, eating lunch with the teacher, or extra time to draw) after they have earned the required number of tokens. This approach gives students some autonomy and also recognizes that they may be motivated by different things on different days. We think that sending these messages (I see you, I am paying attention to your interests, I think you are capable of choosing what motivates you) is a way to increase high-quality interactions with students, which is an important component of building positive relationships with students.

Finally, fostering a positive relationship with students is largely dependent on the student's perception (see Chapter 1). Carefully selecting backup reinforcers that align with students' preferences is an excellent way to increase the likelihood that students will perceive these interactions to be authentic.

How Do I Implement Token Economies in My Classroom?

Implementing a token economy requires a bit more planning and preparation than some of the other strategies described in this book, but once the preparation is complete and the system is ready to implement, it is straightforward and fairly simple to use a token economy in the classroom. There is a general consensus that there are six main components to effectively implementing a token economy system that is focused on the positive reinforcement of target behaviors (Ackerman et al., 2020; Ivy et al., 2017; Kim et al., 2022), and we describe these components in the six steps below. Note here that we are focusing on positive reinforcement. We point this out because in some cases, there are seven components to token economy systems (e.g., Kim et al., 2022), in which teachers may incorporate a procedure known as response cost. In a response cost procedure, students can lose tokens that have been earned when they fail to meet a given expectation.

In general, we encourage the teachers we work with to avoid using response cost if possible and we make this recommendation for a few reasons. First, our philosophy is grounded in the belief that the most effective behavior management strategies are those that are positive. Second, the response cost procedure can be quite complex and can actually cause disruptive or problematic behavior to escalate, which is the opposite of what most teachers are hoping to accomplish in their classrooms. In our experience, students with or at risk for disabilities that impact their behavior have a particularly hard time with response cost systems; frankly, we believe that in most cases teachers can achieve the same, or better, results without taking tokens away. For example, rather than taking a token back from a student after they have earned it, teachers can simply withhold distribution of the next token depending on the schedule of reinforcement being used (more on that in just a moment). Finally, we worry that when a response cost procedure is in place, it may actually decrease the effectiveness of the overall token economy system, especially for students who have more difficult or challenging behaviors. Consider your own work and the example we used at the beginning of this chapter related to paychecks. Imagine how you would feel if you came to work one morning and had a really great day for the first six hours, but then, at the end of the day, you encountered a challenging situation and perhaps engaged in behavior that is less than ideal (e.g., conflict with a parent, heated disagreement with your boss). How would it feel to have some portion of the money you earned earlier in the day taken back because of a problem you encountered later in the afternoon? We think that not only would most people agree this would be a negative experience, but that it might influence behavior, attitudes, and motivation going forward in less than ideal ways. Although this is an exaggerated example, think about this in terms of your students. Students may feel less motivated to earn tokens if they know that a misstep later in the day could lead to the tokens being taken back, and the likelihood of missteps later in the day is particularly high for students with challenging behavior. In the sections that follow, we share ideas for how to structure a token economy system for students with challenging behavior without needing to use a response cost procedure.

Step 1: Define Behaviors

The first step in implementing a token economy is to define the behaviors that will lead to students earning tokens. The easiest way to do this at a class-wide level is to simply align token distribution with the class-wide or school-wide expectations (see Chapter 2). We think of this as a system to "catch students meeting expectations" in which students can earn tokens when they are seen demonstrating behavior that, for the sake of an example, is safe, respectful, or responsible. In this situation, it is most common for teachers to use a variable reinforcement schedule. We discuss this type of schedule in more detail in Chapter 13, but put simply, it means that students are not reinforced every single time they demonstrate a target behavior (that would be a lot of reinforcement for teachers to keep up with for most students!), but rather, they are reinforced periodically throughout the period or day.

For students who have more intensive behavioral needs, we suggest that teachers align token distribution with the student's behavioral goals. These goals may be formally outlined in an Individualized Education Program (IEP) or Behavior Intervention Plan (BIP), or they may be identified through your own observations. For these students, we suggest reinforcing the target behaviors as often as possible in the beginning. In all cases, teachers should be sure that anyone who is responsible for the distribution of tokens (co-teachers, paraprofessionals, parent volunteers) is familiar with the behaviors that can earn tokens and that students have been explicitly taught how to demonstrate these behaviors.

Step 2: Select and Teach Tokens

The next step is to figure out what will be used as "tokens" for reinforcement. Tokens can take many different forms. In many cases, teachers use raffle-type tickets that they either purchase or print themselves. Another common token is the use of play money. Again, this money can be purchased so that it looks real, or it can be printed and given a clever name, such as "bonus bucks," "dolphin dollars," or "Collins cash." We encourage teachers to select tokens that will be easy for students to store without taking up too much space, such as in an envelope that is kept in their binder or desk.

After determining what will be used as a token, the next thing to do is to teach students about the token economy system. Typically, this can be done fairly quickly, without taking up too much instructional time and can usually be done in about ten minutes or less. When teaching students about the tokens, it is important to teach students (a) what behavior will earn a token (Step 1), (b) how often tokens will be distributed (Step 2), and (c) how tokens can be exchanged (Steps 3–5). We think it is a good idea to create a poster that has this information on it and that can serve as a visual reminder for students, especially in the beginning.

Step 3: Identify Backup Reinforcers

An important aspect of any token economy system is the backup reinforcers and here is where you, as the teacher, will want to rely on your own knowledge of your students. In our experience, when we ask teachers to name what their students' interests or favorite preferred activities are, most teachers can do so for their class as a whole and for their students on an individual level. Teachers know which students prefer reading for pleasure versus having extra time to work on an art project, which students would get a thrill out of having lunch with them versus which students would be highly motivated by some extra time on the playground after finishing their lunch. Similarly, teachers know the latest and greatest interests of their students to know what might be appealing in class store, such as candy, fidgets, or even small trinkets or trading cards. In some classrooms, students might all receive the same backup reinforcer (such as candy) and in others, students might get to choose from a few items or preferred activities. The choice is entirely up to the teacher based on what is most feasible for you and your classroom

Of course, providing backup reinforcers can come with an added expense, so there are several ways teachers can reduce or eliminate out-of-pocket costs. The first option is to use preferred activities. The key here is to find a time that does not interfere with instructional time and that also does not punish students who may not have earned enough tokens to exchange. For example, perhaps one morning, students who have earned enough tokens can be excused from the bell work and select an activity of their choice. Another way to reduce the cost of backup reinforcers is to ask for donations from parents or other community members. Teachers can create online wish lists for their classroom and share those lists with parents, friends, neighbors, etc. We have seen teachers have great success by sharing their lists online, through social media platforms. A few other "tricks of the trade" are to gather things that might be in your own home that you are no longer using, purchase holiday candy after it goes on sale, and gather promotional items from conferences – the little hand sanitizer or pocket highlighter type trinkets that can be found sprinkled around exhibit tables at professional developments can make excellent items for your class store. Regardless of how you choose to accrue backup reinforcers, it is helpful to remember that they don't need to be elaborate or expensive. Sometimes students are motivated by the simplest of things, like a fun pen or cool pencil.

Step 4: Determine Exchange Schedule
Next, it is important to think about how often tokens will be exchanged for backup reinforcers. Again, this is entirely up to

you and every classroom will vary. We have seen token economies work in classrooms where the exchange happens as infrequently as once per quarter and we have seen success where exchange happens much more often, such as once a week. Again, we encourage teachers to use their own judgment here to find the sweet spot of providing exchange times often enough that it is reinforcing, but not so often that it loses appeal or novelty. In some classrooms, students have the option not to exchange and to roll their tokens over to the next exchange period; for some students, "banking" their tokens is itself highly motivating.

But what about some of the students in your classroom who have behavioral needs that are a bit more intensive – students who may be prone to demonstrating challenging behaviors if they don't earn a token or if they don't have enough tokens to exchange when the time comes? We think this concern is very real. We have experienced students we taught having meltdowns or worse, and these scenarios are among the most frequently asked questions we get from the teachers with whom we work. Here are a few suggestions we have found to be helpful. First, we encourage you to reinforce these students as often as possible, especially at the beginning of implementation. Earlier, we talked about "catching" students when they are demonstrating behaviors that can earn a token and this is especially important for students with more challenging behaviors. We know from both research and experience that students who need reinforcement the most often receive it the least, so it can be helpful to have these students on your radar and make a concentrated effort to reinforce their behavior. Another strategy that can be helpful is to have an individualized token economy system for those students you believe will struggle with even the basics of a class-wide token system. We recognize that doing this for every student would be a classroom management nightmare, so please know that is not what we are suggesting. That said, for students who have more intensive needs, this type of individualized support can be extremely helpful. Token economies can be individualized in a few ways. First, you can reduce the number of tokens needed to exchange for a backup reinforcer; instead of needing ten tokens before an exchange can occur, perhaps this student can exchange after three or five tokens at first. Another option is to create a subsystem of reinforcement, in which students earn different tokens for their individualized needs. In this system, students usually exchange these tokens for a backup reinforcer more frequently (at minimum, once a day, but we have seen this done even more often; once after the morning, before lunch, and again at the end of the afternoon). Note here that in these cases, students still participate in the class-wide token economy system. Finally, if you are aware that a student does not have enough tokens to exchange for a backup reinforcer, we suggest implementing precorrection (Chapter 8) and offering the opportunity to earn tokens for successfully navigating this situation. For example, a teacher may say "Eliza, today is exchange day and unfortunately, you don't have enough tokens to exchange for a granola bar. But, if you can remain calm during exchange time and refrain from yelling or cursing, then you will earn two tokens that you can put toward next week's exchange."

Step 5: Determine Rate for Token Exchange

The last step for implementing a token economy in your classroom is to determine the exchange rate. In some classrooms, the exchange rate is the same for all backup reinforcers. This works especially well if students are exchanging tokens for a preferred activity or for the same tangible item, such as a piece of candy. In other classrooms, teachers may choose to create a class store, where each item has a different cost. This works well in token economy systems where students are allowed to wait on exchanging tokens to save up for a certain item from the store. Again, we encourage teachers to think about what will work best for their students and their classrooms, and to develop an exchange rate that is reasonable and attainable for students to meet.

What Do I Need to Begin Implementing a Token Economy?

The obvious needs for implementing a token economy include the tokens and the backup reinforcers. But to implement a token economy successfully you also need to have clear rules and expectations established in your classroom (see Chapter 2), as these expectations will be the foundation for determining what behaviors can earn tokens. In addition, you will need to have a plan in place for the exchange system, including both a schedule for when exchanges will occur (Step 4) and a rate at which the tokens will be exchanged for backup reinforcers (Step 5). At the end of this chapter, we have included a planning template (Figure 11.2) that will guide you in thinking through the various components of a token economy and we have provided a completed planning template as an example (Figure 11.1). We have also included a self-assessment checklist (Figure 11.3) to support your implementation of a token economy.

What Do Token Economies Look like in a Classroom?

As we have mentioned several times throughout this chapter, the implementation of token economies can vary across classrooms. In the sections below, we provide two examples of how token economies can look depending on the different needs of the teachers and students in the classrooms.

Elementary Example

Ms. Steingut is a second grade special education teacher who has been asked to provide some additional support to one of her students, Kay. Kay has individual behavioral goals, mostly related to communication and management of her feelings. Several times a day, Kay will engage in verbal outlashes toward her teachers and peers, and when she becomes angry or frustrated, she has a tendency to rip her papers or break materials. Ms. Steingut decides to implement a token economy system for Kay, in which she will have the opportunity to earn tickets for engaging in her replacement behaviors (e.g., instead of cursing at the teacher, Kay should say "I am so mad right now and I need a break"). In addition, Kay will earn tickets for demonstrating positive peer interactions and for completing assignments without damaging any materials. She is given one ticket for each positive interaction or assignment completed. Kay is in an inclusion classroom and since Ms. Steingut is the co-teacher, she is able to structure the token economy system so that Kay can earn a preferred activity twice a day: before lunch and before dismissal. In the beginning, Kay will need to have five tickets to exchange for five minutes of a preferred activity of her choice, either drawing or time on a tablet, both of which she loves. Ms. Steingut structures the day into two separate blocks, so that after lunch, Kay turns her tickets in to Ms. Steingut and starts over. This way, if she doesn't earn her morning reinforcement, she has a chance to start over for the afternoon. Ms. Steingut plans to gradually increase the number of tickets Kay needs to exchange to earn the backup reinforcer.

Secondary Example

Mr. Anderson is an eleventh grade English teacher. For the most part, his students demonstrate behavior that reflects the school- and class-wide expectations. His students arrive on time to class, they are courteous to one another and to him, and they complete their assignments on time. However, he has been trying to facilitate rich discussions about the novels they read and for some reason, the students in his second period class are reluctant to participate. He provides them with discussion questions ahead of time so that they can prepare and jot down notes before the discussion. Since the students turn their notes in at the end of class, Mr. Anderson can tell that they have completed the assigned reading. In an attempt to increase participation, Mr. Anderson decides to implement a token economy (see Figure 11.1 for his completed planning template). Since it's an English class, he makes fake money that he decides to call Bonus Bucks. Mr. Anderson doesn't want to spend much on backup reinforcers, but since his class period is only 90 minutes, he doesn't have a lot of time he can allocate to letting students choose preferred activities. Luckily, Halloween just passed, so he is able to score some large bags of assorted candy for 75% off! Mr. Anderson explains to his students that every time they participate in the class discussion, they will have an opportunity to earn a Bonus Buck. He tells them that he isn't worried about their answer being "right" or "wrong," but rather that they are attempting to engage with him and their classmates about the book. Once the class has

Token Economies Planning Template

General Considerations – What schoolwide/classwide expectations or rules have generally been difficult for your class or for specific students?

2nd period really struggles to participate, even when they've come in prepared with the reading.

Economy Components

Describe all components in specific detail and how they will be introduced to the students.

	BEHAVIORS THAT EARN TOKENS	TOKENS & INSTRUCTION	REINFORCEMENT SYSTEM		
			BACKUP REINFORCERS	EXCHANGE SCHEDULE	EXCHANGE RATE
ALL STUDENTS	Any form of participation in our class discussion about the readings—doesn't matter if right/wrong	Book Bucks earned after participation. Will go over Book Bucks process at the start of class Monday to explain how it works—highlight that they don't have to be correct, just attempt to participate. Bonus Book Buck for asking their own questions	Assorted Halloween candy	End of each novel or major unit, takes about three weeks	3 Bucks = 1 candy
SPECIFIC STUDENTS	No individual students need a tailored token system as of now. Will see how this works with the whole class first.				

Data Collection Plan

Describe the specific behavior(s) targeted for improvement:
Student participation answering questions and asking their own questions
Describe the metric (e.g., % of time on-task) and method for data collection:
Frequency – tally count of participation on the seating chart to make sure all students are participating more

FIGURE 11.1 Completed Example of Token Economy Planning Template

finished reading the current novel (which should take about 3 weeks), students will have a chance to trade in their Bonus Bucks for candy. Specifically, for every three Bonus Bucks they trade, they can choose a piece of candy. Mr. Anderson reinforces students every time they participate, and when students answer his questions and then pose a question of their own, he throws in a Bonus Buck. Student participation skyrockets and eventually, Mr. Anderson is able to move to an intermittent schedule (see Chapter 13) for reinforcing participation.

Final Thoughts

In this chapter, we described the basic components of a token economy and we explained how those components can be varied to meet the needs of teachers and students. We outlined five steps for successfully implementing a token economy and we hope that we've made it clear that although these components are necessary, teachers have a great deal of leeway in how they choose to carry out this system. We recognize that using a token economy requires more resources than most of the other strategies in this book, but it is our hope that with the suggestions we've made for reducing costs and the materials we've provided for planning, you will find implementation to be both manageable and successful.

References

Ackerman, K. B., Samudre, M., & Allday, R. A. (2020). Practical components for getting the most from a token economy. *Teaching Exceptional Children*, 52(4), 242–249.

Ayllon, T., & Azrin, N. (1968). *The token economy: A motivational system for therapy and rehabilitation*. Appleton-Century-Crofts.

Ferster, C. B., & DeMyer, M. K. (1962). A method for the experimental analysis of the behavior of autistic children. *American Journal of Orthopsychiatry*, 1, 87–110.

Ivy, J. W., Meindl, J. N., Overley, E., & Robson, K. M. (2017). Token economy: A systematic review of procedural descriptions. *Behavior Modification*, *41*(5), 708–737.

Kazdin, A. E., & Bootzin, R. R. (1972). The token economy: An evaluative review 1. *Journal of Applied Behavior Analysis*, *5*(3), 343–372.

Kim, J. Y., Fienup, D. M., Oh, A. E., & Wang, Y. (2022). Systematic review and meta-analysis of token economy practices in K-5 educational settings, 2000 to 2019. *Behavior Modification*, *46*(6), 1460–1487.

Maggin, D. M., Chafouleas, S. M., Goddard, K. M., & Johnson, A. H. (2011). A systematic evaluation of token economies as a classroom management tool for students with challenging behavior. *Journal of School Psychology*, *49*(5), 529–554.

Soares, D. A., Harrison, J. R., Vannest, K. J., & McClelland, S. S. (2016). Effect size for token economy use in contemporary classroom settings: A meta-analysis of single-case research. *School Psychology Review*, *45*(4), 379–399.

Token Economies Planning Template

General Considerations – What schoolwide/classwide expectations or rules have generally been difficult for your class or for specific students?

Economy Components
Describe all components in specific detail and how they will be introduced to the students.

	BEHAVIORS THAT EARN TOKENS	TOKENS & INSTRUCTION	REINFORCEMENT SYSTEM		
			BACKUP REINFORCERS	EXCHANGE SCHEDULE	EXCHANGE RATE
ALL STUDENTS					
SPECIFIC STUDENTS					

Data Collection Plan
Describe the specific behavior(s) targeted for improvement:

Describe the metric (e.g., % of time on-task) and method for data collection:

FIGURE 11.2 Token Economy Planning Template

Token Economy Steps & Self-Assessment	
0→Not in Place 1→Partially in Place 2→Fully in Place	
STEPS	**How Did I do?**
1. Define behaviors.	☐ 0 ☐ 1 ☐ 2
2. Select and teach tokens.	☐ 0 ☐ 1 ☐ 2
3. Identify backup reinforcers.	☐ 0 ☐ 1 ☐ 2
4. Determine exchange schedule.	☐ 0 ☐ 1 ☐ 2
5. Determine rate for token exchange.	☐ 0 ☐ 1 ☐ 2
Notes & Reflection:	

FIGURE 11.3 Token Economy Implementation and Self-Assessment Checklist

12
Positive Group Contingencies

In this chapter, we explain how and why positive group contingencies can be used to improve student behavior. We begin by providing a definition and description of this strategy, followed by a brief overview of the research that supports the use of this strategy. Next, we explain how positive group contingencies can build positive relationships with students, particularly those who demonstrate challenging behaviors. Finally, we describe how to implement this strategy and provide two examples of what this practice might look like in a classroom. The supplemental resources for this chapter include a planning template (one blank for your use and one completed as an example) and a self-assessment checklist to support implementation fidelity.

What Is a Positive Group Contingency?

In technical terms, a group contingency is a classroom management strategy in which the reinforcement for students in a particular group is dependent on whether another student, or students, meet behavioral expectations. In a group contingency, both the behavioral expectations and the reinforcement are predetermined. A less technical way to think about a group contingency is that students are trying to earn some kind of reinforcement, either a preferred activity or item. But, earning that reinforcement depends not just on their own behavior, but on the behavior of others. For example, if a teacher says, "if everyone has their science book open to page 37 by the time my timer goes off in twenty seconds, I will add a handful of marbles to the marble jar," she is implementing a group contingency. In many ways, a group contingency is similar to a token economy (see Chapter 11). Typically, the group earns points (or tickets, or some other type of reinforcement) and then once the group has earned a predetermined number of points, they receive either a preferred activity (such as extra time at recess or a movie day) or a preferred item (such as a piece of candy or a small item, like a bouncy ball). There are many variations of group contingencies, and we will briefly provide an overview of some of the differences. However, in this chapter, we will primarily focus on the basic concept of what a group contingency can be and highlight the approaches that, in our experience, have been most effective.

You may notice that the title and focus of this chapter is on a specific type of group contingencies – *positive* group contingencies. We point this out because there are group contingencies in which students lose reinforcement (e.g., loss of points or tickets) based on their behavior and/or the behavior of others. Ultimately, this decreases their chances of accessing the preferred activity or item. We hesitate to promote this type of group contingency for a few reasons. First, our belief is that the most effective classroom and behavior management strategies are those that are positive, preventative, and instructional in nature. Second, negative group contingencies, in which students lose access to reinforcement, can often have the opposite effect of what teachers are trying to achieve. In many cases, especially for students who display serious challenging behavior, this type of contingency can lead to behavioral outbursts that actually make classroom management more difficult. For example, a student who has his head down on his desk and is refusing to take out his materials and get to work may end up demonstrating an escalation is his behavior from noncompliance to disruption (e.g., yelling at the teacher, throwing materials on the ground). Finally, a negative group contingency can isolate and put pressure on students who have a difficult time demonstrating behavioral expectations. In some cases, students with severely challenging behavior will purposely engage in disruptive or noncompliant behavior in order to sabotage the overall group. Note that this should not imply any deep motivation to cause problems – the reality is simply that for students with challenging behaviors, escaping a task or receiving attention from their teacher or peers (even if it is negative attention) is often more reinforcing than an item or activity that the group is working toward. One reason for this is that escape and attention are more immediate, whereas receiving the preferred activity or item is typically delayed (more on that in a moment). This issue is also related to another important component of group contingencies: determining what constitutes the groups.

When implementing positive group contingencies, there are two ways a group can be defined. The first option is to divide the class into smaller groups. These groups are usually based on physical location (think of all students sitting at the same table, or simply dividing the room in half). In this situation, groups can either work at their own pace to earn the reinforcement or groups can work in competition against one another. In the first scenario, one group's success does not impact with another group earning reinforcement once they also meet the designated criterion. Each group works toward earning the predetermined number of points needed to earn the preferred item or activity, and they start over once they have earned it. In the competitive approach, once one group meets the designated criterion, members of that group earn the reinforcement, and all groups start over. This competitive approach means that even though students *within* the groups are working together, the groups are working against each other.

Yet another option is that the entire class can constitute a group. In this situation, the whole class is reinforced for demonstrating behavioral expectations and is working toward earning the predetermined activity or item. Both approaches are effective, but we encourage teachers to select a group contingency model that is not competitive because this approach is the most inclusive. As we've mentioned, students with challenging behavior can have a difficult time with group contingencies anyway, so reducing competition can be especially helpful for these students (and indeed the entire group).

It's probably important to acknowledge one common criticism of using preferred activities (e.g., extra time outside, ten minutes of free time at the end of the period, or a movie) as reinforcement in positive group contingencies. One concern about this approach is that it results in a loss of instructional time. However, in classrooms where student behavior has been disruptive or noncompliant to an excessive level, a lot of instructional time is probably lost every day due to classroom management issues. In this sense, successfully implemented positive group contingencies will actually free up *more* instructional time because there are fewer disruptions and behavioral issues to deal with. Another way to minimize this concern is to think of creative ways that preferred activities can still be educational and connected to learning standards. For example, students could complete a graphic organizer about the plot and theme of a movie as they are watching it. Or students could watch the movie version of a text that they've read, and complete a Venn Diagram to compare and contrast the two. It is also generally advisable to provide preferred activities in short windows, such as five or ten minutes of free time at the end of the period or extra recess. Many students will find an extra 10 minutes of recess highly rewarding, and in our experience, merely adding more time – offering 20 or 30 minutes of extra recess – won't necessarily enhance the "power" of the reinforcer all that much. We encourage teachers to think creatively about how time for preferred activities can be incorporated into the implementation of a group contingency without significantly impacting schedules or disrupting the time needed to provide high-quality instruction.

How Do I Know Positive Group Contingencies Work?

The effectiveness of group contingencies on improving student behavior has been widely researched and findings have been consistent over time. Several different research teams have reviewed the forty-plus years of research related to group contingencies. In all of the reviews, group contingencies in general education, special education, and resource classrooms are consistently associated with positive impacts on student behavior and academic engagement (Beaver et al., 2023; Little et al., 2015; Maggin et al., 2017). This strategy is also effective for improving the behavior of young students in preschool settings (Pokorski et al., 2017).

One of the most commonly applied and researched type of group contingencies is known as the Good Behavior Game (GBG). In the original version of the GBG (Barrish et al., 1969), the class was divided into two teams, or groups of students. The teacher presented a list of behavioral expectations for students, such as remaining in their seats and refraining from talking unless given teacher permission. If any student on the team was seen violating one of the rules, then the team was given a point. At the end of the period, the team with the *fewest* points would earn special privileges for the last thirty minutes of the day, while other students continued to work on assignments. Members of the winning team also earned stars by their names on a "winner's chart" (p. 121) and were allowed to wear "victory tags" (p. 121) and be the first to line up for lunch. Importantly, even in this original version of the GBG, if *both* teams had fewer than five marks, then both teams earned the rewards. (Thus, while there was an element of competition, both teams could "win"). You may note that important elements of the GBG may seem contrary to the themes of this book (being positive, preventive, building relationships, etc.). The original GBG did set up competition, could clearly have a winning team and a losing team, and maybe most obviously, focused on defining and counting negative behaviors. You would not be alone in wondering about these elements.

Although the GBG showed very consistent positive effects for improving a wide variety of behaviors, including disruption, engagement, rule following, and externalizing behavior (e.g., cursing or yelling; Flower et al., 2014), researchers addressed questions about the focus of the GBG by modifying certain elements, including most obviously focusing on students following behavioral expectations, rather than violating them. Maag (2019) described a version of the GBG based on his previous research in 2018, in which students earned three points for demonstrating behavior that aligned with expectations and lost one point for demonstrating behavior that violated the rules. Clearly, this approach is more aligned with our philosophy that the most effective behavior and classroom management strategies are those that are positive. However, it still includes students competing against one another. While this works for most students, we've shared our concerns about competition for students who have severe and chronic challenging behavior, as well as taking points away (see Chapter 11). Later in this chapter, we describe how a teacher can modify the GBG even more, to remove the competition and focus only on positive behaviors, without students losing points for violating expectations.

How Do Positive Group Contingencies Build Positive Relationships with My Students?

A critical component of effectively implementing a group contingency is that students are reinforced for their demonstration of behavior that aligns with classroom expectations. As with any strategy that includes reinforcement, this helps build relationships with students because it is a way of letting them know that you, the teacher, see and appreciate their efforts. Further, in most group contingencies, students are working to earn access to a preferred item or activity. This is a way that teachers can show students they have been paying attention to the things students like and enjoy. In applications of *positive* group contingencies, students are awarded points (or something similar) when they are observed demonstrating the behavioral expectations. We suggest that teachers pair this type of reinforcement with behavior-specific praise (Chapter 10), such as "I'm awarding a point to the group because I can see that everyone is on-task and focused on completing the assigned math problems." When implemented correctly, group contingencies provide students with clear expectations and rules (Chapter 2), which we believe are important for students to feel safe and to set-them up for success. Finally, when we think of group contingencies, we think of the adage about all work and no play. Of course, students are in school to learn, but implementing a positive group contingency can create a fun learning environment where, ideally, students are working together for a common goal and are rewarded with a little "downtime" or desired item for their hard work.

How Do I Implement Positive Group Contingencies in My Classroom?

As with most of the strategies we've described in this book, implementing positive group contingencies begins with setting clear expectations about what behaviors students will need to demonstrate to be successful; to earn points, tickets, etc. There are two approaches for determining expectations. First, teachers can simply refer back to the class-wide expectations that are already in place (see Chapter 2). In this case, students simply earn points for demonstrating any of these expectations. Another option is for teachers to identify specific expectations that have been trouble-spots in the classroom. For example, students might do an excellent job being safe (e.g., using materials appropriately) and responsible (e.g., turning in work on time), but as a whole the class may be struggling with being respectful (e.g., raising a hand and waiting to be called on). In this scenario, the teacher may choose to only focus the group contingency on reinforcing behavior that demonstrates respect to adults and peers. In either case, if the behavioral expectations are not already clearly posted in the classroom, teachers should be sure to post them in an area that is clearly visible to students.

After determining the behavioral expectations, the next thing to do is to figure out what will be used to reinforce meeting behavioral expectations in the short term (e.g., points or tickets) and how to determine what students are working toward (what the points or tickets will earn). For the short-term reinforcement, it is important that students can see their progress toward meeting the goal. This can be done by tallying points on a board, hanging tickets, or dropping marbles in a jar. For simplicity, we will use the term "points" from here on out but know that this can be any type of visible, token reinforcement that you choose. For the preferred item or activity, there are several options teachers can use to select what students will earn. The most obvious option is that teachers can simply make decisions here based on their knowledge of students and the constraints of their own schedules. Maag (2019) suggested that teachers can write the item or activity on a piece of paper and place it in an envelope labeled "mystery motivator" (Rhode et al., 1992) that is then opened once students have earned it. Some teachers might not have time to offer access to a preferred activity, and therefore may choose to let students select a small piece of candy from a few options. In other cases, teachers may allow students to choose from a few preselected options of a brief period activity at the end of the period or day, such as playing a board game or working on art. Or teachers may have students work toward a longer preferred activity, such as a movie. The length of time for some preferred activities will likely impact how often teachers are able to offer the activity. A movie, for example, might be something that students work toward monthly, whereas ten minutes for a simple preferred activity could be offered daily.

This brings us to the next step, which is determining how long students will work toward earning points before they will have access to the preferred activity or item. In some classes, this may be determined by a specific time interval. For example, the teacher may count the points at the end of a set time-frame – a single-period, day, week, or month to determine if students have met the criterion for earning their reward. If so, they earn the preferred activity or item; if not, they start over, working toward the next opportunity. In other instances, the reward is simply given whenever students earn the predetermined number of points, regardless of how long it takes. When making this decision, teachers will likely need to consider their schedule, how long they have students in the class, and whether students can earn the reinforcer within a reasonable amount of time – especially for some students, the power of any reinforcer may be lost if students have to wait days or weeks to enjoy the desired items or activities. As you can imagine, this will likely look different for a teacher in high school, who only has students in their class every other day for ninety minutes, than in an elementary school, where teachers have students in their class all day long.

Once you have determined how often you will offer a preferred activity or desirable item, the next step is to figure out how often you will reinforce students for meeting behavioral expectations, and if this will happen all day or only during a specific period of time when behavior has been most challenging. It is not reasonable to constantly reinforce students (except perhaps in very rare cases), so we encourage teachers to think about a reasonable schedule of reinforcement for distributing points. Again, this will likely depend on how long students are in your classroom – it would be exhausting, and likely become repetitive to do this every three minutes all day long, but every three minutes for a 30-minute period of time might feel doable. Regardless of your choice, we suggest using a fixed schedule of reinforcement (see Chapter 13) in the beginning. This means that every X-minutes (you choose), a timer alerts the teacher to scan the classroom and determine if students are meeting expectations. If so, they would provide behavior specific praise and students would receive a point. Over time, teachers may remove the prompt and move to a more intermittent, or sporadic, schedule of reinforcement.

After all of the planning decisions have been made, it is time to teach the intervention to students. Instruction should begin by reviewing behavioral expectations and then simply explaining how the group contingency will work. Specifically, teachers will want to explain what students need to do to earn points, how often points can be earned, and when the points will be counted to see if students have earned the preferred activity or item.

The last part of implementing a group contingency is a recommendation that comes both from basic principles of reinforcement as well as our own experience using this strategy in a variety of settings. Like with many interventions or new strategies you might try, but especially when first implementing a group contingency, it is really important for students to be successful early on in the implementation. One obvious reason for this involves buy-in – we want students to enjoy the strategy, be excited about it, and actively participate in striving to meet expectations and earn points. In fact, with some strategies that work well with students finding early success, we find students literally asking to use it more often or in other contexts (e.g., "can we do the point system during math, too?"). For classrooms where there is a high level of disruptive or noncompliant behavior, this means that you might have to work a little harder to catch students demonstrating behavioral expectations. It also might mean that you may need to look for opportunities other than when the timer goes off to award points. For group contingencies to be most effective, students need to experience success and believe that earning the preferred item or activity is attainable. As the teacher, you are completely in control of the distribution of points, so you can and should manipulate things a bit if necessary to contrive situations where students are successful

What Do I Need to Begin Implementing Positive Group Contingencies?

At the end of this chapter, we have included a planning template (Figure 12.2) that will help you plan for the decisions that need to be made to successfully implement a positive group contingency (described in the previous section). We have also provided a completed planning template (Figure 12.1) to serve as an example. In addition to these materials, you will need whatever items you choose to use for reinforcement. If using points or tickets, you will want to make sure that you have space on the board where they can be permanently displayed. If using other materials, like marbles, you will want to be sure that you have a clear container for collecting them. You will also want to make sure that you have preferred items (e.g., a variety of candy, colored pens) and any materials needed for preferred activities (e.g., coloring books, movie). Finally, you will need a timer to prompt you to scan the room and award points if students are demonstrating the desired behavior. Once your plan is in place and you have the necessary materials, you are ready to begin! We have included a self-assessment checklist (Figure 12.3) at the end of this chapter to support your implementation of this strategy.

What Do Positive Group Contingencies Look like in a Classroom?

There are many ways that teachers can implement positive group contingencies in their classrooms, and as we've described, this strategy can vary in many ways. In this section, we describe two different types of group contingencies, including one example that represents a variation of the GBG that is strictly positive and does not include student competition.

Elementary Example

Ms. Florez is a second grade, general education inclusion teacher. She and her special education teaching partner, Ms. Fergusson, learned about positive group contingencies at a recent professional development presentation and they thought it would be fun to implement in their classroom. Their students sit at desks that are clustered in groups of four throughout the classroom and during independent work times, they tend to be quite chatty. Recently, several students have started to get out of their seats and wander during these periods as well. So, the two teachers decide they would like to implement a positive group contingency for the small groups that are already in place (see Figure 12.1 for their completed planning template). The teachers decide to use marble jars for their immediate reinforcement, and they place the jars at the front of the classroom in an area that students can see, but is generally out of reach. Each jar is labeled with a number, to match the team numbers that are assigned to the groups of desks. Since there are a few students in the class who have intensive behavioral needs, they recognize that having the groups compete against one another would probably not be the best approach. Since they are focusing on independent work time, they decide that when students are at their desks, they will set a timer to go off every three minutes. When the timer goes off, they will scan the room and each group that has all students sitting quietly at

Positive Group Contingencies Planning Template

Behavior to Improve ☒ Disengagement ☐ Disrespect ☒ Disruptiveness ☒ Following Directions ☒ Other: **Describe challenges:** *Out of seat, walking around, talking instead of working on task*	**Context** (class, time of day, activity where problem behavior is likely): *Any independent work time*

Group Contingency Components
Describe all components in specific detail and how they will be introduced to the student.

Expectations	Describe the specific behaviors you want to see from students: *Staying in seat* *Quiet/following the voice level* *On-task attempting the work*
Short-term Reinforcers	Describe the immediate reinforcement method (e.g., tickets, points) and any needed materials: *Student groups earn 5 marbles in their numbered jar. Need marbles and 1 labeled jar per group*
Culminating Reinforcer	Describe the preferred activity or item students will work toward: *10 minutes free time with activity choices: reading, drawing, coloring, puzzles, or educational games on tablet.*
Reinforcement System	Describe the criteria students will have to meet to earn the preferred activity/item, including whether students will be grouped (or competing), & how often you will deliver short-term reinforcers for meeting expectations: *Free time earned for a group whenever their jar is full, based on their table groups. No competition; each group goes at their own pace. Will use a 3-minute timer during independent work to check groups and award marbles.*
Ensuring Success	Describe ways to ensure students experience early success, including any necessary considerations for specific students: *Will use prompts and precorrections to set students up. Intermittently award bonus marbles in between the timer going off for students following expectations. Pay close attention to Tables 3 & 6, since they struggle the most, and remind them of the marbles. Set marble jars in visible places to remind students. Make changes over time (like size of jar or timer interval) to tweak the system.*

Data Collection Plan
Describe the specific behavior targeted for improvement:
Being in-seat, quietly working on tasks

Describe the metric (e.g., % of time on-task) and method for data collection:
Percentage of intervals each group is in-seat, quietly on-task; will track throughout week on seating chart

FIGURE 12.1 Completed Example of Positive Group Contingencies Planning Template

their desks, on-task, will earn five marbles for their jar. Once the jar is full, students in that group will earn ten minutes of free time at the end of the day and will be allowed to choose from reading a book for pleasure, drawing or coloring, working on a puzzle, or playing an educational game on a tablet. Each group will work at their own pace to earn free time, which the teachers hope will reduce the feeling of competition. Since this is their first time implementing this strategy, the teachers know that they will need to reevaluate how things are going after a few weeks. They may need to change the size of the jars, reduce the number of marbles added for reinforcement, or change the interval at which the timer alerts them to scan the room to find the "sweet spot" that works best for their students and their schedule.

Secondary Example

Mr. Wilson and Ms. Vanderwerf are co-teachers in a ninth grade science class. While their students are generally well behaved, things start to feel out of order when they are running experiments, which happens once a week. Specifically, students begin to talk loudly, chat about things that are off-topic, and use materials in ways that are unsafe. After talking with Ms. Wolfe, one of the instructional coaches in their school, the teachers decide to implement a variation of the GBG. In this variation, the entire class will be one group and they will be working against the teacher to earn more points by the end of each period in which there is an experiment. Specifically, students will need to be on-task and using materials appropriately. The notion of working against the teacher – class against teacher – has been described in some models of groups contingency, and as you might imagine, this could be *very* motivating for *some* groups of students (imagine the teacher saying, "oh my gosh, you kids are amazing – I bet you're going to beat me!"). Of course, we've also taught groups with whom we would NOT use a competition with the teacher. In any case, Mr. Wilson and Ms. Vanderwerf decide that this type of arrangement would totally work in their specific context.

Ms. Wolfe also suggests that the teachers play classical music at a low volume to help monitor noise control; one of the expectations will be that the teachers should be able to hear the music playing when they scan the room to award points. Their class period is ninety minutes, and the experiments usually take between thirty minutes to an hour to complete. The teachers decide to set a timer to go off every three minutes. When they scan the room, if students are meeting behavioral expectations, they will earn a point. If not, the teachers will earn a point. Points will be displayed on the board at the front of the room and the teachers will use behavior-specific praise when awarding points to students ("everyone is on-task, working safely, and we can hear the music, so the students get a point") and corrective feedback if needed ("we can't hear the music so the teachers earn a point; remember to use a whisper"). The teachers have agreed that they will not point out any student in particular, but rather will speak to the group collectively. If any individual students need more support, they will provide that feedback as privately as possible. The teachers also recognize that although this version of the GBG, it does come with a risk of conflict because students could become upset at the one or two students who may not be meeting expectations and therefore, prevent the whole class from earning a point. If conflicts become an issue, the teachers will try another variation of the game, in which the students are simply working to earn a predetermined number of points by the end of the experiment period – in this version, the teachers will not earn points if students are not meeting expectations. In all versions of the GBG in their classroom, students in their class will be working to earn the choice of a healthy snack (e.g., a small bag of trail mix, granola bar).

Final Thoughts

In this chapter, we described positive group contingencies and discussed the research that supports this strategy as well as a variety of ways this strategy can be applied in classrooms. In closing, we reiterate two very important takeaways related to this strategy. First, we strongly encourage teachers to start with group contingencies that are positive – that is, contingencies that reinforce students for demonstrating behavior that aligns with expectations rather than penalizing them for demonstrating behavior that is disruptive or noncompliant. The other important takeaway is that implementing group contingencies effectively depends on many factors. Teachers have different classroom schedules and routines that impact how a group contingency can be implemented. It is also important to consider contextual variables in individual classrooms, and to make decisions about exactly what a group contingency will look like initially, as well as to remember that you may need to adapt the strategy after you've started implementation to make sure it works well for your schedule and your students.

References

Barrish, H. H., Saunders, M., & Wolf, M. M. (1969). Good behavior game: Effects of individual contingencies for group consequences on disruptive behavior in a classroom 1. *Journal of Applied Behavior Analysis*, *2*(2), 119–124.

Beaver, B. N., Ré, T. C., Griffith, A. K., Zhang, D., & Schoener, M. A. (2023). A systematic literature review of group contingencies within general education classrooms. *Contemporary School Psychology*, 28, 1–14.

Flower, A., McKenna, J. W., Bunuan, R. L., Muething, C. S., & Vega Jr., R. (2014). Effects of the Good Behavior Game on challenging behaviors in school settings. *Review of Educational Research*, 84(4), 546–571.

Little, S. G., Akin-Little, A., & O'Neill, K. (2015). Group contingency interventions with children—1980–2010: A meta-analysis. *Behavior Modification*, *39*(2), 322–341.

Maag, J. W. (2018). *Behavior management: From theoretical implications to practical applications* (3rd ed.). Cengage Learning.

Maag, J. W. (2019). Why is the good behavior game used for bad behavior? Recommendations for using it for promoting good behavior. *Beyond Behavior*, *28*(3), 168–176.

Maggin, D. M., Pustejovsky, J. E., & Johnson, A. H. (2017). A meta-analysis of school-based group contingency interventions for students with challenging behavior: An update. *Remedial and Special Education*, *38*(6), 353–370.

Pokorski, E. A., Barton, E. E., & Ledford, J. R. (2017). A review of the use of group contingencies in preschool settings. *Topics in Early Childhood Special Education*, *36*(4), 230–241.

Rhode, G., Jenson, W. R., & Reavis, H. K. (1992). *The tough kid book: Practical classroom management strategies*. Sopris West.

Positive Group Contingencies Planning Template	
Behavior to Improve ☐ Disengagement ☐ Disrespect ☐ Disruptiveness ☐ Following Directions ☐ Other: **Describe challenges:**	**Context** (class, time of day, activity where problem behavior is likely):
Group Contingency Components Describe all components in specific detail and how they will be introduced to the student.	
Expectations	Describe the specific behaviors you want to see from students:
Short-term Reinforcers	Describe the immediate reinforcement method (e.g., tickets, points) and any needed materials:
Culminating Reinforcer	Describe the preferred activity or item students will work toward:
Reinforcement System	Describe the criteria students will have to meet to earn the preferred activity/item, including whether students will be grouped (or competing), & how often you will deliver short-term reinforcers for meeting expectations:
Ensuring Success	Describe ways to ensure students experience early success, including any necessary considerations for specific students:
Data Collection Plan Describe the specific behavior targeted for improvement: Describe the metric (e.g., % of time on-task) and method for data collection:	

FIGURE 12.2 Positive Group Contingencies Planning Template

Positive Group Contingencies Steps & Self-Assessment	
0→Not in Place 1→Partially in Place 2→Fully in Place	
STEPS	**How Did I do?**
1. Set clear expectations about desired behaviors.	☐ 0 ☐ 1 ☐ 2
2. Determine short-term reinforcement method and culminating preferred activity or item.	☐ 0 ☐ 1 ☐ 2
3. Establish criterion (e.g., time interval, points earned) for accessing preferred activity or item.	☐ 0 ☐ 1 ☐ 2
4. Decide how often to reinforce students for meeting behavioral expectations.	☐ 0 ☐ 1 ☐ 2
5. Review expectations and teach students how the group contingency will work.	☐ 0 ☐ 1 ☐ 2
6. Ensure students are successful early on when first implementing the group contingency.	☐ 0 ☐ 1 ☐ 2
Notes & Reflection:	

FIGURE 12.3 Positive Group Contingencies Implementation and Self-Assessment Checklist

Part V
Responding to Intensive Behavior Support Needs

13

Differential Reinforcement

In this chapter, we explain how and why differential reinforcement can be used to improve student behavior. We begin by providing a definition and description of this intervention, followed by a brief overview of the research that supports the use of this intervention. Next, we explain how differential reinforcement can build positive relationships with students, particularly those who demonstrate challenging behaviors. Finally, we describe how to implement this intervention and provide two examples of what this practice might look like in a classroom. The supplemental resources for this chapter include a planning template (one blank for your use and one completed as an example) and a self-assessment checklist to support implementation fidelity.

What Is Meant by Differential Reinforcement?

If you've read even some of the other chapters in this book, it should be clear that we're big fans of positive procedures, and further that virtually all of these include very straightforward ways of delivering *reinforcement* – a consequence (usually positive or desirable) that results in an increase in the behavior it follows. This would have been perhaps most obvious in terms of *behavior-specific praise* (Chapter 10). For example, suppose James has trouble entering the classroom and getting to work most days. One day, when James takes a seat upon entering the class and starts his morning work, the teacher notices and says, "great job taking a seat and getting started, James. Thank you." She notices that James does the same the next day, and she reinforces him again ("you're working so hard, James! You came in and sat down and got right to work."). She then notices (because she takes data on such things) that James has entered the classroom and begun his work on his own on seven out of ten days over the past two weeks. She concludes that her praise indeed served as a reinforcer for James entering the room and getting to work. So that's reinforcement.

But what about those times when behaviors that are interfering with success become a teacher's greater concern? In other words, what if it's not just what James might *not* be doing, but what he *is* doing. The concern might not be merely that he's not coming to class on time, or completing his work, or keeping quiet while others are working. Maybe the concern has become that instead of those things, he's running in the hallways, loudly disrupting others, even destroying materials (like ripping up a paper when he's frustrated with an assignment). Is a positive procedure like behavior-specific praise enough to overcome these?

A concern we often encounter when those troubling behaviors become the greater concern is the call from some professionals to implement some sort of swift punishment. Fortunately, advocates of positive procedures – like us – have a second line of procedures with a solid evidence base to turn to first in these cases. These fall under the category of *differential reinforcement*. Differential reinforcement in fact was often referred to as simply "positive procedures for reducing behavior" (e.g., Deitz & Repp, 1983) when this classroom research was first evolving. And as we note in a later section, differential reinforcement has consistently been supported by good evidence of effectiveness (e.g., Tiger & Hanley, 2021). In short, while we recognize that there are indeed times when a negative consequence may become necessary and appropriate (e.g., a loss of points or privileges, as would be the case in a *response cost* procedure), one of the first things we recommend when simpler antecedent, positive procedures may not be quite enough is differential reinforcement. So, what exactly is *differential reinforcement*?

In simple terms, differential reinforcement really just means that we want reinforcement to occur when students meet expectations, and as much as possible *not* to occur when they are not meeting expectations. We'd like for students' successful efforts and behaviors to be reinforced so that those behaviors occur more often or are at least maintained. We don't want those behaviors to go unnoticed (i.e., to be ignored, even if it's unintentional). Likewise, we'd hope that many of those random behaviors we might not want to see more of are *not* reinforced (which can also happen unintentionally). The kid who cracks a joke (especially one that's actually funny) right in the middle of a lesson might get reinforced if others laugh, but as teachers we'd strive to NOT reinforce that behavior; to basically withhold reinforcement for the moment. Differential reinforcement might help. We think of differential reinforcement having what we call a general approach, as well as some very specific variations. We describe the general approach first, and then elaborate on several variations that allow for some very specific applications.

Differential Reinforcement: The General Approach

We use the term *differential reinforcement* all the time when we teach introductory behavior management classes, or when working with teachers in any context around issues of classroom and behavior management. The reason for this is we believe this basic concept – what we call the general approach of differential reinforcement – underlies a lot of what goes on in classrooms. This includes both those things that work well, and in helping to explain where things break down. A term we think captures this core, general concept in differential reinforcement is *praise and ignore*. An example may highlight what we mean by this:

Teacher begins group lesson: "OK, guys, all you need is your graphic organizer and a pencil; now I need eyes on me."

Several students have the organizer and a pencil out and are looking at the teacher; but several others are fishing in their desks, or talking to peers without any materials out

Teacher: "Good job Kayla, Marcus, and Devin... I see your organizers out and eyes on me; you guys are ready!"

Britani, who had plopped down on the floor beside her desk to rifle through her things, and Freddie, who had just been chatting with her and laughing, finally both locate everything, and look up at the teacher

Teacher: "I see Britani and Freddie are ready. Good job, guys."

This example may seem simple, but when we teach this concept, we like to highlight several things. First, what was the teacher's *first* response? She acknowledged those students who were on task – meeting the expectation. And she did this as soon as she could. Second, what did she *not* do? We think it's really important that at least for an instant, she didn't really give any attention at all to Britani and Freddie. This exemplifies a key element of praise and ignore; we encourage teachers to first acknowledge those students whose behavior is meeting expectations, which by default means that at least for a moment they are ignoring those who are not meeting expectations. We stress here that "ignore" should NOT carry negative connotations. For one thing, you're not ignoring for any length of time – typically this is literally a matter of only a few seconds. And besides – suppose you chose to attend to Britani and Freddie first, by saying, for example, "C'mon, Britani and Freddie – find those graphic organizers so we can get started." In that moment, it's critical to note that while you're talking to Britani and Freddie you are in fact also *ignoring* Kayla, Marcus, and Devin, who happen to be the only students who are meeting expectations. Second, we point out that the "ignore" part of this sequence is often referred to as *planned ignoring* – you're not just randomly giving attention to some kids but completely ignoring others. Rather, you have carefully planned out that for some specific behaviors in specific contexts, you will intentionally NOT attend to those failures to meet expectations before you first give attention to those who are meeting expectations.

We describe this to our teachers in training as "tipping the balance" – just change how you attend by a few seconds, so that the *first* thing you do is acknowledge those who are meeting expectations, before moving on to prompt or otherwise support those other students who are not yet meeting the expectation (perhaps using any number of the other strategies in this book). Finally, note one more thing this teacher did *not* do. She did not respond to Britani and Freddie with a negative response (e.g., "what are you doing Britani? You should have had that organizer in your notebook").

Another way we describe how to use praise and ignore to teachers is to think about using it *across* students as well as *within* students (both were evident in our example above):

Across students: In a small group or whole class context, attend first to those students who are meeting expectations. Just scan the group and offer praise and acknowledgment to those students first (e.g., "I see Kayla is ready; Marcus also has his notebook out; good job guys"). For the moment, simply ignore (don't attend to) those who are not yet meeting the expectation.

Within students: As noted in this example, you'd be withholding attention – briefly – from students who are not yet meeting expectations, but *as soon as they begin* engaging in the behaviors needed, acknowledge that effort with behavior-specific praise.

Here are a couple of notes on why we like this distinction, as well as important disclaimers. First, we think attending *first* to students who are meeting expectations conveys that positive behaviors are noticed and appreciated (more on that under "relationships" below). From a behavioral theory perspective, attending to these with positive teacher attention will help those behaviors increase or at least maintain. But we're equally fond of the commonsense perspective, and perhaps you've observed this. Suppose a student consistently meets expectations, but gets no acknowledgment for it. Worse, what if while they're meeting those expectations, the teacher is consistently across the room talking away with students who are not meeting expectations. Behavioral theory certainly predicts what might happen in those cases (what behaviors will continue, and what behaviors will stop or fade away). But we frankly also worry about what students will think and feel. In short, why work hard and behave in a way that meets expectations if no one cares or even notices?

A second point we harp on is that teachers are NOT ignoring students for any significant length of time! Indeed, praise and planned ignoring often means withholding attention for only an instant. One way we phrase this is to suggest that teachers simply acknowledge those students who are meeting expectations ("I see Kayla and Marcus are ready; great job; can you guys can fill out the top line of your organizer?") literally while they are walking over to offer more supports to those who are not ("Freddie and Britani, I need you to have your organizer and one pencil out," perhaps adding in any number of our other suggestions from this book; e.g., Behavioral Momentum (Chapter 5), Instructional Choice (Chapter 6), or Precision Requests (Chapter 9)). Again, the key point here is that the teacher acknowledged those who were meeting expectations before moving on to these additional supports.

As you might guess, the use of praise and ignore is especially important for students whose behavior is maintained (i.e., reinforced) by adult attention. Most teachers are well aware that some students are reinforced by adult attention – they seek it out and will do so in whatever manner works for them (i.e., with positive or negative behavior). Moreover, they will do this even if the attention they get is not necessarily what we might think of as positive attention (e.g., a verbal reprimand or warning). Consider Freddie and Britani from the example in the previous paragraph. In some cases, immediately turning teacher attention to these students may unintentionally reinforce the off-task behavior, even if that teacher attention is a redirection, rather than specific praise. In contrast, withholding that teacher attention by briefly ignoring the behavior and instead using specific praise to reinforce those who are following directions, gives Freddie and Britani a chance to hear what is earning teacher attention and adjust their behavior accordingly.

Finally, if not obvious, teachers cannot and should not ignore students when their behaviors are seriously disruptive or dangerous to themselves or others. Praise and ignore is obviously not a go-to strategy if the behaviors of those not meeting expectations include racing around the room, physical aggression of any kind, or profane rants toward others. Those scenarios obviously demand more intensive interventions and supports for those students. Still, both research and our experience suggest that the far more common instructional challenges teachers face involve less extreme examples of some students meeting expectations, but many others not, and in these cases praise and ignore is a good first step we highly recommend.

Specific Forms of Differential Reinforcement: DRI, DRL, DRA, DRO

We mentioned above that we use the term differential reinforcement all the time in the context of the general case – praise and ignore – when working with beginning teacher education students or beginning teachers. Similarly, when we teach an advanced course in behavior management, or work with teachers on how to deal with more specific issues around challenging behavior, we dive right into the more formal ways differential reinforcement can be applied. Because of its flexibility, adaptability, and the simple logic behind it (it's all really still variations of praise and ignore, so if that makes sense, these will too), we like the following strategies a lot. We highly recommend that all teachers are at least familiar with them, such that you can draw upon them and apply them as needed to your own contexts. The four we consider are differential reinforcement of incompatible behavior (DRI), differential reinforcement of alternative behavior (DRA), differential reinforcement of low rates of behavior (DRL), and differential reinforcement of other behavior (DRO).

Differential Reinforcement of Incompatible Behavior (DRI)

We especially like DRI because, as the name implies, the teacher is set up to reinforce behaviors that not only meet expectations, but make it literally impossible that the problem behavior that has become a concern will occur. Think for a moment how simple and logical this can be. Suppose you're concerned that a child is out of his seat a lot. This might include wandering around the room, obviously not working, and perhaps bothering others as well. But the basic problem, the premise, is that he's out of his seat. With DRI, the logic would say to start simply with reinforcing an incompatible behavior – one that is essentially the opposite of what he's currently doing. In this case, it should be obvious that being *in his seat* is the incompatible behavior. If he's in his seat, he simply *cannot* be out of this seat at the same time. Thus, DRI would suggest the teacher set up a simple reinforcement program (with behavior-specific praise (Chapter 10), or something like tokens (see Chapter 11) if stronger reinforcement is needed) designed to increase "in-seat behavior." Notice, too, that if this works, even a little – if his in-seat behavior increases by 10 or 20% – then by definition his "out of seat" behavior *decreases* by a similar amount.

But note too why we so strongly recommend these strategies; namely the praise and ignore element. Differential reinforcement in all forms, including DRI, suggests that when the teacher implements the strategy, the idea is to reinforce the behavior that meets expectations – the incompatible behavior of "being in seat" in this case – while essentially ignoring the behavior we want to see diminish. We described above that this student who's out of his seat may be getting into lots of other trouble as well – e.g., bothering others, interrupting the teacher's instruction – but in using DRI the teacher would *not* draw significant attention to these (e.g., by loudly correcting the student, engaging in lengthy discussions about why he needs to sit down, threatening or implementing a specific consequence, like loss of points or privileges). At most, the teacher would typically provide a judicious reminder or prompt. In fact, this is sometimes best offered to the entire class; for example, if Johnny wanders out of his seat, the teacher might say to the whole class, "Remember the expectation that we stay in our seats while working quietly on these problems." Then, whenever she catches Johnny *in* his seat, she makes certain to offer that reinforcement with behavior-specific praise at minimum, or additional reinforcers if appropriate (i.e., "I see Johnny's in his seat, working hard; good job, Johnny, you've earned a point for morning work"). We provide additional examples of logical, incompatible behaviors a teacher might reinforce in Table 13.1.

TABLE 13.1 Example of Behaviors to Target in DRI

Behavior of concern	Possible incompatible behaviors to reinforce
Out of seat	♦ In-seat behavior
Talking out	♦ Raising hand and remaining quiet until called on ♦ Working quietly at desk
Running in hallways	♦ Walking
Physical aggression (pushing, shoving in line)	♦ Keeping hands to self ♦ Standing still in line ♦ Standing arm-length away from others

Differential Reinforcement of Alternative Behavior (DRA)

As much as we recommend DRI, we have to say that DRA comes equally highly recommended for classroom applications. The definition will make it obvious why this should be a go-to strategy for many teachers. In DRA, the teacher will reinforce a behavior that provides a more appropriate alternative to achieve the same goal the student was trying to achieve with his negative behavior. An example should highlight how this works. Suppose a student seeks teacher attention frequently by just shouting out. Further, even though hand raising has been established as a classroom expectation, his failure to meet that expectation is made worse by how egregious some of his demands are (e.g., "Hey teacher – get over here! I said I need help!"). The teacher decides that with DRA she will reinforce him when he demonstrates a more appropriate way to get her attention. And note that while hand raising is the ultimate expectation, she decides she will reinforce any alternative behavior that more appropriately seeks her attention or assistance. The first day she implements DRA, the student does raise his hand, although instead of waiting for her, he quickly says, "I need help on these problems." She notes that he does say this in a proper tone and voice level, so she immediately comes over, says she will be happy to help him, and adds, "and thanks for raising your hand; next time, let's work on waiting to be called on." She did this because he has displayed a much more appropriate alternative to his usual shouting out inappropriate demands (e.g., "get over here!") without hand raising.

TABLE 13.2 Examples of Alternative Behaviors that Might Be Reinforced in a DRA Implementation

Behavior that does not meet expectations	Possible alternative behavior to reinforce
Physical aggression to get toy or materials from another child	♦ Asking to borrow materials ♦ Asking to join in a game others are playing
Destroying materials or throwing on floor when frustrated with difficult assignment	♦ Asking for help when he doesn't understand how to do an assignment ♦ Requesting a break when frustrated
Calls out loudly during class for any request (e.g., to use restroom)	♦ Raises hand and waits to be called on before making request

Two additional notes about DRA: first, remember that by definition DRA must involve reinforcing not just any alternative to an inappropriate behavior of concern, but one which achieves the same goal or objective (like gaining the teacher's attention) as the unacceptable behavior we hope it replaces. We offer additional examples of alternative behaviors a teacher might reinforce using DRA for a few examples of clearly inappropriate or unacceptable behaviors in Table 13.2. And a last note about DRA – true of all variations of differential reinforcement – is to remember the ignore part of the praise and ignore equation. Continuing our example, suppose that even after one "better" example of requesting teacher assistance, the student above reverts the next day to shouting out inappropriately (i.e., "I need help!"). If she is sticking with DRA (as we'd recommend) the teacher should *ignore* this behavior at least for the moment. In our experience, when students realize the teacher is not responding or reacting to their negative requests, they will often try a more appropriate alternative, at which point the teacher should respond with reinforcement – by meeting the student's request – as quickly as possible.

Differential Reinforcement of Low Rates of Behavior (DRL)

DRL is an excellent and powerful strategy, designed – as its name implies – to help lower rates of behaviors that are occurring at high rates and are interfering with students' ability to meet expectations. Consider an example (a real one we have encountered). Suppose

Sonny is a young child – a kindergartener – who has adopted a very colorful vocabulary that includes many words that can only be described as profanity. He uses these when angry or frustrated, which may be understandable, but he's also taken to just using them conversationally, as part of this everyday language (e.g., at lunch, "wow, did you see how many $@%^&!# french fries they gave me!"). After some simple counting, we learn he's using profanity an average of 27 times a day. Because this happens in many contexts (bus, hallway, cafeteria, as well as classroom), his parent and teachers have decided that while they don't want to overreact, they realize this may create problems for Sonny down the line, so they have brainstormed ways to help him use more contextually appropriate language, and less profanity in contexts where it might cause him problems. Because his special education teacher has some basic training in behavior management, she has recorded his "baseline levels of profanity," and because everyone agrees this rate is way too high, she suggests to the group they use DRL. In using this, they are going to reinforce Sonny when he uses less profanity *less than* 27 times a day; they set his initial target at 15.

While we love and have used DRL effectively in many practical contexts, we have also encountered some educators (and administrators or even parents) raising questions or concerns about it. The main ones are usually variations of this: "You're really going to reinforce him when he cusses at someone 15 times a day!?" Our answer, of course, is "Yes." But what we really mean and try to explain is that what we are reinforcing is not "using profanity," but his ability to actively control and reduce his use of profanity. And we make that clear to both the student and anyone raising these concerns. When reinforcement is provided, it's paired with praise for that very effort – e.g., "look how you were able to reduce your use of bad words; you met your goal!" (Note: We are aware that the term "bad words" carries lots of implications – we use it here only to highlight that teachers will have to define what profanity is for a given child, as well as the complex idea that contexts in which some words are not appropriate can vary – for very young kids, we have indeed used the phrase "bad words" as that's a term many of them readily understand, and in fact is how they often describe their own language).

When concerns are raised about DRL, we usually also have to add that we too have a goal of helping students reduce certain behaviors to zero – e.g., yelling profanity at a teacher. We just have to justify and explain that if a given behavior is happening at extremely high rates, eliminating that behavior entirely – dropping it to zero – in the short term is simply not a logical or feasible goal. A significant reduction, sometimes any reduction, will be an important accomplishment.

A final note on DRL, which we hope is also obvious. It cannot and should not be used for dangerous behaviors – e.g., physical aggression toward others. A good way to think of DRL is this: is this a behavior that we (ourselves as teachers, as well as parents, classmates, and the student himself) can tolerate still occurring *some of the time* as we work to reduce it? If a behavior doesn't meet that criterion, DRL is probably not the right strategy.

Differential Reinforcement of Other Behavior (DRO)

We saved the last procedure, DRO for last, for the simple reason that we think it may be slightly less applicable for likely readers of this book. As we've tried to stress, we hope all teachers fully embrace *praise and ignore*, and the concepts of DRA, DRI, and DRL, as we believe these have common, if not almost everyday implications for classroom practice. In contrast, DRO tends to be used more often for very serious concerns, like physical aggression or even self-injury. The definition of DRO highlights why this is so: in using DRO to address a negative or challenging behavior of concern, the teacher would reinforce the student when they engage in *any* other behavior besides the targeted behavior. Carry the example of physical aggression forward; suppose we have a student who will physically harm (i.e., hit or punch; push or shove) other students when he feels provoked or slighted. If a teacher chooses to address this with DRO, she would reinforce him periodically (e.g., with behavior-specific praise, perhaps in addition to tokens or other tangible reinforcers) as long as he was *not* engaged in physical aggression. You can probably see both the potential benefits and uses of DRO, as well as some of the limitations. On the plus side is simply that it can work – if a student is engaging in high rates of seriously concerning behaviors like physical aggression or self-injury that are truly impacting the safety and well-being of self or others, this would limit the student's ability to participate in many typical school routines. In such cases, DRO can be an invaluable tool. But, as we have noted, DRO is not typically thought of as a go-to for more common behavioral concerns in classrooms. The main reason we say this is because DRO does not generally result in the improvement of any specific behaviors; it doesn't help the student learn what to do instead (as would happen in DRA, for example). Note that a student could be sitting at his desk working, or doodling on a notepad, or even just putting his head down. The teacher using DRO for physical aggression would still reinforce him for *any* of these other behaviors – including just putting his head down on his desk – because he was NOT engaged in physical assault of another student.

How Do I Know Differential Reinforcement Works?

Differential reinforcement is built upon the simple foundation of positive reinforcement, which we described at the beginning of this chapter and elsewhere in this book (e.g., Behavior Specific Praise, Chapter 10). Despite occasional criticisms in the popular press, there is simply no question that positive reinforcement works – it describes why some behaviors increase or continue to occur and others do not, and more importantly can be used by teachers to support students in learning and more consistently displaying behaviors that help them meet the expectations in any environment in which they find themselves. The benefits of positive reinforcement have been supported by one of the most extensive bodies of research in all of education; moreover, this has been evident for many decades (e.g., Walker & Buckley, 1968), and remains foundational in most recommended models of support for students (see Alberto et al., 2022; Center on PBIS, 2024).

The idea behind praise and ignore – combining positive reinforcement in the form of praise with other procedures more systematically – also has a long history and is supported by highly consistent research over time. As early as the 1960s, school-based researchers were learning not just of the positive effects of reinforcement, but of the additive effects of combining praise with planned ignoring. Consider this quote from Madsen and colleagues, after they studied the effects of a simple routine that included three parts: creating and posting rules, ignoring inappropriate behavior, and praising appropriate behavior:

> The main conclusions were that: (a) Rules alone exerted little effect on classroom behavior, (b) Ignoring inappropriate behavior and showing approval for appropriate behavior (in combination) were very effective in achieving better classroom behavior, and (c) Showing approval for appropriate behaviors is probably the key to effective classroom management.
> (Madsen et al., 1968, p. 1)

Deitz, Repp, and colleagues conducted and summarized much of the early work on the forms of differential reinforcement we describe in this chapter (DRA, DRI, DRL, DRO) (e.g., Deitz & Repp, 1983) and this too has been consistently supported over time (e.g., Tiger & Hanley, 2021). In short, we have no reservations at all in recommending positive reinforcement as a foundational component of all classroom management routines. And, because we also know from both research and experience that teachers must have some means of dealing with excesses of behaviors that clearly do not meet expectations, we are equally comfortable recommending differential reinforcement as a first response to help students reduce or limit those concerning behaviors that keep them from being successful.

How Does Differential Reinforcement Help Build Positive Relationships with My Students?

We hope it goes without saying that positive reinforcement contributes to more positive teacher-student relationships.

Acknowledging behavior that meets an expectation or demonstrates success is almost universally appreciated. Do note that we say *almost* universally appreciated because some students will have clear preferences that even their most successful behaviors *not* be called out in a public or demonstrative way. We implore teachers to be sensitive to cultural or familial norms, or just individual preferences in this regard, but we note further that doing so can in and of itself enhance relationships. To us, demonstrating that you know and remember that Cassius doesn't like public praise, so instead you give him a quiet nod when you see him put away his things properly and get prepared for class can be doubly beneficial. You've shown Cassius that you see and appreciate his behaviors, but also that you get that he doesn't like public praise, so you delivered your acknowledgment subtly.

However, since this chapter is about not just reinforcement, but *differential* reinforcement – it's important to explore how this added component can contribute to relationships. We think the main benefit lies in the basic concept we described in the context of *praise and ignore*. Recall how we noted what teachers do, and do not do, in this context. Failure to meet an expectation is not the first thing teachers point out – they are not merely scanning the room, looking for behaviors to correct or students to call out for misbehavior. In fact, we think the most effective teachers overlook minor transgressions (i.e., briefly ignore them) with perhaps only a supportive prompt at first. As we tell our pre-service teachers all the time, if you're scanning the room (a good idea) to keep an eye out for behavior, please do so like the teacher in Table 13.3 Column A, rather than Column B.

In short, we think statements like Teacher A offered create a positive environment in which students will feel noticed and appreciated. Differential reinforcement as we have described here provides teachers with a framework we hope can help with establishing that perception. We hope it helps teachers be more intentional about acknowledging positive efforts to meet expectations and drawing less attention to failures to meet those expectations. The sum of this, we believe, can only enhance teacher-student relationships.

TABLE 13.3 Examples and Nonexamples of Effective Differential Reinforcement

Scenario: Teacher scans room during a brief period of independent seatwork. Carlos, Tammy, and Alberto get right to work. The room is mostly quiet, and Angelique raises her hand and waits quietly for the teacher. Three students, however, have not started working. Dennis and Darius don't even have the right materials out; Jared has simply put his head down on his desk and appears to be falling asleep.

Teacher A	Teacher B
"I see Carlos working hard. So is Tammy, and Alberto too. Nice job, guys."	"Jared, don't put your head down; it's not time to sleep."
"You guys are all working so quietly; great job everyone!"	"Dennis and Darius, why don't I see any materials on your desk?"
"I'll be right there, Angelique. Thank you so much for raising your hand."	"Anyone who doesn't finish these problems by 10:15 will not be joining us at recess."

How Do I Implement Differential Reinforcement in My Classroom?

Implementing the most basic form of differential reinforcement – praise and ignore – is simple. Or at least, the idea is simple. We find that teachers struggle most with simply making sure they remember to do it. Recall that we described one way to think about praise and ignore is in "tipping the balance" – remembering to first acknowledge behaviors that are meeting expectations with behavior-specific praise, and then move on to supports, prompts, or even more intensive interventions (when needed). Some of this just demands practice, but we also recommend any sort of reminder that is helpful to the individual teacher. For example, a 3x5 card on your clipboard, or some other note-taking reminder on your phone, tablet, or laptop that serves as a prompt and reminder to acknowledge when expectations are met. This can be a simple generic prompt (to "acknowledge successes"), or a slightly more formal chart, like a simple row of boxes to check each time you offer behavior-specific praise for meeting expectations. If using the latter, you can also set a goal by either choosing a number (e.g., ten times per lesson), or perhaps just keep track of how many times you reinforced meeting expectations, with a goal of maintaining or improving upon the previous day's rate. These instances of praise may be especially helpful at the beginning of the day or class period as students enter or begin a lesson, as well as during transitions. As a prompt during instruction specifically, we recommend making an explicit note somewhere at the beginning of a lesson plan or guide (e.g., "acknowledge those who meet expectations for having materials ready").

Implementing the more formal applications of differential reinforcement (DRI, DRA, DRL, and DRO) will naturally require some more thought and at least a little planning. Again, though, we include differential reinforcement in this book because this planning is still relatively simple and logical and should not take much time. We include a broad planning template (Figure 13.3) at the end of this chapter but list the key elements or decisions a teacher needs to make before using differential reinforcement here in Table 13.4. We describe each step a bit more in the next sections.

TABLE 13.4 Planning for the Use of DRI, DRA, DRL, and DRO

Step	Notes
1. Define the target behavior that is interfering with meeting expectations (the behavior that needs to be reduced).	♦ This should be a well-defined, specific behavior. ♦ Good examples: • "tears papers/destroys materials when frustrated with a task" • "uses profanity loud enough to be heard by teachers and other students" ♦ Poor examples: • "acts out" • "is disrespectful"
2. Define the behaviors that will be reinforced instead of the behavior targeted for reduction	♦ For DRI – define *incompatible* behavior(s) ♦ For DRA – define acceptable *alternative* behaviors *that achieve the same goal.* ♦ For DRL – determine a goal *rate* that will earn the reinforcer; most important point here: *set an achievable goal.* ♦ For DRO – be sure that DRO is the right choice! That is, be certain your intent is to reinforce the student for engaging in *any* behavior other than the behavior targeted for reduction
3. Determine a reinforcement plan	Think about what reinforcers you will use, and how frequently you will issue reinforcement

Step 1. Define the Target Behavior that Is Interfering with Meeting Expectations

The whole point of differential reinforcement is that a behavior needs to be reduced; this should be a well-defined, specific behavior that is somehow interfering with a student's ability to meet expectations. At this step, the critical element is simply identifying and defining that behavior. As we noted, broad behavioral concerns (e.g., "is disrespectful," "disrupts class") will not be useful here. As you'll see in the next steps, well-defined behaviors that warrant reduction will help specify exactly how the teacher proceeds.

Step 2. Define the Behaviors that Will Be Reinforced Instead of the Behavior Targeted for Reduction

If the logic thus far has made sense, you know that we're talking basically about praise and ignore here – in differential reinforcement we're going to reinforce a behavior(s) we want to see more of, while simultaneously withholding reinforcement from the behavior that's been problematic. At this step we just need to carefully define those behaviors that *do* meet expectations in this context. These vary only slightly across the different forms of differential reinforcement:

For DRI – define incompatible behavior(s); these are essentially the opposite of the behavior of concern (e.g., "sitting in seat" is incompatible with "gets out of seat and runs around room").

For DRA – define acceptable alternative behaviors: what is the most appropriate alternative to the negative behavior that achieves the same goal? (e.g., "raises hand and remains quiet until called on" is an alternative to "yelling out *I need help*" in order to get teacher attention).

For DRL – determine a *goal rate* that will earn the reinforcer; some researchers recommend using the lowest number observed during a baseline phase (e.g., if Sammy has yelled profanity five, eight, four, seven, and six times this week, his daily goal might be no more than four. Another rule of thumb for some behaviors is to cut the rate in half. In this

example, Sammy used profanity an average of six times a day, so a goal rate might be no more than three. Perhaps most critical here is to set an achievable goal.
- *For DRO* – again, be sure that DRO is the right choice! For example, is it really your intent, and is it acceptable, to reinforce the student for engaging in any behavior other than the behavior targeted for reduction? For example, if using DRO to reduce hitting, you reinforce the student periodically (maybe every 5 minutes) for not engaging in hitting, regardless of whether he's working, talking, or putting his head down on his desk. DRO can be appropriate in many cases, most obviously things like aggression or self-injury; just be sure to consider alternatives and possible drawbacks.

Step 3: Determine a Reinforcement Plan

This need not be elaborate and can often fit into existing management routines if things like a point or token system is in place. Perhaps the main question is *when* to deliver reinforcement. In some instances, you would aim to reinforce the student every time the behavior occurs. Suppose in using DRA you are supporting the student in raising his hand (the alternative behavior) and waiting for help, rather than yelling out "I need help!" (the behavior we hope is reduced). In this case, you'd reinforce hand raising basically every time it occurs. In contrast, consider a use of DRI in which you want to reinforce Sabrina for staying in her seat during work times, rather than getting up and wandering around the room. In this case, you might issue reinforcement every five minutes that Sabrina is *in* her seat (e.g., "good job, Sabrina; you're in your seat and working hard").

What Do I Need to Begin?

We described the four basic steps in using differential reinforcement above and listed them in Table 13.3. We include a simple planning template (Figure 13.3) at the end of this chapter that will help teachers think through each of these steps and plan their use of differential reinforcement; we have also provided a completed planning template as an example (Figure 13.1). Again, we don't believe any of these are complicated, and in most cases a teacher can be ready to use differential reinforcement as long as they can clearly define (a) the problem (a behavior that occurs too much and interferes with meeting expectations), and (b) a behavior that essentially replaces this behavior of concern (usually an incompatible or alternative behavior). We have provided a self-assessment checklist (Figure 13.4) at the end of this chapter to support your implementation of differential reinforcement.

What Does Differential Reinforcement Look like in the Classroom?

We've described both the general approach to differential reinforcement (praise and ignore) as well as four separate applications of differential reinforcement in DRI, DRA, DRL, and DRO. We hope that the general approach is clear and easy to understand, so in this section offer classroom examples of DRI and DRL we hope teachers can relate to, and possibly adapt for their own use. First is an elaboration on Sonny, the kindergartner we referred to earlier who used profanity – a lot – and how his teacher used DRL to reduce that behavior. The second is a secondary example where Ms. Hartigan used DRA to help George, a ninth grader in her math class, seek help more appropriately and thus to be more successful in her class.

Elementary Example – Mr. Langlow

Mr. Langlow is an elementary school teacher who has a kindergarten student, Sonny, in his class. Mr. Langlow learned on the first day of school that Sonny used a lot of profanity, but it didn't take long for most adults in the school building (teachers, the office secretary, lunchroom staff) to start reporting that they were shocked to hear some of the words Sonny uses. They'd appear in Mr. Langlow's doorway at times, asking, "Do you know what Sonny called me today?" In any case, it became clear even through informal observations and reports that Sonny was using a lot of profanity, at a very high rate. Because Mr. Langlow was with Sonny most of the day, he decided first to take baseline data – he had learned some informal data collection techniques in his behavior management class, and thought he might be able to identify patterns if he collected enough data. After only three days, however, he realized the concern was frequency above all else. Sonny used profanity in every location in which Mr. Langlow observed – his classroom, the hallways, lunchroom, even the playground. What Mr. Langlow found striking was the sheer volume – Sonny used profanity an average of 27 times per day in his class alone – and that was just the morning block. He decides to start there, and remembering as well from his behavior management class that DRL was recommended for high-rate behaviors, he decides to try this out (see Figure 13.2 for Mr. Langlow's completed planning template).

He uses the following steps to start his plan:

1. First, Mr. Langlow meets briefly with Sonny in the morning before school. Mr. Langlow knows that Sonny is well aware of his language; both Sonny and the other kids often refer to his use of "bad words," which Sonny also calls "cuss words." Mr. Langlow says that he has seen Sonny getting in trouble for his use of cuss words and wants to help him not get into trouble so much. Sonny laughs at first, but then agrees that he does not like "getting in trouble all the time."
2. Mr. Langlow shows Sonny a chart that shows his profanity, and says matter-of-factly – "well, look, I've been keeping track of how many times you use bad words. Here's the last three days," he says while showing Sonny the line indicating how many times he has "cussed" (the solid line in the chart below).
3. Mr. Langlow then draws a line (the dotted line on the chart) and says, "but I think we can get it lower – do you think you can get your cussing below this line?" He explains that the new line represents 20 instances and tells Sonny that if he can use "nicer words" instead of cuss words, and get below this line, he will earn two points toward

Differential Reinforcement Planning Template	
Student: Sonny	**Context** (class, time of day, activity where problem behavior is likely): Throughout the day and school, anywhere there is another person to hear him
Differential Reinforcement Components *Describe all components in specific detail and how they will be introduced to the student.*	

Problem Behavior	Define the specific target behavior that is interfering with meeting expectations: Sonny uses high rates of profanity (27/day during morning block in class alone)	
Behavior to Reinforce (choose best form of differential reinforcement)	**DRI** Define incompatible behavior:	**DRA** Define acceptable alternative behavior:
	DRL Define a goal rate of behavior: Sonny will use fewer than 20 instances of profanity during morning block, using "nice words" instead. Will show Sonny a chart with baseline and the goal, and walk through the goal. Will keep track with tallies on an index card. I'll change the goal once he's successful.	**DRO** Ensure DRO is an appropriate fit:
Reinforcement Method	Describe how the desired behavior will be reinforced and when to deliver reinforcement: When Sonny meets the goal, he will earn 2 extra points for our class store. We will go over his amount of profanity after each morning block and compare it to his goal. Sonny can exchange points before lunch (right away) or at the end of the day to get his favorite snacks or another reinforcer.	
Data Collection Plan Describe the specific behavior targeted for improvement: Amount of Profanity Describe the metric (e.g., % of time on-task) and method for data collection: Frequency of profanity during morning block. I'll tally it on an index card and graph it.	

FIGURE 13.1 Completed Example of Differential Reinforcement Planning Template

their classroom store. We note that Mr. Langlow chooses the terms he uses because this is how Sonny and the other kids talk about their language. They all know well what a cuss word is, and to them the opposite of a cuss word is a "nice word," so Mr. Langlow uses this same language. Mr. Langlow reviews a few alternative words and phrases that Sonny can use (e.g., "darn it"; "freaking") and while these are not the end goals, Mr. Langlow thinks it's helpful to provide Sonny with language that is more acceptable than what he was using to begin with.

4. Sonny agrees, so they start the program that very day. Mr. Langlow carries a simple 3x5 card on his clipboard and records each instance of Sonny using profanity. Notably, Mr. Langlow doesn't intervene any differently when he hears profanity (unless it's part of a larger conflict or disruption, in which case he prompts or redirects Sonny and others back to work or other appropriate activities). Otherwise, he just records the behavior.

5. At the end of the morning block, Mr. Langlow calls Sonny over and records the total for the day (18 instances of profanity) on his chart. Because it is below their target line, Mr. Langlow quickly says, "See? You did it! Nice job, Sonny; you used more nicer words and not so many cuss words today. You earn two points."

6. Because it has been established that Sonny (and all kids) can "buy" things at the school store either right before lunch or at the end of the day, Mr. Langlow asks Sonny if he wants to exchange his points now or save them. Mr. Langlow has also just added a few of Sonny's favorite snacks to the store in hopes this would also be motivating to Sonny. Sonny is very excited to have earned his points and exchanges them for a small snack he takes with him to lunch.

A few final notes on Mr. Langlow's use of DRL with Sonny:

- Mr. Langlow set an initial goal of 20 for Sonny because he was optimistic this was achievable. He knew about the rule of thumb for DRL to think about a 50% reduction – but Mr. Langlow knew it was important for Sonny to meet his goal the first day, so he set it at a more manageable 20.
- Another rule of thumb in DRL is that the goal changes – is lowered – as students demonstrate mastery in decreasing their behavior. Mr. Langlow's plan (which he knows may

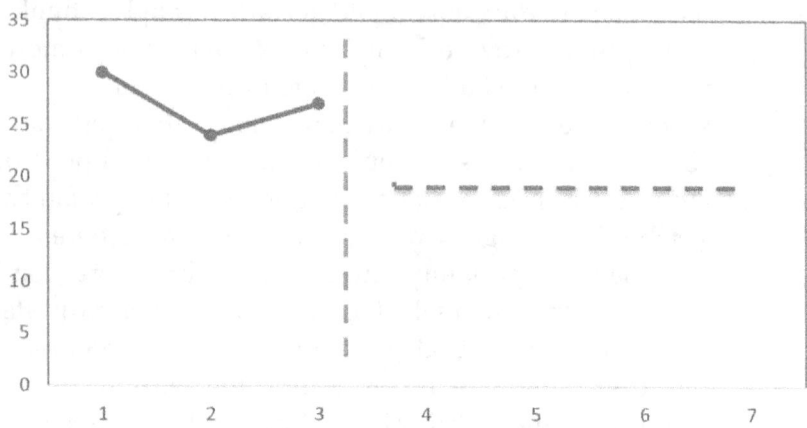

FIGURE 13.2 Example of Differential Reinforcement Student Data

have to be modified) is that after Sonny reaches the goal of 20 or less for three consecutive days, he will lower it, by saying, "Sonny, look, you have been doing great at keeping this below 20, but I think we can get even lower. Do you think you can make it all the way under 15?" Like the initial goal, the steps should be lowered by manageable amounts, and, if necessary to achieve success, reinforcers may need to be adjusted slightly.

Secondary Example – Ms. Hartigan

Ms. Hartigan teaches ninth grade math, and most of her classes run very smoothly, except for fifth period. She has very organized routines in her classes and high expectations for both academic work and behavior, but in fifth period, a number of students struggle to meet those expectations. She chats with the special education consultant teacher about this class, and they realize that Jeremiah is one student she ends up in confrontations with a lot. After the consulting teacher observes her class, they agree that a trigger for these confrontations occurs when Jeremiah doesn't understand something. They note that he almost immediately just calls out, often in a tone that can best be described as defiant or angry (e.g., "I don't know how to do this!" or "These problems are impossible!"). They further decide that DRA may be a good option to try. It seems obvious to them that they have identified the behavior they'd like to help Jeremiah reduce (calling out for help in very loud ways), as well as a more appropriate alternative for getting the teacher's attention (using a signal that he needs help).

Ms. Hartigan uses the consulting teacher's advice to try to show Jeremiah a strategy he can use. They prepare a small round circle cut out of card stock that is colored red on one side and green on the other. Ms. Hartigan shows Jeremiah before class one day that she will place the circle on his desk with the green side facing up when they begin an assignment, and that will indicate that he is working hard and understands what he is supposed to do. Then, if he reaches a point where he is lost or confused, he can just turn the circle over, and when Ms. Hartigan sees the red side, she will know to come over to see how she can help him. He agrees to try this, and she agrees that she will do her best to get right over to him when he signals for help.

After they discuss the strategy, she tries it out the first day with a very short assignment that includes some review problems. Jeremiah is able to complete them all, so the card stays green side up, and they both assume all is well. But the next day they have an assignment at their desks, there are more challenging problems and Jeremiah doesn't know what to do. He instinctively just says out loud, "these are really hard," but before he escalates into louder protesting, Ms. Hartigan just gestures toward the green circle without saying a word. Jeremiah flips the circle over to red, and Ms. Hartigan immediately heads over and helps him. She works through two problems with him, and then says, "can you try the next one on your own?" She feels like they have found some tentative success, but she also has in the back of her mind that ultimately she wants Jeremiah to just raise his hand when he needs help. The consulting teacher agrees but suggests that for now the green and red circles might serve as a good prompt or reminder for Jeremiah to seek help instead of calling out, so for the time being they agree to keep using this approach until Jeremiah is experiencing consistent success.

Final Thoughts

In this chapter, we described differential reinforcement. This included our strong recommendation that teachers use and rely on the basic concept – what we called the general approach to differential reinforcement, sometimes referred to as "praise and ignore." To highlight this, we used the example of teacher attention and encouraged teachers to think about this when teaching group or whole class lessons: (a) briefly attend first to those students who are on task/engaged, while essentially ignoring for the moment those who are not engaged; but (b) for individual students, attend to them positively when – and as soon as – they are attending. The concept of differential reinforcement suggests that students receive reinforcement when and only when they meet a given expectation in that context.

In addition to the general approach, we described four specific variations of differential reinforcement that can help reduce the occurrence of specific behaviors that interfere with meeting expectations: DRI, DRA, DRL, and DRO. Recapping:

- DRI means the teacher has identified and reinforces behaviors that are directly incompatible (cannot occur at the same time) with the targeted behavior of concern;
- DRA means that teachers reinforce a positive behavior that meets the same goal (function) as the behavior of concern (we used the example of reinforcing hand raising to hopefully replace yelling out, "hey! I need help!");
- DRL means that the student is reinforced when he achieves a goal of engaging in a behavior at or below an established target rate. DRL was described as useful for behaviors of concern that occur at very high rates (we used the example of profanity), and for which all can agree that some level of the behavior can still be tolerated as the team works to help reduce its occurrence; and finally
- DRO was described as the case in which *any* behavior other than the targeted behavior of concern is reinforced – essentially, the student is reinforced whenever he is not engaging in this behavior. While DRO has good evidence

of effectiveness for many applications, we described it as more often appropriate for limited cases of extreme behavior (e.g., physical aggression or self-injury) where almost any other behavior is preferred to the behavior of concern.

We hope that teachers understand, appreciate, and can use the general approach to differential reinforcement as we described it – *praise and ignore* – as we see this as an essential ingredient in creating and maintaining a positive and successful learning environment. The more positivity teachers create, especially in frequently acknowledging student's successful efforts, the better we think teacher-student-relationships will be. We also believe that the more specific applications of differential reinforcement (especially DRI, DRA, and DRL) only add to this in that they provide essentially positive means for teachers to address behaviors that have become concerning without resorting to harsh or punitive procedures as a first line of defense.

References

Alberto, P. A., Troutman, A. C., & Axe, J. (2022). *Applied behavior analysis for teachers* (10th ed.). Pearson.

Center on PBIS. (2024). *Supporting and responding to Student's social, emotional, and behavioral needs: Evidence-based practices for educators* (Version 2). Center on PBIS, University of Oregon. www.pbis.org.

Deitz, D. E., & Repp, A. C. (1983). Reducing behavior through reinforcement. *Exceptional Education Quarterly*, 3(4), 34–46.

Madsen, C. H., Becker, W. C., & Thomas, D. R. (1968). Rules, praise, and ignoring: Elements of elementary classroom control. *Journal of Applied Behavior Analysis*, 1, 139–150.

Tiger, J. H., & Hanley, G. P. (2021). Differential reinforcement procedures. In W. W. Fisher, C. C. Piazza, & H. S. Roane (Eds.), *Handbook of applied behavior analysis* (2nd ed., pp. 237–251). Guilford.

Walker, H. M., & Buckley, N. K. (1968). The use of positive reinforcement in conditioning attending behavior. *Journal of Applied Behavior Analysis*, 1(3), 245–250.

Differential Reinforcement Planning Template

Student:	**Context** (class, time of day, activity where problem behavior is likely):

Differential Reinforcement Components
Describe all components in specific detail and how they will be introduced to the student.

Problem Behavior

Define the specific target behavior that is interfering with meeting expectations:

Behavior to Reinforce (choose best form of differential reinforcement)

DRI	DRA
Define incompatible behavior:	Define acceptable alternative behavior:

DRL	DRO
Define a goal rate of behavior:	Ensure DRO is an appropriate fit:

Reinforcement Method

Describe how the desired behavior will be reinforced and when to deliver reinforcement:

Data Collection Plan
Describe the specific behavior targeted for improvement:

Describe the metric (e.g., % of time on-task) and method for data collection:

FIGURE 13.3 Differential Reinforcement Planning Template

Differential Reinforcement Steps & Self-Assessment

0 → Not in Place 1 → Partially in Place 2 → Fully in Place

STEPS	How Did I do?
1. Define the target behavior that is interfering with meeting expectations.	☐ 0 ☐ 1 ☐ 2
☐ DRI – Define incompatible behaviors that are essentially the opposite of the target behavior.	
☐ DRA – Define acceptable alternative behaviors.	
☐ DRL – determine a goal rate for less of the target behavior.	
2. Define the behaviors that will be reinforced instead of the behavior targeted for reduction.	☐ 0 ☐ 1 ☐ 2
3. Determine a reinforcement plan.	☐ 0 ☐ 1 ☐ 2
Notes & Reflection:	

FIGURE 13.4 Differential Reinforcement Implementation and Self-Assessment Checklist

14

Check-In Check-Out

In this chapter, we explain how and why check-in check-out can be used to improve student behavior. We begin by providing a definition and description of this intervention, followed by a brief overview of the research that supports the use of this intervention. Next, we explain how check-in check-out can build positive relationships with students, particularly those who demonstrate challenging behaviors. Finally, we describe how to implement this intervention and provide two examples of what this practice might look like in a classroom. The supplemental resources for this chapter include a planning template (one blank for your use and one completed as an example) and a self-assessment checklist to support implementation fidelity.

What Is Check-In Check-Out?

Check-in check-out (CICO) is a strategy developed to help students who need additional, more intensive behavioral support to demonstrate behavior that aligns with the school-wide and classroom expectations. In multi-tiered systems of support (e.g., PBIS), this strategy is typically considered a "Tier 2" strategy, meaning that it is not a strategy recommended or necessary for all students, but rather one that should be reserved for students who are not consistently responding to the universal, or "Tier 1," strategies that are in place. Typically, this will be about 15–20% of students. One reason this strategy is not recommended for all students is that it is a bit more time-consuming than many of the other strategies suggested in this book; so, if students are responding well to the Tier 1 supports, there is probably no need to devote significant teacher time (which we all know is already limited) to implementing a more intensive intervention.

So, what exactly is CICO? The crux of the strategy is actually quite simple and it includes several of the other strategies presented in this book, such as behavior contracts (Chapter 15), precorrection (Chapter 8), behavior-specific praise (Chapter 10), and in some cases, a token economy (Chapter 11). CICO has five core components (Crone et al., 2010), which we describe in detail later. Briefly, these components are (1) checking-in, (2) completing a daily progress report (DPR), (3) providing adult feedback, (4) checking-out, and (5) communicating with parents or guardians. As you read this chapter, we hope you will notice how CICO is by design a multi-component intervention, and the inclusion of several of the strategies we described in the first section of this book (e.g., behavior-specific praise, precorrection, token economies) is natural and logical.

In CICO, students first check-in with a teacher, paraeducator, or another adult (such as a guidance counselor or even a custodian) with whom they have established rapport at the beginning of the day or period, depending on the student's needs. During the check-in, the student's behavioral goals are typically presented on a piece of paper, the daily progress report (commonly referred to just as a DPR), that includes an area for each teacher to indicate whether the goals were met. After checking in with the adult, the student goes about their day, carrying the DPR with them. At the end of the relevant periods (such as lunch or math class) or the end of the day, the student asks their teacher to indicate whether their behavioral goals were met for that period. Then, at the designated time at the end of the day, the student checks-out, preferably with the same adult who did the check-in. We suggest that for most students, the check-out will occur at the end of the day. However, some students may benefit from having their day chunked, in which case they may have multiple check-ins and check-outs throughout the day. For example, a high school student might check-in and check-out with their respective teachers for each period. Other students may benefit from a morning check-in and midday check-out (e.g., before lunch), followed by another check-in (e.g., after lunch) and an end of day check-out. In many versions of CICO, the student takes their DPR home to have a parent or guardian sign off that they have seen their progress toward their goals. In many cases, there is a corresponding goal that the student returns the signed DPR the next day. One great thing about this component of CICO is that it encourages communication between home and school, and more specifically provides parents or guardians with information about the student's day in a quick and easy-to-read format – teachers don't need to worry about sending an email or making a phone call because the information is all on the student's sheet. However, there are a few things to consider when implementing this as part of CICO, which we describe in detail a bit later.

How Do I Know Check-In Check-Out Works?

In addition to CICO being a positive and preventative strategy, we have chosen to highlight it in this book because it is supported by a rich body of research evidence, and has been found to be especially effective for students whose challenging behavior is maintained by adult attention (Wolfe et al., 2016). This makes sense, considering that adult-student interaction through checking-in and checking-out is foundational to this strategy. A particularly appealing aspect of CICO is that it is generally effective for reducing challenging behaviors for students in a wide-range of grades, including elementary through high school (Maggin et al., 2015). Moreover, the core components of this strategy have been adapted in several different research studies (Majeika et al., 2020). Even when adapted, CICO can be effective. For example, a fairly common adaptation involving having peers conduct the check-in and check-out sessions has shown to be a promising approach for improving behavior

(Collins et al., 2016; Dart et al., 2015; Melius et al., 2015). The effectiveness of adapted versions of CICO (and really any intervention) is important because this means that teachers can vary the intervention slightly to meet their students' individual needs and, as long as the core components are implemented, they can have confidence that the intervention will likely lead to improved student outcomes (Cook & Rao, 2018).

How Does Check-In Check-Out Build Positive Relationships with My Students?

The connection between CICO and student-teacher relationships may be among the most obvious of all of the strategies presented in this book because an integral part of implementing CICO is literally that the student and teacher purposefully connect with one another. When the teacher is the person who is conducting the check-ins and check-outs, it is very clear how this strategy lends itself to building a positive student-teacher relationship. However, we mentioned that any adult (not necessarily the student's teacher) can conduct the check-in and check-out process. In some cases, it may actually be best for the adult to be someone who already has a positive and trusting relationship in place with the student – someone that the student seems to have connected with and with whom there is mutual respect (e.g., guidance counselor, baseball coach, custodian). There is also reason to believe that CICO may even help to maintain such a relationship, which is in itself a good thing. That said, even if it is not the teacher who is conducting the check-ins and check-outs, there are still opportunities for this strategy to help create a more positive relationship between the student and teacher. For example, even if the person conducting the actual check-ins is the guidance counselor, the student must present their DPR to the teacher at the end of a designated period, and the teacher must complete the DPR to indicate if the student met their goals.

During the time the teacher is completing the DPR, there is a built-in opportunity to acknowledge, support, and encourage the student. While the teacher is completing the DPR, the student should receive positive feedback on the goals that they met ("Excellent job remembering to turn in all of your work today, Joaquin!") and encouragement on the goals that they were not met ("Erica, you didn't keep your hands to yourself during PE today, but tomorrow is a new day, and we will go over some better strategies again before PE tomorrow. I know you can do it!"). The difference in this type of communication, rather than simply completing the DPR and handing it back to the student is small, and does not take much more time, but the difference in *tone* is monumental. Consider how a student might feel if their teacher simply completes the DPR and hands it back to them, versus a teacher who acknowledges their effort and shows an interest in the student's achievement by saying something along the lines of, "You met four out of five goals today, Erin! Mr. Price is going to be really proud of you when he sees this during your check-out. How do YOU feel?!" This type of exchange aligns with some of the characteristics of a high-quality student-teacher relationship (warmth, reciprocal communication, verbal engagement) and helps lay a foundation for other characteristics (closeness, security, higher-quality and more organic interactions).

How Do I Implement Check-In Check-Out in My Classroom?

There are five core components of CICO (listed in Table 14.1). As we mentioned, these components may be adapted slightly to meet the individual needs of students but, with the exception of component 5, all of the components must be present in some form. Before beginning the CICO procedure, however, four things must happen. First, the student's behavioral goals must be identified. We encourage teachers to include their students in identifying the behavioral goals that need to be addressed; more often than not, students are aware of their own trouble spots throughout their day. Second, teachers should teach students about CICO. This doesn't need to be a lengthy conversation, but just a brief overview that gives students a run-down of what CICO is and how it is going to work for them. Third, teachers must determine the reinforcement that students will be working

TABLE 14.1 Core Components of CICO

Component	Considerations
1. Daily Progress Report (DPR)	♦ Each teacher targeted for CICO completes the DPR (for students who change classes); or ♦ Teacher completes DPR at end of each identified segment (for students who do not change classes) (e.g., literacy block, math, science; or morning and afternoon blocks) ♦ Each teacher completing DPR indicates clearly whether each behavioral goal was met
2. Check in	♦ Review behavioral goals on the DPR ♦ Provide specific precorrects as needed ♦ Review criteria for reinforcement
3. Provide adult feedback	♦ Each teacher completing the DPR should provide positive feedback as appropriate, as well as prompts about how to better meet goals going forward ♦ Adult conducting check out, as noted below, also provides positive feedback
4. Check out	♦ Review goals ♦ Provide behavior-specific praise for those met ♦ Provide prompts, as appropriate, as to how to meet goals tomorrow ♦ If earned, provide access to the reinforcer
5. Communicate with parents/ guardians	♦ Consider whether adding the home-school communication component is helpful for the student and feasible for the parents/guardians ♦ If so, explain CICO with parents/guardians and answer any questions ♦ If agreed upon, include space on the DPR for parent signature and a way to document if the previous day's DPR was returned

for. Again, we encourage teachers to collaborate with their students to identify what might be motivating and then provide them with some options to choose from, noting that reinforcement can vary day to day or week to week. Fourth, teachers will need to figure out the logistics of the check-in and check-out process, including how often students will check-in and check-out, which adult will be responsible for conducting the meetings, and where the check-ins and check-outs will occur (i.e., will the student come to the adult or will the adult come to the student?). We have provided a planning template (Figure 14.2) that aligns with these considerations at the end of this chapter. Finally, teachers will need to communicate with any other teachers or adults that will be responsible for completing the student's DPR throughout the day. Once these preliminary planning steps are complete, CICO can be implemented using the five core components. We elaborate on each step or component in the following sections.

Component 1: The DPR

In most versions of CICO, the DPR is a physical sheet of paper that the student is responsible for carrying throughout their day. Depending on the technology available, the DPR could also be an electronic document but the student should still maintain responsibility for delivering it to their teachers throughout the day. The DPR outlines the student's behavioral goals and the different periods of the day that the student needs to get feedback from their teacher. As we mentioned, this will look different for different students, especially when considering how different the structure of an elementary school day is compared to that of a high school day. For students who are with the same teacher all day, the goals might be broken up into time periods (e.g., 9 am–11 am) or subject areas (e.g., reading, math, art). For students who change classes, the goals will usually be broken up by periods (e.g., first period, second period).

The DPR should have the students' behavioral goals clearly represented in a way that is useful to the student. For students who are English learners, it may be best to include both their first language *and* the English translation on the goal sheet. For students who have a difficult time reading, using visual supports such as icons or pictures can be extremely helpful. The DPR should also have the criterion that the student is working toward (four out of five goals met in four out of seven periods) and what their reinforcement will be.

Component 2: Check-In

During the check-in, the adult reviews the student's behavioral goals on the DPR. These goals are related to trouble spots a student has been experiencing throughout their day and can be specific to certain contexts (such as lunch, a specific class or subject area, or a time of day) or can pertain to an entire school day. During the review of behavioral goals, the adult should offer a form of precorrection (also see Chapter 8). For example, during the check-in with a student who has a hard time following the expectations in the cafeteria, the adult may say something along the lines of "Cameron, one of your goals is to use food, eating utensils, and anything you may have during your meal appropriately. This means that when you are finished with your lunch, you keep everything on your tray until it is time to throw away or recycle what you didn't use." Of course, Cameron's teacher should provide another precorrection immediately before Cameron enters the lunchroom, but it's always good to have additional reminders. After reviewing the student's behavioral goals for the day, the adult should review the target criterion needed for the student to earn reinforcement. If a student has five behavioral goals, perhaps they need to meet three of the five goals to earn reinforcement. Note here that the criterion will likely increase as the student's behavior improves, but it should start off attainable – we don't expect a student who is having a difficult time meeting five behavioral expectations to suddenly meet them all as soon as CICO begins; like anything, it will take some time and we want the criterion to be reasonable so that students can experience success early and often. The reinforcement can be connected to the classroom or school-wide token economy, in which case a student may earn points, tickets, or play money to use at a later time. Or, the reinforcement can be more individualized, and students can earn access to a preferred activity, such as five or ten minutes of free time in the gym or library before dismissal.

Component 3: Positive Adult Feedback

Positive adult feedback is delivered at several points throughout the CICO strategy, which we have described in detail in several sections of this chapter. The key here is that students receive verbal and written feedback at the designated checkpoints throughout their day when the DPR is completed and then again during the check-out period. If various teachers are completing the DPR throughout the day, we encourage those teachers to include any notes about the student's progress that could be helpful to the student and/or to the adult who is conducting the check-out. This can include positive notes – "Carlos did SO great in P.E. today!"

Component 4: Check-Out

During this time, the adult who is tasked with the check-in and check-out process reviews the student's goals, offering behavior-specific praise for the goals that were met ("Wow, Annnabeth! You did a great job keeping your hands to yourself during recess today. Let's do it again tomorrow."). For goals that were not met, adults can have a brief discussion with the student about what they might do differently to improve for the next day. During the debrief, it is important not to dwell on the student's challenges; this is not the time for disappointment, or a lecture (e.g., no need to say, "Gosh, Jerome! I can't believe you didn't make it to Algebra on time today. It's not that hard if you would just quit stopping to socialize on your way to class"). Rather, now is the time to keep the conversation positive and productive ("Jerome, I see you didn't meet your goal of getting to algebra on time today. What happened?...What might you do tomorrow to help you meet this goal?"). At the end of the debrief, the adult provides the student with access to the reinforcer ("Trista, you met four out of five of your goals today, so you earned a Dolphin Dollar. Great work.") or with information regarding why they didn't earn the reinforcement ("You came really close to meeting all of your goals today, Donovan, but you needed to meet all five to earn free time in the gym. I bet you can meet them all tomorrow!").

Component 5: Parent/Guardian Communication

The last component of CICO requires careful consideration, and as noted is the only component that might be skipped or eliminated, depending on the following factors. First, it is always important to consider the student's wellbeing. If there is any reason to believe that the child may receive harsh criticism or punishment for not meeting their goals, we think it is best to leave this component out of the CICO procedures. Second, it is important to think about the individual characteristics of the student. Students with or at risk for disabilities that impact their behavior may be more likely to engage in problem behaviors related to this approach (i.e., their behavior may worsen *because* they didn't meet their behavioral goals). We have also had students change their teacher's ratings on their DPR or "lose" the behavior goal sheet on the way home. For these students, we think it can be counterproductive to even include the home-school connection piece of CICO, at least at first. Doing so with some students may only set them up to engage in behavior (e.g., lying) that will lead to more conflict. For these students, teachers can omit the home-school connection or can email a parent a copy of the student's progress at the end of the day or week. In all situations, we are hesitant to make returning the signed DPR the next day a behavioral goal because in reality, meeting this goal is not entirely up to the student. There are plenty of reasons parents or guardians may not be able to sign the DPR – they may be working multiple jobs, running their kids from one activity to another, or just downright forget because – like most people, they just have a lot on their plates. Finally, it is critical to consider any other barriers that might impact communication with home. Teachers should think about the parent or guardian's first language, and whether they read English. If not, the information should be translated. Related, and regardless of first language, written communications, if used, should be brief and straightforward. As always, it is important to be sensitive in thinking about the numerous factors that may impact home-school communication and consider these factors carefully when determining whether or not to implement the home-school connection.

What Do I Need to Begin Implementing Check-In Check-Out?

We have included a planning template (Figure 14.2; see Figure 14.1 for a completed example) and an implementation and self-assessment checklist (Figure 14.3) at the end of this chapter. In addition to these materials, you will need a DPR to implement CICO. We have provided an example of a DPR (Figure 14.4) at the end of this chapter; please note that this example has a space for the parent/guardian connection, but depending on your student's needs, you may decide to remove this section. If using tangible reinforcers, you will need to obtain any materials (e.g., tickets, candy) that will be used for reinforcement.

What Does Check-In Check-Out Look like in a Classroom?

In this chapter, we have emphasized that implementation of CICO will likely look different depending on the student's needs and schedule. We have also described that a benefit of CICO is that teachers can adapt *how* the core components are implemented. To help illustrate these points, we provide two examples that show how a fifth and ninth grade teacher chose to implement CICO in their classrooms.

Elementary Example

Ms. King is a fifth grade, general education teacher who is regarded by her peers as having excellent behavior and classroom management skills. She has clear routines and procedures in place, implements a token economy in her classroom that aligns with school-wide expectations, and makes a conscious effort to provide behavior-specific praise to her students. Her classroom typically runs so smoothly that her principal often has new teachers observe her! This year, however, Ms. King has been having a hard time with one student in particular. Lainey is a high-energy student who is performing above grade level academically but has a difficult time with her social behaviors. Lainey's behavior during instructional time is manageable; Ms. King implements a combination of several antecedent interventions (see section 1 of this book) that really seem to help. However, Lainey really struggles during less structured time, notably on her bus ride to school (her grandma picks her up after school), and during recess, lunch, and PE Ms. King talks to one of the behavior specialists in her building and, after learning about CICO, she decides to implement this strategy with Lainey (see Figure 14.1 for her completed planning template). Ms. King and Lainey talk about the strategy and work together to identify some goals that Lainey should work on across the different parts of her day that are a challenge. They agree that across all environments, Lainey needs to work on keeping her hands to herself and using kind words with her peers. On the bus and in the lunchroom, Lainey needs to work on staying in her seat. And at recess and PE, Lainey needs to work

	Check-In Check-Out Planning Template		
Student: *Lainey*	**Context** (class, time of day, activity where problem behavior is likely): *Less structured time (bus, recess, lunch, PE)*		**Behavior to Improve** *Out of seat and area, touching other students and their things, talking disrespectfully to other students, not following directions*
Ways to Include Student: *Set goals and reinforcer together*			
	Check-In Check-Out Components *Describe all components in specific detail and how they will be introduced to the student.*		
Goals	Describe the specific behavior you want to see from the student: *Hands to self; respectful words; staying in seat/area; following directions; using PE gear safely*		
Instruction	Describe the skills student needs to acquire or improve and method of instruction: *Very brief modeling, role play, or discussions with Lainey during check-ins to help her understand all the behavioral goals*		Describe details (who/what/how/when) for teaching student Check-in Check-out: *I'll meet with her to go over the goals and the Daily Progress Report before we start.*
Reinforcement	Describe possible reinforcers for meeting behavioral goals and criteria for earning them: *Extra Parrot Points in our classroom token economy. Earn 2 extra if she meets 2 or more goals on the bus and at lunch and 3+ goals in recess or PE*		
Logistics	Determine frequency of check-ins/outs: *After arrival (after bus ride) check-in, and at end of day check-out*	Which teacher/adult will conduct check-ins/outs: *I will since we already have a good relationship*	Where will check-ins/outs occur？ *In class at my desk*
Communication	Describe communication plan for sharing with other teachers/adults: *Meet individually with bus driver, all cafeteria monitors, and our PE teacher*		Describe communication plan for sharing with parents/guardians (if appropriate): *Check in with Lainey's dad (room parent) to make a plan to collaborate, especially around reinforcing Lainey's success*
Data Collection Plan *Describe the specific behavior targeted for improvement:* *All behavioral goals listed above* *Describe the metric (e.g., % of time on-task) and method for data collection:* *Percentage of goals met each day on the Daily Progress Report; I'll graph this to determine Lainey's progress*			

FIGURE 14.1 Completed Example of Check-In Check-Out Planning Template

on following directions, staying in the designated activity areas, and using equipment safely. In all, Lainey has four environments that they will target; she has three goals for the bus and in the lunchroom and five goals for recess and PE To earn her reinforcement, which Lainey has expressed as wanting to earn two extra Parrot Points (the tickets Ms. King uses in her token economy), Lainey will need to meet at least two goals on the bus and in the lunchroom and three goals in *either* recess or PE As Lainey starts to improve, she will need to meet more goals to earn extra Parrot Points, but as the criterion increases, so will the amount of Parrot Points that Lainey can earn. Ms. King already has a pretty solid relationship with Lainey, so she will do the check-in and check-out each day. She prints off several DPRs for Lainey to keep in her folder so that she has one to start her day every morning on the bus. Ms. King recognizes that this means the check-in won't happen until after the bus ride, which represents her first goal area of the day, but she thinks that will work for Lainey because she's an exceptionally smart kid who seemed to understand CICO when Ms. King first explained it to her. Finally, Ms. King considers the home-school connection. She actually taught Lainey's sister a few years ago, and Lainey's dad is one of the room parents, so she has a great relationship with Lainey's parents. She decides that she *will* send the DPR home each day and Lainey's parents have actually agreed to provide additional reinforcement at home. They assure Ms. King that Lainey won't lose any privileges, but rather she will earn ten extra minutes of time on her gaming system. Ms. King communicates the plan to the bus driver, cafeteria monitors, and PE teacher and gets ready to implement the plan!

Secondary Example

Mr. Albertson is a high school special education teacher. One of his ninth grade students, Diego, has been demonstrating some behavioral challenges that are consistent across his school day. Diego is tardy for most of his classes every day, including first period. Mr. Albertson knows that Diego rides the bus to school, so unless the bus is late, Diego gets to school with plenty of time to make it to his first period class. All of his teachers have shared similar concerns about Diego's behavior in class: he often refuses to even attempt independent work, even though he is academically capable; when prompted to start his work, he becomes angry and "lashes out," which means that he curses and sometimes stands up, flips his chair, and tries to leave the classroom. Mr. Albertson meets with Diego's teachers and comes up with a plan to try and support Diego. First, all of Diego's teachers agree to increase their use of some of the Tier 1 strategies that have worked with Diego in the past, including precorrection, precision requests, behavioral momentum, and of course, behavior-specific praise. While the classroom teachers focus on these strategies, Mr. Albertson develops a CICO plan for Diego and meets with Diego to review the behavioral goals that he's come up with based on feedback from Diego's teachers. Diego agrees that arriving to each period on time, *attempting* to complete his work (starting his work and working for at least ten minutes), using school-appropriate language, and staying in the classroom are reasonable goals. Mr. Albertson develops a DPR to reflect these goals; Diego is a Spanish-speaking student, so Mr. Albertson uses Spanish on the DPR (with English printed below). Mr. Albertson and Diego agree that meeting at least three goals for three out of four periods a day is achievable. If Diego accomplishes this, he will be allowed to have ten minutes of time at the end of the day to get a head start on some track drills he is working on with his coach. Mr. Albertson knows that all of the ninth graders on the track team are assigned an upper class peer-mentor, so he meets with Diego's team mentor and asks if he would be willing to help with the check-in and check-out period. Diego's teammate agrees, and Diego loves this idea. At first, Mr. Albertson, Diego, and his teammate will participate in the meetings while Mr. Albertson models the procedures; then Mr. Albertson will fade his support and Diego's teammate will take the lead on providing feedback. Mr. Albertson talks with Diego's parents about his latest plan and asks if they would like to receive a copy of Diego's DPR each day. Diego's parents share that they are actually working on some different behavioral goals at home, with the help of a behavioral therapist. They would like to know about Diego's progress, but they don't want to add yet another thing to their plate to have to "enforce" at home. They have realized that it is better for Diego to "start fresh" when he comes home, rather than carry over any issues that he had in school. Mr. Albertson understands and agrees to send home the DPRs at the end of the week. Of course, Diego's parents want to be notified if anything major happens, but otherwise they are comfortable with a weekly update that doesn't need to be signed and returned. Mr. Albertson gets ready to implement CICO and is prepared to collect data along the way to determine if any modifications might be needed.

Final Thoughts

In this chapter, we described CICO as a multi-component, Tier 2 intervention that includes five components: (1) checking-in; (2) completing a DPR; (3) providing adult feedback; (4) checking-out; and (5) communicating with parents or guardians. We discussed several ways that this strategy can be adapted to meet the needs of students and the context of both the learning and home environments. Although planning for CICO is a bit more involved than some of the other strategies presented in this book, the time needed to plan for implementation is still relatively minimal and the time needed for implementation is relatively small – in fact, check-in and check-out meetings should be able to be conducted in as little as two minutes (i.e., they are not meant to be lengthy talk or debriefing sessions). For these reasons – the flexibility that allows for individualization and minimal use of time – as well as the potential of the strategy to build and strengthen student-teacher relationships, we believe CICO is an ideal strategy for many students who require more intensive behavioral supports.

References

Collins, T. A., Gresham, F. M., & Dart, E. H. (2016). The effects of peer-mediated check-in/check-out on the social skills of socially neglected students. *Behavior Modification, 40*(4), 568–588.

Cook, S. C., & Rao, K. (2018). Systematically applying UDL to effective practices for students with learning disabilities. *Learning Disability Quarterly, 41*(3), 179–191.

Crone, D. A., Hawken, L. S., & Horner, R. H. (2010). *Responding to problem behavior in schools: The behavior education program* (2nd ed.). Guilford Press.

Dart, E. H., Furlow, C. M., Collins, T. A., Brewer, E., Gresham, F. M., & Chenier, K. H. (2015). Peer-mediated check-in/check-out for students at-risk for internalizing disorders. *School Psychology Quarterly, 30*(2), 229.

Maggin, D. M., Zurheide, J., Pickett, K. C., & Baillie, S. J. (2015). A systematic evidence review of the check-in/check-out program for reducing student challenging behaviors. *Journal of Positive Behavior Interventions, 17*(4), 197–208.

Majeika, C. E., Van Camp, A. M., Wehby, J. H., Kern, L., Commisso, C. E., & Gaier, K. (2020). An evaluation of adaptations made to check-in check-out. *Journal of Positive Behavior Interventions, 22*(1), 25–37.

Melius, P., Swoszowski, N. C., & Siders, J. (2015). Developing peer led check-in/check-out: A peer-mentoring program for children in residential care. *Residential Treatment for Children & Youth, 32*(1), 58–79.

Wolfe, K., Pyle, D., Charlton, C. T., Sabey, C. V., Lund, E. M., & Ross, S. W. (2016). A systematic review of the empirical support for check-in check-out. *Journal of Positive Behavior Interventions, 18*(2), 74–88.

Check-In Check-Out Planning Template			
Student: **Ways to Include Student:**	**Context** (class, time of day, activity where problem behavior is likely):		**Behavior to Improve**
Check-In Check-Out Components *Describe all components in specific detail and how they will be introduced to the student.*			
Goals	Describe the specific behavior you want to see from the student:		
Instruction	Describe the skills student needs to acquire or improve and method of instruction:		Describe details (who/what/how/when) for teaching student Check-in Check-out:
Reinforcement	Describe possible reinforcers for meeting behavioral goals and criteria for earning them:		
Logistics	Determine frequency of check-ins/outs:	Which teacher/adult will conduct check-ins/outs:	Where will check-ins/outs occur?
Communication	Describe communication plan for sharing with other teachers/adults:		Describe communication plan for sharing with parents/guardians (if appropriate):
Data Collection Plan *Describe the specific behavior targeted for improvement:* *Describe the metric (e.g., % of time on-task) and method for data collection:*			

FIGURE 14.2 Check-In Check-Out Planning Template

Check-In, Check-Out Steps & Self-Assessment	
0→Not in Place 1→Partially in Place 2→Fully in Place	
STEPS	**How Did I do?**
1. Develop a Daily Progress Report that includes the student's behavioral goals and feedback periods.	☐ 0 ☐ 1 ☐ 2
2. Check in with the student to review goals.	☐ 0 ☐ 1 ☐ 2
3. Provide positive adult feedback while completing the DPR throughout the school day.	☐ 0 ☐ 1 ☐ 2
4. Check out with student, reviewing goals and providing reinforcement.	☐ 0 ☐ 1 ☐ 2
5. Communicate with parents/guardians.	☐ 0 ☐ 1 ☐ 2
Notes & Reflection:	

FIGURE 14.3 Check-In Check-Out Implementation and Self-Assessment Checklist

DAILY PROGRESS REPORT

Student Name: _____ | **Date:** _____

SCHEDULE (time/period)	BEHAVIORAL GOALS (2 = Met, 1 = Partially Met, 0 = Unmet)					NOTES
	2 1 0	2 1 0	2 1 0	2 1 0	2 1 0	
	2 1 0	2 1 0	2 1 0	2 1 0	2 1 0	
	2 1 0	2 1 0	2 1 0	2 1 0	2 1 0	
	2 1 0	2 1 0	2 1 0	2 1 0	2 1 0	
	2 1 0	2 1 0	2 1 0	2 1 0	2 1 0	
	2 1 0	2 1 0	2 1 0	2 1 0	2 1 0	
	2 1 0	2 1 0	2 1 0	2 1 0	2 1 0	
	2 1 0	2 1 0	2 1 0	2 1 0	2 1 0	

Goal Criterion to Earn Reinforcer: _____   **Reinforcer for Meeting Goal:** _____

_____   _____
Parent/Guardian Signature   Date
(optional)

FIGURE 14.4 Check-In Check-Out Daily Progress Report Example

15

Behavior Contracts

In this chapter, we explain how and why behavior contracts can be used to improve student behavior. We begin by providing a definition and description of this intervention, followed by a brief overview of the research that supports the use of this intervention. Next, we explain how behavior contracts can build positive relationships with students, particularly those who demonstrate challenging behaviors. Finally, we describe how to implement this intervention and provide two examples of what this practice might look like in a classroom. The supplemental resources for this chapter include a planning template (one blank for your use and one completed as an example) and a self-assessment checklist to support implementation fidelity.

What Are Behavior Contracts?

It is often the case that students behave better when teachers explicitly describe and teach their expectations, and that is especially the case when students have a say in potential reinforcers, they can earn for making improvements. Behavior contracts serve as simple formal agreements between a student and teacher, and often involve other relevant stakeholders such as caregivers or administrators. These contracts clearly define expected behaviors, rewards for meeting those expectations, and methods for evaluating student success. Behavior contracts are more than just tools for targeting student problem behavior; they represent a proactive approach to behavior management that emphasizes collaboration, mutual respect, student voice and buy-in, and personal responsibility.

At their core, behavior contracts help students take ownership of their actions by providing them with a clear roadmap of what is expected and what they will gain from adhering to the agreement. For teachers, behavior contracts offer a structured way to address specific behavioral issues while reinforcing positive behaviors in a consistent and systematic manner. Though practical and quite simple, contracts support teachers to be more intentional in laying out clear expectations and reinforcement systems with students while helping students better understand what is expected of them and what they have to gain from it.

Behavior contracts can be especially effective in situations where traditional classroom management methods have been insufficient to yield desired student outcomes. For students who may be resistant to authority or struggle with self-regulation skills, behavior contracts are akin to instructional choice (see Chapter 6), providing a sense of agency and control by giving the student voice and choice, helping them to internalize the importance of their behavior in relation to their success in the classroom.

How Do I Know Behavior Contracts Work?

Behavior contracts are rooted in well-established principles of behavior, including the use of positive reinforcement, that are supported by a vast array of research. The effectiveness of behavior contracts lies in their ability to support making behavioral expectations explicit, while simultaneously providing tangible incentives for students to meet those expectations.

Behavior contracts have been demonstrated to have a positive impact across a wide variety of students and target behaviors. Bowman-Perrott and colleagues (2015) synthesized findings from 18 studies of contracts and found a positive impact on reducing problem behaviors, such as disengagement and destructiveness, as well as on improving desired student behaviors, such as appropriate social interactions, active engagement, task completion, and correct academic responses.

Over 50 years of research have demonstrated the benefits of behavior contracts as a practical, yet effective strategy for improving student behavior (e.g., Bailey et al., 1970). Numerous studies have shown that when students are actively involved in collaboration to negotiate their own goal behaviors and the consequences of their actions, they are more likely to comply with behavioral expectations. The cooperative nature of behavior contracts, where students participate in the creation of the contract, leads to increased buy-in and a sense of ownership over the process. For example, Schrieber and colleagues (2023) implemented behavior contracts with high school students who had been identified by a school-wide screener for finding students with challenging behavior who may need more support. The researchers conducted a simple interview with students to better understand their challenging behaviors (e.g., calling out, being out of seat, playing games on a laptop, sleeping in class) and what would motivate the students to improve. Simply by setting up a basic contingency through behavior contracts, the researchers demonstrated significant improvements in students' engagement with academic tasks and reductions in their off-task and disruptive behaviors. Moreover, the students and their teachers reported positive experiences with the intervention.

How Do Behavior Contracts Build Positive Relationships with My Students?

One of the most significant benefits of behavior contracts is their ability to foster positive relationships between teachers and students. The process of developing a behavior contract is inherently collaborative, requiring open communication and mutual respect. Rather than teachers alone exerting their authority to determine what students need to improve and what they will gain from doing so, students also have a voice in the development of an intervention that is intended for their benefit, which is an approach students with challenging behavior may not experience much in schools. This collaborative approach helps to break down barriers between teachers and students, creating a partnership that is focused on the student's success.

When a behavior contract is introduced, it involves a discussion where both parties can voice their concerns and expectations. This dialogue is an opportunity for teachers to listen to their students, understand their perspectives, and work together to find solutions. By involving students in the decision-making process, teachers show that they value the students' input and are committed to their growth and well-being. Whereas students with challenging behavior often experience negative interactions with their teachers as well as punitive measures, students involved in a behavior contracting process have opportunities to experience teamwork with their teachers through this dialogue focused on a unified goal of their own behavioral success.

Additionally, students with challenging behavior, especially those from certain subpopulations (e.g., students with disabilities), may struggle to pick up on implicit cues about classroom behavior expectations and end up frequently running afoul of them without ever understanding why. This may seem quite unfair and frustrating to these students and lead to increasing conflicts with their teachers. However, behavior contracts remove any need for guesswork as specific expectations for appropriate behavior are explicitly defined in the contract. This structure supports better understanding from students of what is expected from them, allowing them to have a much greater chance at successful participation in their class. These experiences of success allow for more positive interactions between these students and their teachers (as well as their peers), which are the foundation of strong, positive relationships.

The use of positive reinforcement within the contract further enhances the relationship between teacher and student. When students see that their teacher is not just an enforcer of rules, but also someone who is invested in their success and willing to reward their efforts, it builds trust and rapport. This positive dynamic can lead to improved classroom behavior, as students are more likely to respond positively to a teacher they feel connected to and supported by. Moreover, behavior contracts can serve as a foundation for ongoing communication between teachers and students. Regular check-ins and progress reviews provide opportunities for teachers to offer praise, encouragement, and guidance. These interactions help to maintain a positive and supportive atmosphere in the classroom, reinforcing the idea that the teacher is a partner in the student's journey toward meeting their goals.

How Do I Implement Behavior Contracts in My Classroom?

Behavior contracts are relatively simple to implement and require little preparation. The heart of the process involves a meeting with the student to engage in open, collaborative dialogue to clarify expectations, set goals, and identify reinforcers, all toward a mutual goal of student success. We have broken down the process for implementing behavior contracts into five simple steps, which we describe briefly in the next subsections.

Step 1: Identify the Target and Expected Behavior

The first step in implementing a behavior contract is to consider students whose behavior warrants more support and identify the specific problem behaviors that need to be addressed. These behaviors should be clearly defined and measurable to ensure that both the student and teacher have a mutual understanding of what needs to be addressed. Additionally, we recommend focusing in on the behavior you most *want* to see from the student, clearly defining positive expectations for what behavior the student should engage in.

Step 2: Collaborate with the Student to Set Clear Expectations and Goals

Once the target and expected behaviors are identified, engage in a meeting with the student. This meeting could involve other stakeholders (e.g., other teachers, parents/caregivers) who can support student success with the intervention. Begin by identifying the expected behavior and collaborating with the student to set clear, achievable goals. This step is crucial, as involving the student in the goal-setting process increases their buy-in and commitment to the contract. It is especially helpful to come up with a concrete, clear goal for the type and amount of appropriate behavior. For instance, instead of setting a vague goal like "improve behavior," a more effective target would be "remain seated during class" or "complete homework assignments on time." The goals should be specific, realistic, and time-bound, allowing for easy tracking and monitoring. For example, a goal might be, "Stay on task, attempting to complete your work, for at least 80% of the class period." When setting expectations and goals, we recommend considering what skills the student may be missing or need growth in and making a plan for teaching these skills.

Step 3: Help the Student Identify a Reasonable Reinforcer for Meeting Expectations

Work with the student to identify what is in it for them to make these behavioral improvements. It can be helpful to ask the student to brainstorm a variety of possible rewards for achieving the identified goal so that you can pick what seems most realistic and appropriate yet still valuable to the student. If the student struggles to come up with ideas, you might ask them questions about their interests (with the added benefit of further strengthening the relationship) or point out things you have noticed them doing often in their free time (such things can often function as reinforcers if we harness their power).

Step 4: Monitor Student Progress and Provide Feedback and Reinforcement

Regularly monitor the student's progress and provide feedback regarding their progress toward the goal. This can be done through daily check-ins, progress charts, or other tracking methods. The reinforcement identified in the contract should be given consistently when the student meets the contract's expectations. It's essential to celebrate small successes along the way, as this encourages the student to continue working toward their goals.

Step 5: Review and Adjust the Contract as Needed

Behavior contracts should be flexible and open to adjustments. If the student is consistently meeting the goals, consider revising the contract to include new targets or more challenging criteria to meet goals or fading out the intervention altogether. Conversely, if the student struggles to meet the goals, use this as an opportunity to provide constructive feedback and make necessary adjustments to the contract to help them succeed. This might involve modifying the rewards to increase student motivation, providing additional resources or support to address gaps in students' skills, or breaking down the goals into smaller, more manageable steps.

What Do I Need to Begin Implementing Behavior Contracts?

One of the greatest advantages of employing behavior contracts is how very little advanced preparation or resources are needed to implement them. We recommend a basic foundation of rapport with the student through positive interactions as an ideal way to set the stage for dialogue with the student around a contract to go well (we provide practical ways to do this throughout this book, such as positive greetings at the door; see Chapter 4). If rapport is still a work in progress, it can be helpful to invite another teacher or adult who has an established positive relationship with the student.

Additionally, effective implementation of behavior contracts requires the teacher to have a collaborative mindset and to foster a collaborative spirit with the student. The success of a behavior contract depends heavily on the student's involvement in the process. Plan to have a direct discussion with the student to create the contract together, ensuring they understand and agree to the terms. This collaboration not only increases the likelihood of the student's compliance but also fosters a sense of responsibility and ownership over their behavior.

Finally, teachers may benefit from taking a brief period of time to plan ahead for their student meeting. We have provided a behavior contract planning template to help think through some primary considerations (see Figure 15.2). Additionally, although a specific template for the actual contracts is unnecessary (i.e., contracts could be jotted down on a piece of paper on the fly), it can be quite helpful to have a simple template to guide the conversation and to lay out the terms clearly for both teacher and student. Clarity allows for better collaboration and a greater likelihood of successful student outcomes. To support this, we have provided a simple behavior contract template that can be adapted to individual needs (see Figure 15.3). An example of a completed planning template (see Figure 15.1) is also included. Finally, we have included a self-assessment checklist (see Figure 15.4) that includes each step for implementing behavior contracts to maximize your probability of success with your students.

What Do Behavior Contracts Look like in a Classroom?

In the following sections, we provide two examples illustrating teachers supporting students with behavior contracts in elementary and secondary classrooms. In the first example, you will read about Ms. Acklin, a third-grade teacher who uses a behavior contract to support a student who seems to constantly disrupt the class by blurting things out and leaving his seat. In the second example, you will learn about Mr. Hance, a tenth-grade science teacher who has often been concerned about students who seem apathetic about school. Mr. Hance uses a behavior contract to support one such student who frequently skips class and is missing a growing number of assignments.

Elementary Example
Ms. Acklin, a third-grade teacher, had been struggling with one of her students, Dylan, who frequently interrupted lessons by talking out of turn and leaving his seat without permission. Despite her efforts to manage his behavior through verbal reminders, seating changes, and loss of privileges, Dylan's disruptive behavior improved little and continued to hinder his learning and that of his classmates.

Recognizing the need for a more structured approach, Ms. Acklin decided to try a behavior contract. Before opening any dialogue with Dylan about how to address his behavior, Ms. Acklin takes a few minutes to complete a planning template to help herself prepare (see Figure 15.1 for a completed sample). She scheduled a meeting with Dylan and explained that they would be creating an agreement together to help him stay on

Behavior Contract Planning Template		
Student: Dylan	**Behavior to Improve** ☐ Disengagement ☒ Disruptiveness ☐ Disrespect ☐ Following Directions ☒ Other: ___Out of Seat___	**Context** (class, time of day, activity where problem behavior is likely): *During whole group instruction or independent work; any time he has to be seated and quiet*
Contract Components *Describe all components in specific detail and how they will be introduced to the student.*		
Desired Behavior	Describe the specific behavior you want to see from the student: *I'd like Dylan to raise his hand and wait to be called on before he says anything unless there's a different voice level expectation for him to follow. I'd also like him to stay in his seat or his assigned area and to ask for permission before leaving it.*	
Potential Reinforcers	Describe possible reinforcers to propose to the student: *I plan to ask him what he might like, but I know he loves playing on his computer or an iPad, playing tag at recess, reading books about animals, and spending time with a few other students in our class.*	
Instruction	Describe the skills student needs to acquire or improve and method of instruction: *I plan to engage in modeling, guided practice, and independent practice with Dylan to help him learn to raise his hand and wait to be called on.*	
Other Considerations	☐ Parent/Caregiver involvement ☒ Communication with other teachers ☐ Connections to existing IEP or Behavior Intervention Plan ☐ Other Describe any necessary considerations to address: *Dylan's related arts teachers have also expressed concerns about his disruptiveness, so I'll fill them in on the contract he and I make.*	
Data Collection Plan Describe the specific behavior targeted for improvement: *Raising Hand without blurting out and staying in his assigned area* Describe the metric (e.g., % of time on-task) and method for data collection: *Point Sheet/Sticker Chart to measure % of class periods Dylan engages in these appropriate behaviors*		

FIGURE 15.1 Completed Example of Behavior Contract Planning Template

task during class. Dylan was hesitant at first, unsure of what the contract would entail. However, Ms. Acklin took the time to explain the process, emphasizing that the contract was a way for them to work together to help him succeed.

During their discussion, Ms. Acklin and Dylan identified the specific behaviors that needed to change: staying in his seat and raising his hand before speaking. They then set a clear goal: if Dylan could meet these expectations for the whole school day with no more than two errors, he would earn a reward of his choice. They brainstormed possible rewards that might motivate Dylan, who was most excited about the prospect of earning extra time on the computer at the end of the day, which motivated him to agree to the contract.

Ms. Acklin used a simple chart to track Dylan's progress each day. Each period Dylan met the goals without errors, Ms. Acklin placed a sticker on the chart, providing immediate positive reinforcement. They reviewed the chart together at the end of each day, discussing what went well and what could be improved. Over the next two weeks, Dylan's behavior improved significantly. He was proud and excited to earn his reward time on the computer, and the positive reinforcement he received from Ms. Acklin helped him stay motivated.

The behavior contract not only helped Dylan stay focused but also strengthened the relationship between him and Ms. Acklin. By working together on the contract, they developed a sense of mutual respect and trust. Dylan felt supported rather than disciplined, and Ms. Acklin was able to create a more positive learning environment for the entire class through an intervention that did not add extra stress to her day and, in fact, relieved much of her stress due to challenging behavior.

Secondary Example

In his high school science classroom, tenth-grade teacher Mr. Hance faced challenges with a student named Emily, who frequently skipped classes and failed to turn in assignments. Traditional disciplinary measures, such as detention and loss of privileges, had little impact on Emily's behavior. She seemed disengaged from school and indifferent to the consequences of her actions.

Mr. Hance knew that something needed to change, so he decided to introduce a behavior contract tailored to Emily's needs. He began by scheduling a meeting with Emily to discuss her behavior. During their conversation, Mr. Hance took the time to listen to Emily's perspective, asking her why she was skipping classes and struggling to complete her assignments. Emily admitted that she felt overwhelmed by her coursework and found it easier to avoid it altogether.

Understanding that Emily needed a more supportive approach, Mr. Hance worked with her to set specific, manageable goals. They agreed that Emily would attend all her classes for two weeks and complete at least 80% of her assignments. In return, she would earn extra credit points and a pass for one late assignment each week. These incentives were meaningful to Emily and motivated her to commit to trying to meet her goal.

To help Emily stay on track, Mr. Hance made a plan with Emily during their contract meeting for how he could provide additional support to address the overwhelming nature of her coursework. Each day, they had a brief check-in to review her attendance and assignments. During this time, Mr. Hance provided positive reinforcement when Emily attempted or met her goals and offered encouragement and guidance when she faced challenges. The behavior contract was a turning point for Emily. By breaking down her goals into manageable steps and offering incentives that mattered to her, Emily gradually improved her attendance and assignment completion.

The impact of the behavior contract went beyond just meeting academic goals. Mr. Hance's consistent support and encouragement helped Emily regain confidence in her abilities. She began to see school as a place where she could succeed, rather than something to avoid. The positive relationship that developed between Mr. Hance and Emily was instrumental in her turnaround, and she continued to make progress throughout the school year.

Final Thoughts

We described in this chapter how to implement behavior contracts, which are powerful tools for promoting positive behavior and improving student-teacher relationships. By engaging students in collaborative problem-solving, setting clear expectations, and providing consistent reinforcement, behavior contracts help students take ownership of their actions and become more motivated to work toward their goals. These contracts are adaptable to a wide range of situations and can be used to address both minor behavioral issues and more significant challenges.

The success stories of Dylan and Emily illustrate how behavior contracts can make a significant difference in students' lives, paving the way for academic and behavioral success. Whether in an elementary or high school setting, behavior contracts can be tailored to meet the unique needs of each student, leading to a more positive and productive classroom environment. Contracts are of particular benefit to teachers also, given how practical they are to implement and how little they require in terms of time or resources.

Moreover, the collaborative nature of behavior contracts fosters a sense of partnership between teachers and students, building trust and mutual respect. This positive dynamic not only improves behavior but also enhances the overall learning experience, as students feel supported and motivated to succeed. Although on face value, behavior contracts may appear simply to be behavioral strategies alone, the very nature of the contracting process involves collaboration, dialogue, student voice, student interests, and a focus on student success, which are all powerful factors for shaping strong, positive teacher-student relationships.

In conclusion, behavior contracts are not just about managing behavior; they are about empowering students to take control of their actions and achieve their full potential with the proactive, positive support of their teachers. By implementing behavior contracts thoughtfully and consistently, teachers can create a classroom environment that is conducive to learning, growth, and positive relationships.

References

Bailey, J. S., Wolf, M. M., & Phillips, E. L. (1970). Home based reinforcement and the modification of pre-delinquents' classroom behavior. *Journal of Applied Behavior Analysis, 3*, 223–233.

Bowman-Perrott, L., Burke, M. D., de Marin, S., Zhang, N., & Davis, H. (2015). A meta-analysis of single-case research on behavior contracts: Effects on behavioral and academic outcomes among children and youth. *Behavior Modification, 39*(2), 247–269.

Schrieber, S. R., Ware, M. E., & Dart, E. H. (2023). Student interview-informed behavior contracts for high school students identified as at risk. *Behavioral Disorders, 49*(1), 31–45.

Behavior Contract Planning Template		
Student:	**Behavior to Improve** ☐ Disengagement ☐ Disruptiveness ☐ Disrespect ☐ Following Directions ☐ Other: _____	**Context** (class, time of day, activity where problem behavior is likely):
Contract Components *Describe all components in specific detail and how they will be introduced to the student.*		
Desired Behavior	Describe the specific behavior you want to see from the student:	
Potential Reinforcers	Describe possible reinforcers to propose to the student:	
Instruction	Describe the skills student needs to acquire or improve and method of instruction:	
Other Considerations	☐ Parent/Caregiver involvement ☐ Communication with other teachers ☐ Connections to existing IEP or Behavior Intervention Plan ☐ Other Describe any necessary considerations to address:	
Data Collection Plan *Describe the specific behavior targeted for improvement:* *Describe the metric (e.g., % of time on-task) and method for data collection:*		

FIGURE 15.2 Behavior Contract Planning Template

Behavior Contract

| Student: | Date: |

BEHAVIOR
Describe in positive terms the appropriate behavior the student will work on.

I, _____, agree to work on this behavior:

_____
_____
_____

GOAL
Describe in measurable terms the goal for student behavior, including the criteria for earning the reward.

The goal I have for this behavior is:

_____
_____
_____

REWARD
Describe the specific reward(s) the student will receive for meeting the goal and when/how the reward will be provided.

The reward I will receive for meeting this goal is:

_____
_____
_____

REVIEW
Describe the timeline for reviewing the contract to provide feedback and make adjustments if needed.

We will check in on how this contract is going at this time:

_____
_____

_____   _____
Student Signature   Adult Signature

FIGURE 15.3 Sample Behavior Contract

Behavior Contracts Steps & Self-Assessment	
0→Not in Place 1→Partially in Place 2→Fully in Place	
STEPS	**How Did I do?**
1. Identify the target and expected behavior.	☐ 0 ☐ 1 ☐ 2
2. Collaborate with the student to set clear expectations and goals.	☐ 0 ☐ 1 ☐ 2
3. Help the student identify a reasonable reinforcer for meeting expectations.	☐ 0 ☐ 1 ☐ 2
4. Monitor student progress and provide feedback and reinforcement.	☐ 0 ☐ 1 ☐ 2
5. Review and adjust the contract as needed.	☐ 0 ☐ 1 ☐ 2
Notes & Reflection:	

FIGURE 15.4 Behavior Contract Implementation and Self-Assessment Checklist

16

Informal Functional Behavioral Assessment

In this chapter, we explain how and why informal function-based assessment can be used to improve student behavior. We begin by providing a definition and description of this intervention, followed by a brief overview of the research that supports the use of this intervention. Next, we explain how informal function-based assessment can build positive relationships with students, particularly those who demonstrate challenging behaviors. Finally, we describe how to implement this intervention and provide two examples of what this practice might look like in a classroom. The supplemental resources for this chapter include a planning template (one blank for your use and one completed as an example) and a self-assessment checklist to support implementation fidelity.

What Is Meant by Informal Functional Behavioral Assessment?

Functional behavioral assessment (FBA) can be defined as a process for determining what causes challenging behavior to occur. We think the broad idea of FBA has probably become familiar to most teachers. But before we go any further, let's be clear: this chapter will NOT provide a thorough description of how to conduct a full-blown FBA, and we will not dive into the more complex *functional analysis* procedures that fall under the FBA umbrella. There are many great resources teachers can access if they are interested in the logic and process of conducting an FBA (e.g., Borgmeier et al., 2017; IRIS Center, 2024; Umbreit et al., 2024). But remember, this book is intended as a quick overview of strategies *all* teachers can use to prevent or minimize behavioral challenges in their classrooms. And with our focus on positive, preventive strategies that help build and maintain positive relationships, we would be remiss if we did not include discussion of the critical importance of examining *function* when we talk about concerns involving students failing to meet behavioral expectations. So, what is the *function* of a behavior?

In layperson's terms, determining *function* answers this question: what does the student get out of this behavior? We note that sometimes people phrase this question differently, asking simply "why does the student do _____?" We don't recommend focusing on the "why" question – it can lead to vague answers about motivations (e.g., he just wanted to show off), states (e.g., he was stressed), or known and unknown conditions (e.g., he did that because he has ADHD). It's not that these aren't important – we want to know if our kids are stressed, and we want to do whatever we can to reduce that. But we like the first question (what did the student get out of this?) much better because (a) it can usually be answered by some tangible outcome we can see, and (b) knowing this answer helps us directly to design a helpful response. Examples of answers to "What did the student get out of this behavior?" might include: (a) Kayla disrupted my class by yelling profanity at the teacher and got sent to the office; (b) instead of working, Kendrick cracked jokes all during our math lesson, and his peers laughed; or (c) Jason slammed his notebook closed violently and shouted "this is too hard!" and the teacher came over and talked to him quietly.

In each of these cases above, something very specific happened right after the behavior occurred. In these examples, you can hopefully see what the student got out of the behavior, but another key point is that this can mean they literally got, or obtained, something like attention or a tangible item. But what about Kayla, who yelled profanity and was sent to the office? What she "got" was actually escape – she got out of the classroom. In our experience, this happens an awful lot, including at times that may not be obvious. But suppose Kayla hated the class she was in (the content was really hard, she was forced to work in groups, or was simply bored). Acting out in order to escape starts to make sense. If in fact her behavior "worked" to achieve her goal, what is she now more likely to do the next time she is bored or hates a task or assignment she's asked to do? Understanding the function of a student's behavior is important for many reasons, but it is especially important for scenarios like Kayla, when the teacher's response actually reinforced the behavior, making it now more likely Kayla will do the same thing again.

Putting this all together, we're arguing that most behaviors, and certainly most challenging behaviors, occur in order to get something or to escape something; to obtain (access) something or to avoid (escape) something. And note that escape simply means that the behavior results in the student avoiding (or escaping from) a task demand or other context. We think based on our experience that escape may explain an awful lot – maybe a majority – of what goes on in classrooms in terms of challenging behavior. If a student does not like an activity, class, or lesson, they will quickly learn which behaviors to engage in – which buttons to push – to get out of that assignment or task. Note that "escape" can mean just avoiding a task, or literally leaving an environment (e.g., being sent to the office or in-school suspension). In our experience many professionals view discipline referrals or sending kids to the office as punishments – as a way to stop or discourage misbehavior. But if the motivation for that student was to escape, sending them out of the environment may simply be reinforcing their behavior – they got exactly what they wanted.

In short, it seems clear that in most cases a student's behavior is an attempt to communicate a need to access or escape one of the following: attention, a task demand, a tangible item or activity, sensory input, or support or help with a task. We present in Table 16.1 some examples of what it is that students may

TABLE 16.1 Student Examples of Functions of Behavior

Major functions of behavior: To get something or to avoid something

	Student may seek to get or obtain:	Students may seek to avoid or escape:
Teacher attention	♦ Positive teacher attention/praise for meeting expectations ♦ Help from teacher	♦ Verbal reprimands ♦ Public or demonstrative praise
Peer attention	♦ Laughing at jokes or antics; admiration of peers	♦ Negative comments, ridicule, or rejection
Tangible items, tasks, and activities	♦ Preferred activities or games (e.g., time on computer or devices) ♦ Access to toys, food, or objects student likes	♦ Difficult, demanding tasks or entire subject areas (math) ♦ Non-preferred activity; game or activity student is not good at (e.g., kickball game, spelling bee)
Sensory	♦ Toys, devices, or activities that provide sensory input student enjoys	♦ Noisy, crowded, or chaotic environments (pep rallies; assemblies; cafeteria; even large group work or activities)
Support or help from teacher	♦ Specific help on an assignment	♦ Frequent checking from teacher if perceived as negative

try to obtain or escape through their behavior. We note these are only brief examples, and readers wishing to see more and more detailed descriptions can consult sources mentioned earlier (Borgmeier et al., 2017; IRIS Center, 2024; Umbreit et al., 2024).

What we're going to talk about in the remainder of this chapter is framed around the basic processes of conducting an FBA, with a focus on those elements we think most teachers can use in their classrooms. Some refer to this as a practical FBA or simple FBA; we have used the term informal FBA because again – we think the basic elements we describe are both useful and very feasible for most classroom teachers. In brief, we're going to describe four steps: (1) identifying and defining the problem behavior; (2) conducting an A-B-C analysis; (3) developing a hypothesis about the function of behavior; and (4) proposing an intervention to help reduce the problem behavior and replace it with a better option.

How Do I Know Functional Behavioral Assessment Works?

It should not be surprising that when an FBA results in a clear hypothesis about what causes challenging behavior, *and* an intervention that addresses those causes and contributing factors directly is designed and implemented, students tend to be successful. In a summary of research on function-based interventions, Gage et al. (2012) reported that challenging behavior is reduced by up to 70% when such interventions are implemented. A similar review by Walker et al. (2018) found the same thing, but also included the finding that results appeared to be more positive when the FBA was administered by the teacher, rather than by a researcher or therapist. Also important in their findings was that most studies used a descriptive FBA (similar to what we describe in this chapter), rather than a full experimental (or formal) FBA.

In sum, there is plenty of research to support the idea that determining function first before choosing or designing an intervention will greatly enhance the odds of success. We think of this as simple logic – if you don't know what might be causing or contributing to challenging behavior, working to reduce it or replace it with more appropriate alternative behaviors is little more than trial and error. As you have probably seen in other textbooks and resources on behavior management, function-based interventions are highly preferred, and both logic and research support this recommendation.

How Does Functional Behavioral Assessment Help Build Positive Relationships with My Students?

The big idea in this chapter is to focus on *function*. We have no delusions that focusing on function-based interventions alone will directly result in positive relationships between teachers and students. But we do think it's a critical element. Think for a moment about what a function-based orientation or mindset might mean for teachers in their day-to-day interactions with students. As we mentioned earlier in this text, we have all worked extensively with students with challenging behavior, including some with the most serious types of concerns. We have been hit and kicked and cursed to our faces. We have had students sabotage lessons or even just fun activities – a kickball game or a class party. As you might imagine, it was consistently hard in those contexts to remain calm and measured in our responses and reactions (and no, we were not always perfect with this). It was hard to remember that these kids were not "out to get us," did not hate us, and were not just bad kids. Still, their behaviors drove us nuts! Instead, we tried to remove emotion from our reactions, focus on the functions these troubling behaviors were likely serving, and then try to positively support students in finding alternative means to achieve their goals (e.g., for attention, or to escape an activity). And we found that to the extent we were able to do this, we believe our students saw that we had their backs. We were not there to punish them into compliance, but rather to teach them more effective ways to communicate their needs and, in turn, have those needs met. Even in the face of those behaviors that typically send adults over the edge, we calmly (mostly…) tried to help them learn more positive ways to achieve their goals. And we saw payoffs. Most of our students, including those with the most challenging behavior, could not wait to see us in the morning, and often did not want to leave our classrooms. Why? We believe it's partly because they knew we were there to support them in positive, instructional ways toward reaching their goals, and that punishment was not our primary objective.

How Do I Implement Informal Functional Behavioral Assessment in My Classroom?

As we noted in the introduction to this chapter, we are NOT providing a deep dive into FBA. Instead, we have chosen to focus on the key elements of that process we think virtually all teachers can use to help move them toward a more function-based approach to supporting behavior that more consistently meets expectations. Again, we emphasize that when students are engaging in persistent and/or high intensity behaviors that prevent them – and perhaps others – from meeting basic expectations, a more formal FBA process is probably required, including the development and implementation of formal behavior intervention plans (BIP; see Umbreit et al., 2024). The steps we listed above included: (1) defining the problem behavior that has prompted us to conduct an FBA; (2) conducting an informal A-B-C analysis, (3) developing a hypothesis that states when and under what conditions the problem behavior most often occurs, and what the outcomes of the behavior are; and (4) proposing an intervention that involves altering antecedents and/or consequences, or teaches the student a new behavior that might better meet his needs. We elaborate on each step below.

Defining Behaviors of Concern

While we try to stick to our focus on ways to support positive behaviors, there's no way around the idea that the need for an informal FBA arises only when some specific behavior is causing problems. And the first step here is one that should be familiar from previous chapters in this book – we need to define the behavior, and we need to do so using operational terms. Remember that "disrupting others," "being disrespectful," and "acting out" are not really operationally (or clearly) defined behaviors. We need definitions like "talks out loudly enough to be heard across the classroom," or "tears his paper into small pieces and throws them on the floor." As we note in the next section, the operational definition – words that describe exactly what the student did, will be included in the behavior (B) column of the A-B-C form.

A-B-C Analysis

The key to understanding the function a behavior serves is to figure out what happens right before the behavior occurs (the antecedents), and what happens right after it occurs (the consequences). We talk about each in a bit more depth below but note that especially when we can see that these things happen repeatedly – when they represent a pattern – we can start to draw conclusions about what might be causing or at least contributing

TABLE 16.2 Sample A-B-C Chart

Student: Kayla **Date:** October 2, 2025.
Context: Math Class, Mr. Westland

Antecedents	Behavior	Consequences	Notes
9:00 am – Students entering 1st period classroom; bell rings	Kayla takes seat and gets out materials (book, notebook)	Teacher chats with two students in first row	Kayla's appropriate behavior was not acknowledged
9:07 am – Teacher asks for homework to be passed forward	Kayla has no homework; folds arms across chest	Teacher, loudly: "Kayla, do you not have any homework?"	
Teacher, loudly: "Kayla, do you not have any homework?"	Kayla says softly, "nope" and puts her head down.	Teacher: "you've lost your homework points, then; do you want to lose more by putting your head down?"	
Teacher: "you've lost your homework points, then; do you want to lose more by putting your head down?"	Kayla does not raise her head off the desk, but yells through the hood of her hoodie, "I'll put my head down if I want! "&#%@ &#%!"	Teacher says, "very well – you're going to the office, then" and begins filling out a referral.	Kayla's profanity occurred after loss of points, and threat of loss of more; result was referral to office.

to the behavior occurring, and what things determine whether it's likely to continue (occur again). We provide a sample A-B-C chart in Table 16.2 and describe what goes in each column here.

Antecedents. The word antecedent really just means what "comes before" but it's important to note that this can include a few different things. It includes, for example, behavior that the teacher or other students are engaging in, the physical context or locations (at his desk, classroom table, hallway, cafeteria, etc.), and specific task demands or expectations (e.g., the teacher has said "it's time for math," or a more specific request like "you need to write a paragraph of at least five sentences").

Behavior. We talked earlier about operationally defining the behavior, and in the A-B-C logic we need only to record those few words that describe exactly what the student did (e.g., "tore up her paper and threw the pieces on the floor," "pushed all the materials off his desk onto the floor and put his head down on his desk," "got out of his seat and walked around the perimeter of the room shouting profanities").

Consequences. We worry that the word "consequences" is often misunderstood. It really just means "what happened after." We fear the come educators have adopted a definition of *consequences* that implies the teacher administered some punishment – i.e., "gave him a consequence." That is NOT what we're after here. We just need a listing of what happened next, after the behavior noted occurred. Things like "peers laughed," "teacher sent James to the office," or "teacher told James he would lose his points for the morning if he did not stop using profanity" would be sufficient.

Take special note of one wrinkle in the example A-B-C chart in Table 16.2. Note how in some cases, the consequence (C) of one behavior can also then become the next antecedent. In this case, Kayla's teacher responded to her putting her head down with a statement that she's losing points, and a threat to take away more points. While that point deduction and threat were indeed the consequence of the previous behavior, they also now serve as the antecedent to what comes next (and this is simply copied into the A column of the chart). And as we can see, Kayla did not like this at all. After the teacher asks if Kayla "wants to lose more points by putting her head down," Kayla not only becomes defiant ("I'll put my head down if I want to"), but throws in some choice profanity directed at the teacher as well. It would not be a stretch to argue that the teacher's admonition and threat "caused" or at least contributed to Kayla's next behavior. Further, because she was indeed then referred and sent to the office, we might hypothesize that escape from this class or lesson was the function of her behavior.

Forming a Hypothesis

If the term hypothesis sounds technical or complex, we hope an example will make clear that it's really quite simple. In fact, we imagine that teachers form hypotheses all the time, without even knowing that they're doing it – it simply means that they can identify possible patterns and predict when behavioral breakdowns are most likely to occur. Look at the examples below and see if it's obvious how they follow the antecedent-behavior-consequence formula: "Whenever _____, the student tends to _____, which results in _____."

- When asked to work independently on a math problem set, James talks loudly to other students about off-topic matters, and the teacher intervenes by trying to get him engaged with 1:1 support.
- During a literacy lesson when the teacher is calling on students who have quietly raised their hands, Russell makes animal sounds louder and louder until the teacher says, "Russell – we do not need animal sound effects right now."
- In algebra class, as the teacher is modeling how to complete problems on the smartboard, Patrice responds with complaints about homework or makes inappropriate comments by shouting profanities or loud complaints about the teacher; the teacher sends her out and continues with the lesson.

Proposing an Intervention

Once Steps 1–3 are completed, Step 4, proposing an intervention, is also much easier than it might sound. Working from the hypothesis formed in the previous step, the goal now is to help the student engage in a more appropriate behavior that achieves the same goal (i.e., serves the same function) as the behavior that has become a concern. Note that this can involve several pieces, and these align with the A-B-C data we collected:

A. *Antecedents.* The teacher may **alter antecedents**; this would be appropriate if there is an antecedent that both appears to be consistently associated with the behavior *and* is easy to change. For example, if a student exhibits behavior that appears to be designed to avoid difficult math assignments, the teacher might offer instructional choice (see Chapter 6) in which the student can choose where or how to complete the assignment, or perhaps choose only the odd- or even-numbered problems. Another option described in our elementary example later in this chapter uses behavioral momentum (see Chapter 5) to "ease" the student into a difficult or non-preferred assignment.

B. *Behavior.* If the student has rarely displayed the appropriate behavior required in this context, it is almost certain that some simple, ***explicit instruction*** in that skill is required (see Chapter 3). The teacher would first model the behavior, then practice the behavior with the student, and finally provide opportunities for the student to practice the skill independently. Teaching and practicing it in context is of course critical. This can be as simple as "here's how you can ask me for help if an assignment seems really hard; watch me first," followed by "OK, now you show me what you could do if you don't know how to start on your math assignment."

C. *Consequences.* Consequences may be the most important element of a function-based intervention. In addition to modifying antecedents and teaching or practicing the replacement behavior, you must now make certain that ***the desired replacement behavior is reinforced*** – that it serves the desired function – and that the "old" behavior (what the student used to do) is *not* reinforced. Consider a simple example: you have determined through A-B-C analysis that Paulo seems to yell out for attention from the teacher, so you have taught and practiced with him the replacement behavior of raising his hand for attention. Now, during instruction, you should strive to (a) consistently reinforce him each time he raises his hand – i.e., give him attention by calling on him – and (b) *not* reinforce him when he yells out – i.e., simply ignore this behavior. This helps Paulo see that he can get attention with some behaviors, but not with others.

What Do I Need to Begin Implementing Functional Behavioral Assessment?

As we noted, there are really only four key steps to implementing a basic function-based intervention: (1) defining the behavior(s) of concern; (2) conducting an A-B-C analysis; (3) developing a hypothesis about what is causing or maintaining the behavior (i.e., determining the function it serves); and (4) designing an intervention that leads to the student using a more appropriate behavior to serve that function or need. Perhaps the only new or time-consuming element here is using an A-B-C data collection tool to record the behaviors of concern and the events that occur immediately before and after them. We understand that hearing "data collection" may cause some teachers to think there is going to be a complex or difficult task associated with getting started, but the tool that is used to collect this information doesn't need to be fancy or complex – it just needs to have enough space to record multiple examples of the behavior and what happens before and after. We have provided a template (Figure 16.2) at the end of this chapter to make this process as easy as possible; we have also provided a completed planning template as an example (Figure 16.1) and an implementation and self-assessment checklist (Figure 16.3). Once the data is collected, it's time to look for patterns as we previously described – this is really the entire purpose and premise of FBA.

The patterns we're looking for are simply repeated examples of a behavior being preceded or followed by a specific context, event, or outcome. Perhaps we learn that Petra's outbursts have only occurred during math class, or more specifically, when she's asked to complete problems independently at her desk. Perhaps a consequence is part of a pattern– Kendall has been sent to the office three times, and each time it was for physical aggression toward a peer; Kendall may well have learned that physical aggression is an efficient way to escape the classroom or whatever activity is going on.

A function-based intervention is one that provides students with the same reinforcement (access or escape) while teaching them more appropriate ways to have their needs met. Consider a student who rips his math assignment up and curses at the teacher after she assigns independent work; as a result, he is sent to the office. If the data reveal that the student is trying to escape the task, the teacher might respond by teaching the student to request a break – perhaps to have five minutes to read at the back of the room– instead of engaging in those concerning behaviors. Thus, for the time being, he will get to escape the task. Of course, this is not the end goal. Gradually, the teacher will implement other strategies (as described in Sections 1 and 2 of this book) to get the student to engage. While we sometimes get resistance from educators or administrators who think of this as letting students get out of work, or defying teachers' directions to get to work, we view it as a simple choice. Forcing the issue has resulted in meltdowns, conflicts, and sending kids to the office. Approaching the problem with a function-based mindset instead can lead to students' learning more appropriate ways to get their needs met, students remaining in the classroom, and, we believe, in more positive relationships between students and teachers.

What Does It Look like in the Classroom?

In this section, we briefly describe two examples of how teachers used elements of informal functional behavioral assessment to help form hypotheses about the function of a behavior that was causing concern, and how they developed strategies or interventions that addressed those functions.

Elementary Example – Ms. Hawthorne

Carlton is a third grader in Ms. Hawthorne's class, and she observed very soon after the school year started that he was melting down a lot in her classroom – at least two to three times a week. She described these to her grade level team as starting with crying or sobbing at his desk, but that he seemed to escalate to outbursts or tantrums when she tried to support or console him. He would throw himself on the floor, usually taking any materials or books with him as he tumbled out of his desk, and then wail loudly and flail around. After talking things through with her colleagues, Ms. Hawthorne decided to conduct an informal FBA with the goal of getting to the function of Carlton's behavior (see Figure 16.1 for her completed planning template). After about six days of collecting data, Ms. Hawthorne noticed a clear pattern. Carlton's behavioral outbursts occurred

294 ◆ Improving Student Behavior and Cultivating Meaningful Relationships

Informal Functional Behavioral Assessment Planning Template

Student: Carlton **Context** (class, time of day, etc. where problem behavior is likely): In my class throughout the day

FBA
Describe all A-B-C components in specific detail so other adults would recognize it if they saw it.

	ANTECEDENTS	BEHAVIOR	CONSEQUENCES	HYPOTHESIS
PATTERN OF BEHAVIOR	Describe what happens right before behavior occurs: When independent reading, computer instruction, and other activities he enjoys are ending.	Define behavior of concern: Carlton's behavior includes crying, throwing himself (and his stuff) on the ground, flailing around.	Describe what happens right after behavior occurs: I go over to him, talk him through it, try to help him feel better, get him to help me with something, and help him get started on the next thing.	Whenever a preferred activity is ending the student tends to cry and roll around on the floor which results in him getting teacher attention

Intervention
Describe all planned intervention components in specific detail and how they will be introduced to the students and other staff

SUPPORTIVE SOLUTIONS	Alter antecedents to prevent misbehavior or promote appropriate behavior: Set a 3-minute timer to prepare Carlton an activity is almost over. Use behavioral momentum (easy requests; check-in, read the board to me, share what's next).	Explicitly teach new skills and behavior that serves the same function: Practice following through on the easy requests, and using the timer with him and transitioning away from one activity to the next without the problem behavior. May teach him to raise a hand to ask for us too as another way to get attention.	Reinforce desired replacement behavior: Attention from me and Mr. Pitts as he does each thing, including getting to help us pass out papers	Describe the who/what/when/where/how of implementation: I will provide attention during each easy request. Mr. Pitts will too when Carlton shares what's next in class. We'll do this consistently before transitions for a week before assessing how things are going and making changes if needed.

Data Collection Plan
Describe the specific behavior(s) targeted for improvement: Transitioning without crying, throwing himself down, rolling around, etc.

Describe the metric (e.g., % of time on-task) and method for data collection: Percentage of successful transitions at the end of preferred activities. We'll keep a simple chart of the number of transitions and how many were successful to calculate a percentage.

FIGURE 16.1 Completed Example of Informal Functional Behavioral Assessment Planning Template

at the end of certain activities: independent reading periods and computer-based instruction or activities. After reflecting on the consequences, Ms. Hawthorne was able to see that after each time Carlton demonstrated this challenging behavior, she would walk over to him, talk to him for several minutes to try and console him and eventually, she would transition Carlton to the next activity by letting him help her pass out materials. Ms. Hawthorne suspected (and had evidence to support) that the function of Carlton's behavior was access to teacher attention, but that this really only happened at the end of activities that Carlton really enjoyed.

Ms. Hawthorne developed a plan. When there were three minutes left in an activity that Carlton preferred, she would set a timer to start counting down the time to the transition, and she would alert Carlton that there were three minutes left. When the timer went off, Ms. Hawthorne would use behavioral momentum (Chapter 5) to increase the likelihood that Carlton would be able to transition smoothly. She would begin by asking Carlton to come check-in with her (providing a little bit of access to some teacher attention); after that, she would ask him to read the schedule on the board and then repeat back to her what's next (again, a bit more of her attention); next she would ask Carlton to let the teaching assistant, Mr. Pitts, to know what activity is next (again, more teacher attention). After completing these activities, Ms. Hawthorne would prompt Carlton to end the activity and clean up his belongings. If Carlton could clean up his activity without a behavioral meltdown, he would be allowed to help pass out materials, thus continuing to provide teacher attention as the consequence.

Ms. Hawthorn begins to implement this approach, and she is pleasantly surprised at how well it works. When Carlton complies, the entire routine only takes about 60–90 seconds – which is significantly less time than she was spending trying to console him after his meltdowns. The first week, Carlton successfully transitions out of preferred activities on 30% of the occasions. This doesn't feel like a lot to Ms. Hawthorn, but her grade level team reminds her that just last week, Carlton was at 0%. Ms. Hawthorn continues the intervention and after three weeks,

Carlton is transitioning without a meltdown on 75% of occasions. Ms. Hawthorn will continue the intervention and then begin to gradually fade it once Carlton is consistently transitioning without meltdowns.

Secondary Example – Mr. Mercer

Mr. Mercer teaches Biology to tenth-graders, and his 1st period class includes a mix of students he has found to be "very active" and not always interested in doing their work. He blames some of this on the schedule – it's their first class of the day and they have a hard time settling down, but he also knows that several of his students have 504 plans based on ADHD and their difficulties with attention, or who receive support from the special education consulting teacher. He's particularly concerned about Lawrence, who has all these issues (problems with attention and distractibility) but can also be very resistant or even defiant. Almost every time class begins, Lawrence's go-to response has become, "Oh no, Mr. Mercer, I'm not going to be able to do that today." With the help of the consulting teacher, Mr. Mercer collects A-B-C data across three class sessions, and they sit down together to review the data.

From just a quick glance through the data, they see immediate patterns. First, Lawrence's "can't do that" responses always follow specific assignments– only when Mr. Mercer says something like, "so, today I need you to copy down the steps of the experiment, and then…" does Lawrence speak up with his refusal to work. Second, they realize that Mr. Mercer's responses have just been firm re-statements of the assignment, with some mention of consequences (e.g., "Lawrence, yes you can, and you need to finish this, or you will earn no points for today"). What's worse, Lawrence is consistently more defiant when challenged by Mr. Mercer; after the second direction and proposed consequences, Lawrence typically responds quickly with harsher words (e.g., "you can't tell me what to do"). They decide Lawrence has not seemed particularly swayed by consequences, so they will focus first on altering antecedents. They decide on instructional choice (see Chapter 6), and brainstorm several options; these include (a) offering Lawrence an alternate place to work ("you can sit at my desk, your desk, or the back table to work on these"), (b) breaking the assignment into smaller pieces and letting Lawrence choose what to do first, and (c) when possible, allowing Lawrence to choose to do only some portion of an assignment (e.g., from a list of ten vocabulary words, choose five to define and illustrate). Mr. Mercer plans to use one of these strategies in each science lesson with Lawrence (they have science on Blue days, which means two or three times each week).

The next day in Biology they're continuing their introduction to the unit on cells and there is a significant list of vocabulary words to learn. Mr. Mercer has a prepared sheet that includes a cell diagram and a list of ten terms, each with a blank line below it. Students are to define the term in a short sentence and then draw and label what that term represents on the cell diagram. As Mr. Mercer begins just mentioning the assignment – before he's even passed them out – Lawrence sees the worksheets in his hand and says, "hold on, Mr. Mercer, I'm not going to be able to do that today." Mr. Mercer ignores this for the moment, but then as he approaches Lawrence's desk, he leans down and says quietly, "I bet you know some of these already – how about you pick five that you know and just do them." Lawrence is still not happy, but begrudgingly picks up his pencil and mumbles, "well, I might be able to do five…" as he starts drawing on his diagram. Mr. Mercer walks away to circulate around the room, but not before saying softly to Lawrence, "good job tackling those terms, buddy."

Final Thoughts

In this chapter, we tried to focus on two broad points. First is that function matters; whenever there is concern that specific behaviors are interfering with a student meeting basic behavioral expectations, we encourage teachers to think about function first – what is the student getting out of that behavior? The second is that there are simple tools teachers can use and steps they can take to move toward more function-based thinking in how they teach and manage classrooms. An underlying theme in all this is the need to develop a mindset that virtually all behavior has a function, which means at least two important things to us. The first – admittedly easier said than done – is the need to NOT take things personally. We find this a struggle teachers face all the time. The student who spoils the best lesson or activity you have ever planned – one that was going really well for everyone – is not acting out because he's mean, spiteful, or vindictive, or because he hates you. There's surely a purpose – or a function – to this behavior. What's more, we ask teachers in these contexts whether they might have predicted this would happen. Common responses are things like "oh yes, this didn't surprise me," or even more directly, "I kind of knew he might do this; he always does this kind of thing whenever we ____." We remind teachers that if their thinking has brought them this far, they are very close to now preventing these worrisome behaviors, and further that the key lies in altering antecedents (the A in our A-B-C analysis). We cited evidence that function-based interventions are indeed very effective in decreasing negative behaviors (Gage et al., 2012), and thus in helping students more routinely meet expectations. But we hope an underlying message is also that shifting to a function-based mindset not only offers great benefit to teachers in helping students to more efficiently and appropriately meet their needs, but in potentially removing some of the negative emotion that can sometimes evolve around behavioral challenges in classrooms.

References

Borgmeier, C., Loman, S. L., & Strickland-Cohen, M. K. (2017). ABC tracker: Increasing teacher capacity for assessing student behavior. *Beyond Behavior*, *26*(3), 113–123.

Gage, N. A., Lewis, T. J., & Stichter, J. P. (2012). Functional behavioral assessment-based interventions for students with or at risk for emotional and/or behavioral disorders in school: A hierarchical linear modeling meta-analysis. *Behavioral Disorders*, *37*(2), 55–77.

IRIS Center (2024). *Functional behavioral assessment: Identifying the reasons for problem behavior and developing a behavior plan*. https://iris.peabody.vanderbilt.edu/module/fba/

Umbreit, J., Ferro, J. B., Lane, K. L., & Liaupsin, C. J. (2024). *Functional assessment-based intervention: Effective individualized support for students*. Guilford Publications.

Walker, V. L., Chung, Y. C., & Bonnet, L. K. (2018). Function-based intervention in inclusive school settings: A meta-analysis. *Journal of Positive Behavior Interventions*, *20*(4), 203–216.

Informal Functional Behavioral Assessment Planning Template

Student: _____ **Context** (*class, time of day, etc. where problem behavior is likely*): _____

FBA

Describe all A-B-C components in specific detail so other adults would recognize it if they saw it

	ANTECEDENTS	**BEHAVIOR**	**CONSEQUENCES**	**HYPOTHESIS**
PATTERN OF BEHAVIOR	Describe what happens right before behavior occurs:	Define behavior of concern:	Describe what happens right after behavior occurs:	Whenever _____ the student tends to _____ which results in _____

Intervention

Describe all planned intervention components in specific detail and how they will be introduced to the students and other staff

SUPPORTIVE SOLUTIONS	Alter antecedents to prevent misbehavior or promote appropriate behavior:	Explicitly teach new skills and behavior that serves the same function:	Reinforce desired replacement behavior:	Describe the who/what/when/where/how of implementation:

Data Collection Plan

Describe the specific behavior(s) targeted for improvement:

Describe the metric (e.g., % of time on-task) and method for data collection:

FIGURE 16.2 Informal Functional Behavioral Assessment Planning Template

Informal Functional Behavioral Assessment **Steps & Self-Assessment** 0→Not in Place 1→Partially in Place 2→Fully in Place	
STEPS	How Did I do?
1. Define behaviors of concern operationally.	☐ 0 ☐ 1 ☐ 2
2. Conduct an A-B-C analysis.	☐ 0 ☐ 1 ☐ 2
3. Form a hypothesis to describe the pattern of behavior.	☐ 0 ☐ 1 ☐ 2
4. Propose an intervention to support a more appropriate behavior.	☐ 0 ☐ 1 ☐ 2
Notes & Reflection:	

FIGURE 16.3 Informal Functional Behavioral Assessment Implementation and Self-Assessment Checklist

Part VI
Closing Thoughts

17

Final Takeaways

We mentioned in our introduction to this book that we have spent our entire professional careers as teachers, then training teachers at the college level and working with practicing teachers in schools through professional development and consultative support. We find that we typically end our classes or professional development trainings with a message, and it seems like it applies to this book as well. Starting from a premise that we don't pretend to know everything, and would not expect a reader (or teacher in our classes) to remember everything we said or demonstrated anyway, we do hope we have made several points.

First, we hope this book can be kept on a bookshelf as a resource – not a solution to every problem, but as a reminder that there is an array of positive, proactive strategies teachers can easily implement to address their most common behavioral challenges. To possibly help make them more useful, we tried to develop each chapter to serve as a standalone resource. In other words, this book was not meant to be a textbook that can only be read cover to cover, each chapter in order. We hope it is the type of book that you can quickly flip through and find the information you need to address whatever concerns are most pressing for you at a given moment. As you have seen, following the Introduction (Section I), the book is arranged in four sections. In Section II, Teaching Behavior, we highlighted the need to approach behavior just as one would approach academics. Kids have mastered different parts of the curriculum at different levels of mastery, and instruction and supports should be designed and delivered in a way that meets them where they are, and helps them get to the next level. We hope we also made clear the need to actively and directly *teach* behavior! In Section III, Encouraging Appropriate Behavior, we described six strategies that exemplify positive approaches to encouraging behavior that meets expectations, and thus can reduce challenging behaviors. These included Positive Greetings at the Door, Behavioral Momentum, Instructional Choice, Increasing Opportunities to Respond (OTRs), Precorrection, and Precision Requests, and for each we noted not only how they can be effectively implemented, but how they support positive relationships. In Section IV, Maintaining Appropriate Behavior, we described strategies that can be used (ideally with the practices and strategies presented in Sections II and III) to reinforce demonstrations of positive student behavior. Specifically, we discussed Behavior-Specific Praise, Token Economies, and Positive Group Contingencies. Finally, in Section V, we presented a few interventions for students who may require additional support to meet the behavioral expectations in their classrooms and school. We described how Differential Reinforcement, Check-in Check-out, Behavior Contracts, and (Informal) Functional Behavioral Assessment can be used in addition to the practices and strategies presented in Sections II–IV.

Second, we think it is important to circle back to the idea that served as the premise for how we conceptualized this entire book: relationships matter. Our backgrounds included training in, and experience implementing, pretty straightforward behavioral interventions. But as our professional experiences grew, we were increasingly aware that some educators or psychologists seemed to be suggesting that a relationship focus was critical (we totally agree), but further that a relationship-based approach to intervention should be used *instead of* a behavioral approach. Frankly, we've never understood this. It seems clear to us that many behavioral strategies, and we'd argue *most* behavioral strategies that are positive and preventive (i.e., antecedent) in fact are very well aligned with strengthening the exact elements that make for a positive teacher-student relationship. Positive Greetings at the Door (Chapter 4), behavioral momentum (Chapter 5), and instructional choice (Chapter 6) are especially obvious examples of this, we think, but we've described and demonstrated how positive relationships are fostered and maintained by all of the strategies we recommend in this book. We know well that many descriptions of behavioral interventions can seem overly "clinical," but again we hope in this book we have demonstrated how they can be used at minimum as entry points for building positive student-teacher relationships. We also know from both experience and research that teachers often have a difficult time establishing positive relationships with students who exhibit challenging behavior, especially those with and at risk for emotional behavioral disorders. Again, this book was designed with this challenge in mind, and we hope the ease and simplicity of these strategies, as well as the positive impacts they often produce, help in small ways to improve the odds of these positive relationships emerging and strengthening.

Finally, although all of the strategies presented in this book are supported by research, we want to reiterate that no single strategy will be effective every time, for every student. We chose to highlight the strategies we did because they are known to *increase the odds* students will successfully meet expectations. In reality, these odds never reach 100%. But we have been convinced since our own early days of teaching that any meaningful increase in the odds of success is a win. When aggression drops from 60% of the time to 30% of the time, profanity from 27 times a day to three times a day, or staying in one's seat (or even in the classroom) increases from 40% to 50% of the time, life gets better for all concerned. Students are now able to earn more reinforcers, including more behavior-specific praise. The ratio of positive-to-negative interactions by definition increases. As a result, teachers simply have more time for active and positive instructional interactions and students' ability to access academic instruction increases. In short, strategies like these, when well-implemented, will make your job easier, will make your day go smoother, and, we predict, ultimately will increase the quality of teacher-student relationships and student learning, including for those students who may have seemed toughest to teach.

We want to close by stating again that we know firsthand that teaching can be hard, and teaching kids with challenging behaviors can be even harder. In some cases, you may not get it right. We made many mistakes as teachers, or simply missed opportunities to be more positive, preventive, and supportive. But as respected colleagues once noted, if you work with students who display challenging behavior, you will always have more opportunities to practice those skills (Lewis et al., 2017). We hope the strategies and interventions we've described in this book, and the resources that we've included, provide useful examples of some of these skills that can help where challenging behavior is concerned. And we hope they make this part of the job of teaching easier, even if just a little bit at a time.

Reference

Lewis, T. J., Hatton, H. L., Jorgenson, C., & Maynard, D. (2017). What beginning special educators need to know about conducting functional behavioral assessments. *Teaching Exceptional Children*, *49*(4), 231–238.

For Product Safety Concerns and Information please contact our EU representative GPSR@taylorandfrancis.com
Taylor & Francis Verlag GmbH, Kaufingerstraße 24, 80331 München, Germany